9-97

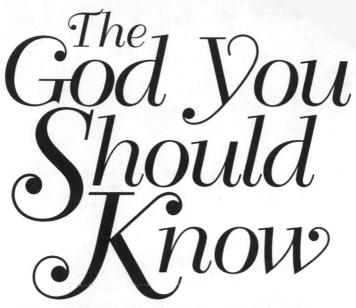

The God You Should Know

How to Have a Dynamic Faith

J. SIDLOW BAXTER

Author of *Explore the Book*

D0681224

kregel
PUBLICATIONS

Grand Rapids, MI 49501

Cover Photo: Art Jacobs
Cover and Book Design: Al Hartman

Library of Congress Cataloging-in-Publication Data

Baxter, J. Sidlow (James Sidlow)
   [Majesty]
   The God you should know / by J. Sidlow Baxter.
     p.   cm.
   Previously published: Majesty. 1984.
   Includes index.
   1. Providence and government of God. 2. God—
Holiness. 3. Trinity. I. Title.
BT135.B36   1993   231—dc20   92-39336
                                             CIP

ISBN 0-8254-2174-8 (pbk.)

1 2 3 4 5 Printing / Year 97 96 95 94 93

Printed in the United States of America

Contents

Explanation

A few years ago it was my privilege to deliver the annual Louis S. Bauman Memorial Lectures at Grace Theological Seminary, Winona Lake, Indiana. Several of the chapters which now comprise this book were first uttered then, though in condensed form. Later they became expanded into a course of lectures covering one entire semester at the California Graduate School of Theology. They were not intended to become a book for publication, but here they are now, in response to warm request, and presented in what I hope may be a useful style and arrangement for the general reader.

This book is quite unpretentious. I have not tried to deal with the subject exhaustively. Whoever *could* treat such a subject exhaustively—a subject measurelessly bigger than the universe itself? I have picked out only those aspects which I think are most needing emphasis or reconsideration today.

So, here is yet another book, like another new vessel being launched on the great wide sea already overcrowded with ships of all sorts and sizes, carrying all kinds of cargo, good and bad. May a kindly Heaven grant that this new little vessel may take the water well, and carry merchandise of spiritual blessing wherever it goes, finding a friendly port in many a human heart.

J.S.B.

Majesty

But Jehovah is the true God,
He is the living God, and an everlasting King:
At His wrath the earth shall tremble,
And the nations shall not be able to abide His indignation.

Thus shall ye say unto them: The gods that did not make the heavens and the earth, they shall perish from the earth, and from under these heavens.

He [Jehovah] hath made the earth by His powers,
He established the world by His wisdom,
And hath stretched out the heavens by His discretion.
When He uttereth His voice there is a multitude of waters in the heavens,
And He causeth the vapors to ascend from the ends of the earth;
He maketh lightnings with rain,
And bringeth forth the wind out of His treasures.
Every man is brutish in His knowledge;
Every founder is confounded by the graven image,
For his molten image is falsehood,
And there is no breath in them:
They are vanity, and the work of errors;
In the time of their visitation they shall perish.
The portion of Jacob (Jehovah) is not like them;
For He is the former of all things;
And Israel is the rod of His inheritance;

Jehovah of Hosts is His name.

Jeremiah 10:10-16

Oh, who can lift enquiring eyes,
And scan the star-bespangled skies,
Yet argue, earthbound as the clod,
Mid wonders such, there is no God?

The flaming splendor of the noon,
The gentler beams of silver moon,
And far-flung systems everywhere
Their wondrous Architect declare.

Yet though His glory they reveal,
Himself, His nature, they conceal;
We grope for Him whom they declare,
Yet can but dimly find Him there.

Oh, love outshining starry gleam,
That He should suffer to redeem!
That He who all the heavens built
Once bled to bear my sin and guilt!

Now skies indeed are softer blue,
And every flower has lovelier hue;
The One whom stars proclaim above
As *Savior* now I know and love.

J.S.B.

1

Time to Rethink

G od is the greatest of all mysteries and the greatest of all realities. He is the infinite mystery behind all reality, and the absolute reality behind all mystery; unimaginably exceeding the profoundest grasp of human comprehension, and beyond all verbal definition. Neither the phenomenal universe nor the invisible universe of thought has any satisfactory explanation apart from God, but the being of God Himself is utterly beyond explanation. He immeasurably outbounds the most distant reach of stars and space in all directions, yet He is so exquisitely close to each of us as to be, in Tennyson's phrase, "closer than breathing, nearer than hands and feet." He is the one "in whom we live and move and have our being," the God "in whose hand our breath is"; the Infinite who fills everywhere. Before all other being began, God already was, or rather, eternally *is*. When He created the universe, He added nothing to Himself, and as He still creates amid His universe adds nothing to Himself, for to the Infinite nothing can be added.

Our human race and the revolving orb on which we live are surrounded by mysteries deep and vast, mysteries awesome and haunting, mysteries intriguing but impenetrable, fascinating yet ever elusive. Our present century is distinctively the epoch of scientific discovery and cosmic exploration; yet any candid scientist will tell you that every new discovery is but another disclosure of undiscovered *further* mystery. Mankind, the earth, the universe, time, space, life, mind are still baffling mysteries to us; and it is well that we should be reminded of that, lest we lose our sense of reverential wonder, or strut around like vain little "know-it-alls" where angels fear to tread. But the mystery of mysteries which ever underlines what infinitesimal specks we are is the inexplicable super-mystery—
God.

How glibly we Christians often speak about God, as though biblical revelation and systematic theology had reduced the Deity

to finite comprehension! Nay, even amid the noonday blaze of completed biblical revelation and of the incarnate Emmanuel, God still
remains sheer mystery as well as the Self-revealed supreme Reality.
Let us ever speak of Him with intellectual obeisance and "godly fear."

Some will tell us, of course, that we are starting these studies
with an unallowable assumption. How do we know that God is? Are
we not assuming what we cannot demonstrate? If God does provenly
exist, then admittedly He is at once the all-transcendent fact; but
is an uncreated Creator an authenticated reality? Are we not starting
with an assumption instead of an argument? Our answer is: Of course
we are, and for a very good reason. We are starting where the *Bible*
starts. It has been argued (but wrongly) that God *cannot* be proved.
It has been replied (and rightly) that God cannot be *dis*proved. Albeit,
there is much more than that. Although God cannot be either opti-
cally or arithmetically demonstrated, I believe that the well-known
ontological, cosmological, teleological and anthropological arguments settle it evidentially that God is, at least to all who are
genuinely open-minded. But do we need to be continually wading
again through all those apologetics when we have scientifically test-
able evidence in the Bible? I refer to the supernatural wonder of
fulfilled prophecy. Clear prediction crowned by exact fulfillment
gives proof positive that God is; for only God knows that which we
human beings call the future. Even one such prophecy, written
plainly and in sufficient detail, designed for fulfillment centuries
later, if fulfilled with complete accuracy, is an unanswerable evidence of God. Well, in the Bible there are scores of such foretellings
and fulfillments;and perhaps more intellectuals have been converted
to the Christian faith by that evidence than by any other.

Our Bible never argues God. It assumes and reveals Him. How
could it argue for God's existence when it is God Himself speaking
through it? The following three postulates have proved true to
thousands of us. (1) The Bible repeatedly *claims* to be the Word of
God. (2) As we let it teach us it *seems* to be the Word of God. (3)
When we thoroughly investigate its credentials it *proves* to be the
Word of God.

But besides that there is the fact of *Christ*. The Lord Jesus
Christ is indeed a "fact," and such an extraordinary fact that He
must be commensurately explained. To ignore or discount such a
supernormal phenomenon of history as JESUS is the unworthy es-
capism of anti-theistic prejudice. No other book and no other person
have ever been scrutinized with such unrelenting scholarly and skep-
tical exhaustiveness as have the Bible and Jesus, especially so during
the past century—but with what result? Not one part of the Bible

has been disproved, either in the Old Testament or in the New. The sixty-six oracles of the Bible outlive all the critics, and in the words of Paul to the Philippian jailer, they say to their most hostile critic today, "Do thyself no harm, for we are all here" (Acts 16:28).

As for the Man, Christ Jesus, the New Testament documents which present Him are now more provenly genuine than ever before. A lie may "travel half way round the world while truth is putting on its shoes," but in the end truth overtakes error, and becomes more obviously true than ever before. That is the position today with both the higher and the textual criticism of the New Testament. Rationalistic criticism has not destroyed the genuine, historical Jesus of the four Gospels. In the end, largely against itself, hostile scholarship has clarified and verified Jesus as the wonderful fact that He is. Thus, more than ever now, the same three postulates apply to Jesus as apply to the Bible. (1) He repeatedly *claims* to be God manifest in the flesh. (2) As we listen and learn of Him He indeed *seems* to be God manifest in the flesh. (3) When we thoroughly investigate Him He *proves* to be God manifest in the flesh.

That, then, is our starting point in these studies. It is so because we begin with the Bible and the fact of Christ, not with secular science or philosophy. We start with the Bible because these expositions are meant, not for atheists, agnostics or skeptics, but for Christians. It may be reasonably presumed that all who travel with us through this series believe that God *is*; that the Bible is the written *Word* of God; and that the God of the Bible is the only *true* God.

In starting there do we not have the endorsement of our very nature as human beings? The fact that God is seems to have an ever-persisting echo in our native humanhood. All the carefully explored evidence seems to indicate that an awareness of God is fundamental and ineradicable in mankind. For some time I doubted that. After contacts with certain aboriginal peoples of the earth, and observation of certain human types in our own civilized society, including some professed atheists, I told myself that in some humans there was not even an inchoate cognizance of God. Lately, however, I have switched back to my earlier persuasion that the idea of God is indeed hereditarily constitutional in men. Such basic God-awareness in us may be resisted, suppressed, twisted almost out of recognition, denied or explained away, but it persists or recurrently resurrects itself. This is demonstrated not only in age-enduring idolatries and world-girdling religions, but in refined philosophies and even in the crude sophistries of recent hippyism.

Experiences have a way of surfacing such God-awareness.

Seven or eight decades ago when my dear mother was on a

voyage from England to Australia, three men on board superciliously mocked her Christian religion. Their versatile raillery indicated that they were volubly "read up." They had mastered the talking points of atheism. However, about halfway across the Indian Ocean one of the ship's boilers burst, and soon afterward one of the worst storms the captain ever remembered hit the limping vessel. All passengers were ordered "below." The next day, at the peak of the storm, passengers were told to keep together in the main lounge so as to be ready for any emergency announcement. Passengers had to cling to whatever was available in the struggle to avoid being flung about. Then what should my mother see but the three atheists prostrated on the floor in panic-prayer, crying out loudly to *God* to intervene and save them! That storm and the unconcealable terror of those three, in contrast with my mother's Christian calmness, tore the disguise from their outward derision.

In the 1940's, during the Second World War, British forces tried to land at Narvik in Norway, but were repelled with much loss under murderous German gunfire. Some time later, in Redford Barracks, Edinburgh, Scotland, a drill sergeant was loudly mouthing his atheism before the men when his eloquent profanity was suddenly interrupted by a young private who called out from the squad, "Sergeant, if you don't believe in God, why did I see you fling yourself down on the beach at Narvik, yelling with terror and begging God to save you?"

On a beautiful, starlit night Napoleon and some of his officers were aboard ship. Some of them were bragging of their disbelief in the existence of God. After listening awhile Napoleon spoke, and pointing to the star-bespangled sky asked, "But, gentlemen, who made all *that*?"

Is it not true that all normal human beings are born with the basic data for God in their very nature? The very fact of our mental rationality in a surrounding universe of corresponding rationality indicates that God made us for faith, not for doubt. We are born to see things as they are and what their real meaning is; and when we let our basic nature guide us that is how we do see them. When the physical wonders amid which our little planet rolls are invested with meanings other than the natural, rational, obviously-intended meaning, that is due to a twist in our own thinking, not to any change in the *real* meaning of things. After John Glenn became the first American astronaut to fly through outer space, some Russian space-fliers asked him sarcastically, "Did you see God anywhere out there?" They might just as sensibly have asked, "Did you see the law of gravitation out there?" There is just about as much reason to disbelieve in the law of gravitation as to disbelieve in God.

That self-existing deity must ever be a subject far beyond the grasp of all creature intelligence. Yet this is equally true, that we may intelligently know and believe that which we do not have the capacity fully to understand. Of this fact there are countless examples. As God alone is the self-existent one, the universe must "have its being" not only *from* Him, but *in* Him. Therefore, God must be *omnipresent*, for creation could not exist apart from Him. He also must be *omnipotent*, for He must continually "uphold all things." He also must be *omniscient*, for all other intelligences derive their intelligence from Him, and it is He who has impressed the harmonious laws of being upon all the interconnected universe. How can we tiny finites grasp such a being? As the Bible says, "He is unsearchable." But we can know what He himself has revealed to us in provably inspired Scriptures and through the Lord Jesus Christ.

The greatest need of the present hour is a movement back to the Bible and to the God of the Bible.

Humanism, with its emphasis on human self-sufficiency, self-determination and self-perfectibility, despite all it has said to us through modern science and philosophy, has not only failed man, it has left him stranded and distraught, morally and spiritually bankrupt. When existentialism took over with its "God is dead," it might just as well have added, "and so is hope," for it has said it bitterly enough since. The late H.G. Wells was such a widely-read interpretative student of history that his melancholy swan song in 1939 has been all the more widely quoted; but I think it worthwhile to quote it again here if only because of the grim endorsement which secular philosophy has given to it during the ensuing thirty-five years.

> There is no creed, no way of life left in the world at all, that really meets the need of the time...there is no reason whatever to believe that the order of nature has any greater bias in favour of man than it had in favour of the ichthyosaur or the pterodactyl. In spite of all my desperation to a brave-looking optimism, I perceive that now the universe is bored with man, is turning a hard face to him, and I see him being carried less and less intelligently and more and more rapidly, suffering as every ill-adapted creature must suffer in gross and detail, along the stream of fate, to degradation, suffering and death.

The same despair was expressed by his brilliant contemporary, Bertrand Russell. Consider the pessimism coming from that genius: "Only on the firm foundation of unyielding *despair* can the soul's habitation henceforth be safely built!" In other words: Do not reckon on anything but the certainty of perishing in the general doom! In his excellent booklet, *Set Forth Your Case,* Professor Clark H. Pinnock says, "Testimonies of this kind from non-Christians awakening to the logic of their own position could be added from an unnumbered host—from Sartre, Camus, Heidegger, Durant, Voltaire, Strauss and many more. The unbounded optimism of western man has reached exhaustion, and he faces his own extinction in his own manufactured hell." Dr. Pinnock notes that the same despair shows itself nowadays throgh novelists like Franz Kafka, and playwrights like Samuel Beckett, Eugene Ionesco, Harold Pinter, and Jean Genet. In varying form they depict life as an enigma of emptiness and futility. Secular philosophy, humanist existentialism, has drained away all meaning and purpose from human life. "The root problem of the non-Christian humanist," as Dr. Pinnock well says, is "the sheer pointlessness of existing in a godless world."

I can vividly recall how different was the outlook when I was a young boy. The tired old nineteenth century had bowed out, and the glamorous-looking twentieth century had stepped in with doffed hat and ingratiating promises of a brave, new era. The apostles of evolution were blandly assuring the public that they were giving mankind at last the really scientific explanation of man—something far better than the Bible myth that man was directly created but had shamed himself by a fall into sin. Man was evolved and is still evolving, they said. Instead of a "fall" downward, we should see man's magnificent struggle upward to kingship of his own achieving. Man is the master of his own fate. He has reached a point now (so they said) from which his development will stride forward with final acceleration to a utopia fulfilling every gallant hope. What old-fashioned religious concepts had failed to do for man in the past, science would now accomplish in the big new push of twentieth-century enlightenment.

Yes, that was my boyhood world. How proudly naive it was! How soon the balloon of its vanity was to be burst! Within the next few decades men were going to learn that science, evolution, Freudianism, psychology, rationalism, higher education, could not find adequate answers to the grim human problems of sin, guilt, hate, greed, lust, fear, sorrow, death. In the first half of the century two world wars were going to write in blood and tears that man's moral problems can be met only by a *spiritual* remedy. The figment of "a war to end wars" would prove a mockery. Soon it would be shouted from wrecked cities and the battlefield graveyards of millions that you cannot wash away human sin with the soldier's blood: It takes a Savior's blood to do that.

Where do we get to know this Savior? These studies will help us to glimpse again the portrait of Him in the biblical revelation. Yet where did those Holy Scriptures get their incomparable photograph of the Almighty, of His character and ways, of His doings and plannings, of His ineffable holiness and outreaching graciousness? Clearly from God Himself. It is worth recalling, how, back in 1643 to 1647, when the famous Westminster Catechism was being drawn up, there came a point of reverent indecision when those assembled divines wanted to frame a concise but worthy definition of God. They resorted to special prayer for guidance, and called on the Reverend George Gillespie to lead them. Gillespie, one of four Scottish members and the youngest man in the assembly, prayed, "O God, who art a Spirit, infinite, eternal, and unchangeable, in Thy being, wisdom, power, holiness, justice, goodness, and truth..." Unanimously it was decided that the answer had been given; so that was the definition which later became permanent in the Westminster Catechism:

> God is a Spirit, infinite, eternal, and unchangeable, in His being, wisdom, power, holiness, justice, goodness, and truth.

Where did Gillespie get that profound, exalted and obviously true concept of the one and only real God? Only from the Bible. Nowhere else do we find the kind of unveiling of God required by human reason.

Through the Bible then we come to know God, not only as an objective *fact*, but as the supreme Father-Savior-Indweller who, in response to human faith, obedience, prayer, communing, makes Himself real to us in our individual *experience*. We may not only learn authentic truth *about* Him, we may directly know *God Himself*, and prove the reality of His Self-communicatings.

Of course, the very thought of knowing *God* may well be stunning, and I can appreciate the incredulity of those who are out of touch with the Bible and do not know the transforming power of the Lord Jesus in their lives. After all, however clearly and fully we may grasp the mighty truths which the Bible teaches us about God, how much can we truly grasp of His incomprehensible infinitudes? How paltry, indeed, are our best-selected words to convey anything of Him who called the stupendous universe into being out of nothing; and with whom a thousand years are as a day; who predetermines to the hour and the minute the revolvings of the planets round the sun; who paints the wayside lily and lights the evening star; who clothes the flashing seraphim with raiment of fire; and just as truly forms the insect which creeps over our garden flower-beds! In that sense God is utterly beyond our knowing; yet that only makes more astonishing and precious His individualizing love toward us, and His expressed desire to be closely known by us.

With such thoughts in mind we now turn to the Bible, to hear its "Thus saith Jehovah," and its "Thus saith the high and lofty One that inhabiteth eternity, whose name is Holy; I dwell in the high and holy place, with him also that is of a contrite and humble spirit, to revive the spirit of the humble, and to revive the heart of the contrite ones" (Isa. 57:15). Above all else, we shall open the treasured pages again realizing that the God of the Bible is supremely revealed and known through the Christ of the Bible. Our golden key will be Hebrews 1:1-3:

> God, who at sundry times and in divers manners spake in time past unto the fathers by the prophets, hath in these last days spoken unto us by His *Son*, whom He hath appointed heir of all things, by whom also He made the worlds; who being the brightness of His glory, and the express image of His person, and upholding all things by the word of His power, when he had by Himself purged our sins, sat down on the right hand of the Majesty on High.

Many of us who have already found that wonderful God through His *written* Word (the Bible) and through the *living*Word (Christ) are already singing —

Strangely I sensed Him everywhere,
The God I ached to find,
Yet could not find Him anywhere,
Above, before, behind.

Myst'ry amazing! Love unknown!
In human form He stands!
He calls with tender human tone,
Uplifting nail-torn hands!

Yes, for in Jesus, God Most High
Has come from heaven above,
To answer all my aching cry
With His redeeming love!

Oh, magnify the Lord with me,
My Savior-King divine!
For in my Savior now I see
Lo, God and heaven are mine!

2

The Sovereignty of God—
The Old Testament Witness

What is the first truth the Bible teaches us about God? Is it His ineffable holiness? His infinite wisdom? His mysterious triunity? His redeeming grace? His essential spirituality? No. Is it His boundless attributes—omnipotence, omniscience, omnipresence, eternality? No. What, then, is it?

In answering that question let me ask another. What is the first book of the Bible? Is it Isaiah, the princeliest of the writing prophets? Or Matthew, the first of the four gospel narrators? Or the Psalms, the race's prayer book? Or the Gospel of John, that immortal account of the Word incarnate? No. It is Genesis. But why? Was Genesis the first book of the Bible to be written? No, there are cogent reasons for believing that the Book of Job is of even earlier antiquity. Why does not Job come first? There is a clear answer. Genesis comes first because it is designed to impress upon us a certain truth about God which we are meant to learn before all else. What is that priority truth? It is the *sovereignty of God*.

In this present study we shall briefly exhibit the sovereignty of God as it is presented in Genesis, the first book of the Bible; then in Isaiah, the first book of the Prophets; then in Matthew, the first book of the New Testament; and then in the Apocalypse, the last book of the Bible. First, then, we turn to the Book of Genesis.

THE BOOK OF GENESIS

Let us quickly review Genesis perspectively. In our English presentation of it there are fifty chapters. All Bible students agree that those fifty chapters break into two clear though uneven parts: part one, consisting of chapters 1 to 11, and part two, consisting of chapters 12 to 50. All are agreed that the call of Abram at the beginning of chapter 12 is the "great divide" which marks off the Book of Genesis into those two major parts. The first part, although much shorter than the second part, covers some two thousand years; whereas the second part covers less than three hundred years.

Part one (the first eleven chapters) tells us about the earliest history of our race; so we may therefore call it *primeval* records. Part two (the remaining 39 chapters) tells us mainly about the first fathers, or patriarchs, of the covenant people, Israel; so we may accordingly call it *patriarchal* records.

Let us imagine ourselves investigating those two parts of Genesis for the first time, open-mindedly seeking to ascertain their principal message. What do we find? First we peruse part one, those first eleven chapters, and after we have gone through them half a dozen times there is a certain feature which impresses us above all else, namely, in those eleven chapters are recorded four tremendous *events*: (1) the Creation, (2) the Fall, (3) the Flood, (4) the Babel Crisis.

Next we read chapters 12 to 50, traversing them observantly over and over again. What is it that becomes evident? It is that all those chapters of part two gather around four outstanding *persons*: (1) Abraham, (2) Isaac, (3) Jacob, (4) Joseph.

So then, in part one we have four tremendous *events*; in part two, four outstanding *persons*. There can be no mistake about it; such is the fourfold contour of those two main movements. That immediately sets us asking: Is there some special significance which we are meant to see in those four super-events of part one, and those four pivotal personages of part two?

We decide to read through part one again, lingering in particular over each of those four extraordinary events, and *now* what do we find? Why, this: Each of them is so narrated as to emphasize one special aspect. Take the first of them: the *Creation.* The whole emphasis is upon what *God* did and said and ordered. "In the beginning God created." "And the spirit of God moved..." "And God said..." "And God made..." "And God saw..." It is all put there to emphasize that God is before all, and above all, and beneath all, and within all, and around all and beyond all. In other words, God is absolutely sovereign in the *physical creation.*

Take the second of those four super-events, i.e., the *Fall.* The same feature is prominent all the way through. The whole weight of emphasis is thrown upon the divine sovereignty. It is God who gives man his being. It is God who places him in the garden paradise. It is God who sets the test and warns of the penalty. It is God who passes sentence on the man, on the woman, on the serpent. In other words, we are meant to see preeminently that God, besides being sovereign in the physical creation, is sovereign in *human probation.* ⌐

Pass to the third event: the *Flood.* How much there is which we could wish had been told us about that long-ago antediluvian era! Yet how severely the narrative excludes everything which would merely gratify prurient curiosity! Seventeen and a half centuries are packed into two and a half pages, so that whatever else we may or may not see, we shall not miss seeing the dramatic connection between the Fall and the Flood. In chapter 3 we read of the Fall, in chapter 4 the Cain line, in chapter 5 the Seth line, in chapter 6 the two lines blur in confusion and corruption, in chapter 7 down comes the judgment of the Flood. The whole fearful drama is so synopsized that we may not miss seeing the sovereignty of God in *historical* ⌐ *retribution.*

Look now at the fourth event: the *Babel Crisis,* with its multiple segregating of the human race, and its diversifying of human language. That tower of Babel, ambitiously started but never completed, centralized the first concerted racial attempt to oppose the will of God. The strange account of its interruption and abortion is so expressed as to put the emphasis once again upon the all-transcendent sovereignty of God. It is God who "came down to view it." It is God who "did there confound their language." It is God who "scattered them abroad upon the face of all the earth." As plainly as can be, we are meant to see that God is sovereign in *racial distribution.* ⌐

So, then, in the first part of Genesis we have those four tremendous events: the Creation, the Fall, the Flood, the Babel tower. In the first we see the sovereignty of God in the physical creation. In the second we see the sovereignty of God in human probation. In the third we see the sovereignty of God in historical retribution. In the fourth we see the sovereignty of God in racial distribution. Or, in alternate wording in those four extraordinary events we have: (1) God's eternal priority, (2) God's moral authority, (3) God's judicial severity, (4) God's governmental supremacy. Could there possibly be four far-reaching events more remarkably objectifying the *sovereignty* of God?

Yet when we look through the second part of Genesis (chapters 12 to 50) and review those four pivotal *persons,* Abraham, Isaac, Jacob, and Joseph, we see, if anything, an even more fascinating presentation of this divine sovereignty. This time it is the divine sovereignty expressed in divine choice, or *election.* √

In Abraham we see divine sovereignty in election, indicated in a supernatural *call.* Abram, later renamed Abraham, was the youngest of Terah's three sons; but, in electing one of those three sons for special purpose and blessing, God bypassed the primogeniture of the first-born son, also bypassed the second son, and selected the *youngest* son of Terah's family. The unusualness of it emphasizes the selective sovereignty of it.[1] Yes, note it carefully: In the case of Abraham we see divine sovereignty in election expressed through a supernatural call—a call such as had never before come to any other member of the human race.

Next, in Isaac we see divine sovereignty in election exhibited through a supernatural *birth*. Just when the divine promise of a son had become seemingly impossible of fulfillment, when Abraham was 100 years old, and his childless wife 90, the lovely miracle happened! Isaac was born! Abraham had said, "Oh, that Ishmael might live before Thee!" but God replied, "In Isaac shall thy seed be called." Thus, in Isaac, we see divine sovereignty in election made clear through a supernatural birth.

Next, in Jacob, we see divine sovereignty in election demonstrated through supernatural *care*. Jacob fled from home to escape the avenging fury of his brother, Esau, but God met him on the moors at dead of night and protected the unworthy fugitive from man and beast until he safely reached his uncle Laban at Padan-aram. There, for twenty years God prospered him despite all the adroit contrivings of his guileful uncle. Then, when he had to flee from the jealousy of Laban's household, and Laban pursued him with evil intent, God intercepted Laban and "suffered him not to hurt" Jacob. Next, when Esau, with long-slumbering revenge, learned that Jacob was back in adjacent territory, and marched against him with four hundred armed men, God suddenly turned Esau's lust for revenge into brotherly affection; and Esau, instead of falling on Jacob's neck with the sword, fell on it with a kiss! So the story goes on until, eventually, when Jacob was on his death-bed and the two sons of Joseph were brought to him for his patriarchal blessing, he said, "The Angel which redeemed me *from all evil*, bless the lads" (Gen. 48:16). It is indeed an eventful story, and all the way through it we see divine sovereignty in election disclosed through supernatural care.

Lastly, in Joseph, we see the same divine sovereignty expressed through supernatural *control*. What a drama was the life of Joseph! What a gem of a man—the loveliest character of the whole record! His life-story moved in three stages: (1) Joseph especially beloved of his father; (2) Joseph rejected, betrayed and sold by his brethren; (3) Joseph exalted to the right hand of the throne as the world's bread-supplier. He was thus a threefold type of our Lord Jesus. But the thing of particular concern here is that those three movements in Joseph's life were a developing unfolding of divine sovereignty in control. They show us how all permitted happenings, even the most contrary, are divinely anticipated and overruled, so that they dovetail into the predesigned plan and bring about the predetermined divine purpose, until at last Joseph himself could only say to his astonished brothers, "It was not you who sent me hither, but *God*" (Gen. 45:8).

That, then, is the Book of Genesis: part 1, four outstanding events; part 2, four outstanding persons. Recapitulate. See those four towering events and those four pivotal persons in their combined force. In the first part: event number one (the Creation)—divine sovereignty in the physical realm; event number two (the Fall)—divine sovereignty in human probation; event number three (the Flood)—divine sovereignty in historical retribution; event number four (the Babel tower)—divine sovereignty in racial distribution. In these we see successively: God's eternal priority; God's moral authority; God's judicial severity; God's governmental supremacy. Then, in the second part of Genesis, we have that successive exhibition of divine sovereignty in election: one, Abraham—supernatural *call*; two, Isaac—supernatural *birth*; three, Jacob—supernatural *care*; four, Joseph—supernatural *control*. Is it not clear that one unifying emphasis runs right through the book? Standing as the leader of the sixty-six documents which comprise the Bible, Genesis would bring us to our knees in reverent obeisance before God as it exhibits to our eyes and thunders in our ears the truth which is to be learned before all others in our approach to God, in our interpretation of history, in our study of divine revelation, in our investigation of the universe, and in our individual seeking of salvation, namely, *the sovereignty of God.*

Yes, hear it again, that is the first big insistence of the Bible: God is *sovereign*; and as we have said, all men and nations today should take careful note of it, for there is no other book like the Bible, no other book which makes such outright claims to be the inspired Word of God, and no other book which has such credentials of divine inspiration.

Let it be repeated: The biggest need of the nations today is to re-learn the biblical dictate of the divine sovereignty. No nation or society can maintain itself for long in true prosperity unless it has some acknowledged authority. Whatever the system of government may be, whether monarchy, oligarchy, democracy, or any other, there must be some definite seat of acknowledged and effective sovereignty. Whether it be military might which is recognized as that authority, or the force of long-established custom, or the voice of the people through a parliament or congress, there must be some sovereignty which society reverences, or else that society perishes.

Back in the 1920s and 1930s, why did the League of Nations fail? It was because there was no recognition of a supreme authority. In our own day, why does the United Nations Organization do so much futile fumbling and plunging from one wordy debacle to another? It is for the same reason. In a committee of nations there needs to be not only the *inter*national, but the *super*-national; that is, a super-national sovereignty in which all minor lordships are subsidiary and unified. But, instead of that, each nation nowadays is a self-styled "sovereign state"; and, strictly speaking, that is an absurd fallacy, for that which is "sovereign" is an end in itself, whereas no human government or state is an end in itself. The state was made for the people; not the people for the state. The state was meant to rule for God, not for its own lordship.

For well over half a century now communism has been the enforced way of managing Russia. It came in with bloody butchery and yelling atheism. It was going to show all other nations how superior communism is to capitalism and free enterprise. But what is the evidence of the past fifty years? Compared with free enterprise, communism has been an economic drag and flop. Everything which repudiates God turns out, sooner or later, to be a failure.

The Communists, like earlier anti-God governments, need to recognize that if you adamantly defy the one true God and the only true Savior of men, you will find, ere long, that you and your ambitious system are broken to pieces on the Rock which no human despots can ever move. In the words of Holy Scripture we say,

O earth, earth, earth, hear the Word of Jehovah (Jer. 22:29).

Jehovah hath prepared His throne in the heavens, and His kingdom ruleth over all (Psalm 103:19).

Hell is naked before Him....He stretcheth out the north over the empty space, and hangeth the earth upon nothing (Job 26:6, 7).

Who hath measured the waters in the hollow of His hand, and meted out the heavens with the span, and comprehended the dust of the earth in a measure, and weighed the mountains in scales, and the hills in a balance? Behold, the nations are as a drop of a bucket, and are counted as the small dust of the balance. Behold He taketh up the isles as a very little thing. Lift up your eyes on high, and behold who hath created these things, that bringeth out their host by number, and calleth them all by name (Isa. 40:12, 15, 26).

The pillars of heaven tremble and are astonished at His reproof.
He divideth the sea with His power, and by His understanding
He smiteth through the proud....Lo, these are but part of His
ways....But the thunder of His power who can imagine? (Job
26:11-14).

What a God! Oh, this great and glorious creator of all! How
wonderful beyond words is His compassion to the humble and His
patience with the prodigal! But how terrible is His anger against
those who defy Him and blaspheme His holy name! As Hebrews
10:31 says, "It is a fearful thing to fall into the hands of the living
God," for He is absolutely sovereign throughout the universe and
from everlasting to everlasting. None can really harm those whom
He protects; and none can ever escape who dare to defy Him.

Oh, this sovereignty of God! Well may it make the ungodly
tremble! But what unspeakable comfort it is to all of us Christian
believers! Whatever may be permitted to happen on this troubled
earth of ours before the present age crashes to its predicted terminus
at Armageddon, the reins of government will never hang loose in
the hands of our heavenly Father's sovereign control. That ever-
watchful God who lights the evening star and paints the wayside
lily, who sees the falling sparrow and counts the hairs of our head,
neither slumbers nor sleeps. His all-controlling watch-care will never
flag for a moment. Especially when times of tribulation break over
us He will be our "very present help in trouble." If we must go
through some seven-times-heated fiery furnace, one like unto the
Son of God will companion us there and bring us through so that
not even the smell of the fire lingers on us. That is our song who to
Jesus belong, for our Savior-God is absolutely *sovereign*.

THE BOOK OF THE PROPHET ISAIAH

We turn now, more briefly, to the prophet Isaiah. There also we
find the sovereignty of God emphasized, and in such a surprising
way that it claims the concentrated gaze of every thoughtful mind.
In a general way Isaiah's accent on the divine sovereignty is representative of all the Hebrew prophets. But the aspect of it presented
through Isaiah is so astounding that when once it is grasped our
thoughts about God can never be the same again.

All of us who are conversant with the prophecies of Isaiah know
what a unique blend of literary genius and supernatural inspiration
they are. Never was grander poetry written than we have in Job
and Isaiah; not poetry in our modern sense of rhyme and rhythm,
but in the form of thought parallelism. I need not take time discussing

whether Isaiah was the sole author of the book which bears his name. Let me simply say (without impropriety, I hope) that Volume 3 of my *Explore the Book* discusses the faultiness of the supposed arguments for a plural authorship, and seeks to show how conclusive are the evidences for one author only, namely, the well-known Isaiah who was the leading historiographer in King Hezekiah's guild of literary experts.

Isaiah's prophecies fall into two distinct series. The first runs through chapters 1 to 35. The second occupies chapters 40 to 66. The overall emphasis is Jehovah, the King who *governs all history*, and in each of the two series there is a key chapter. The key chapter in the first series (chapters 1 to 35) is chapter 6, in which Isaiah describes his transforming vision of the throne of heaven. The key chapter in the second series (chapers 40 to 66) is chapter 53, in which Isaiah describes Jehovah's suffering Servant, "despised and rejected of men." Both are well-known chapters. Read again the opening verses of chapter 6.

> In the year that king Uzziah died I saw also the Lord sitting upon a throne, high and lifted up, and His train filled the temple. Above it stood the seraphim: each one had six wings; with twain he covered his face, and with twain he covered his feet, and with twain he did fly. And one cried unto another and said, Holy, holy, holy is Jehovah of hosts; the whole earth is full of His glory. And the posts of the door moved at the voice of him that cried, and the house was filled with smoke. Then said I, Woe is me! for I am undone, because I am a man of unclean lips, and I dwell in the midst of a people of unclean lips; for mine eyes have seen THE KING, JEHOVAH OF HOSTS! (Isa. 6:1-5).

Every feature of this apocalyptic vision is intensely meaningful, but here I mention two only. The first is very obvious, namely, the high point of the vision is that overpoweringly holy, fire-clad figure seated on that glory-flashing throne; and the center-point of the vision is the prostrate prophet's awed exclamation, "Mine eyes have seen the King, Jehovah of hosts!" The other thing is the remarkable comment on it in the New Testament, in the twelfth chapter of John, verse 41: "These things said Isaiah when he saw *His* [Christ's] glory, and spake of *Him!*" It was none other than our pre-existent Savior before whom those flashing seraphs cried, "Holy, holy, holy," and before whom the very foundation of the heavenly sanctuary trembled. There He was, in that flaming super-throne, reigning in all-transcendent omnipotence as Creater-Controller of the universe, supreme over the histories and destinies of all nations and people—absolutely *sovereign!*

And now pass from that key sixth chapter in part one to the key fifty-third chapter in part two.

> Who hath believed our report? And to whom is the arm of
> Jehovah revealed? For He shall grow up before Him as a tender
> plant, and as a root out of a dry ground: He hath no form nor
> comeliness, and when we shall see Him there is no beauty that
> we should desire Him. He is despised and rejected of men; a man
> of sorrows, and acquainted with grief; and we hid as it were our
> faces from Him; He was despised and we esteemed Him not.
> Surely He hath borne our griefs, and carried our sorrows; yet
> we did esteem Him stricken, smitten of God and afflicted. But
> He was wounded for our transgressions, He was bruised for our
> iniquities; the chastisement of our peace was upon Him; and
> with His stripes we are healed. All we like sheep have gone
> astray; we have turned every one to His own way; and Jehovah
> hath laid on Him the iniquity of us all (Isa. 53:1-6).

To whom does this fifty-third chapter refer? Remarkably enough, that same twelfth chapter of John's Gospel which says that the enthroned Lord in Isaiah 6 was Christ, also tells us that the despised Sufferer in Isaiah 53 was the very same Person. John 12:37, 38 says: "But though He [Jesus] had done so many signs before them, yet they believed not on Him; that the word of Isaiah might be fulfilled which He spake: Lord, who hath believed our report?"

You can tell by the way Isaiah 53 is written that Isaiah was living in it and vividly seeing it. He is writing with a sense of shock. The thing which rivets his eyes is that the one whom he now sees thrashed and bleeding, despised and deserted, execrated and dying in lonely anguish is the one whom he had before seen on that heavenly throne "high and lifted up" in overpowering splendor. Now, amid that stark ugliness of torturous execution, Isaiah recognizes Him and is staggered. And what can *we* say? What can we do? Shall we shudder with horror, that the infinitely holy one who reigned in that ineffable throne of universal sovereignty now languishes bleeding in depthless anguish as our race's sin-bearer? Or shall we shout with utter gratitude and adoring wonder that He loved us to such a sheer "uttermost"?

To see the Crown Prince of heaven hanging naked, shamed, mocked, pain-racked on that cross for you and me, black and blue from fist-blows, with blood cascading down from thorn-scars on His brow, from lacerations in His back, and from nail-holes through His hands and feet, and a gaping gash in His side....!

Does it not leave us dumbfounded? The one who hangs on that cross is *God!*—the God who made the universe! He is the one who, before He became humanly born of the virgin Mary, sat upon that super-throne in the excellent glory! The one who allows Himself to be publicly shamed, spat upon, flogged, and agonizingly pinioned to that splintery cross is the one who is eternally, universally and absolutely *sovereign*! As we have seen, in the Book of Genesis the sovereignty of God is shown in the physical creation, in human probation, in historical retribution, in racial distribution, and in purposive election. But here, in Isaiah, we see the sovereignty of God in *redemption*. Divine sovereignty steps down in vast self-abasement from that all-transcendent throne to that cross of unfathomable grief and self-sacrifice! The King of kings sheds His diadems to be baptized in tears and blood! The Monarch and Controller of all becomes the Servant and Sin-bearer of all!

That cross says something which may well astound us. It is this: God is *humble* Yes, the God by whose creative power and permit all of us human beings exist in our millions, along with all the numberless hosts of angels and all the myriads of other intelligences who may occupy planets and systems thousands of light years away from our own tiny earth, the God who created us all is the *humblest* of us all! Calvary says so. God's words are wonderful, but His deeds are even *more* wonderful, and Calvary is His greatest speech of all. It cost God far more to redeem our world than to create it. God carries the whole universe on His shoulders with ease, but when He carried the cross to Calvary He staggered and fell! God can carry Orion and the Pleiades and the whole Milky Way in the fingers of one hand, but when He carried the burden of humanity's sin and guilt He sweat drops of blood; for (remember!) the heavenly Father suffered in all the sufferings of the incarnate Son.

Look again, then, at that cross in the light of Isaiah 6 and 53. Get the new slant on the divine sovereignty. That sovereignty is not just the activity of the divine will; much less is it the all-embracing grip of a despot. The sovereignty of God must never be thought of apart from all else that God is besides His will. It must never be detached from His holiness, wisdom, goodness, kindness and love, or it can become, at least theoretically, a grinding terror making the whole universe a nightmare. Let it be said again for emphasis: God is far more than an all-dominating will; therefore His sovereignty is not solely a predestinating omnipotence. Let us give thanks for this: the sovereignty of God is the all-controlling expression of His moral and ethical perfection. It is His righteousness, justice, wisdom, sympathy, love and fatherhood in continual operation. As such the divine sovereignty is the moral safeguard of the universe; and therefore it is as comforting to the godly as it is frightening to the wicked. I, for one, am deeply consoled to know that such a God really *is* sovereign. It does much for my peace of mind in days like these.

Again, the sovereignty of God must not be thought of as rigid, like a huge iron vice which holds everything in unrelaxing grip. Certainly, in the physical realm it works through the inflexible laws of nature which are so fixed that they can be expressed in mathematical formulas; but in the moral and spiritual realm of free-willed creatures it operates differently. There is flexibility in it. The sovereignty of God never tramples on human free-will. It continually adapts itself to the responses of human hearts. God created us human beings for fellowship with Himself, and in order to have such fellowship man must be free. There cannot be communion with robots. There is no such thing as automatic fellowship. It must be the volitional, spontaneous reciprocity of free beings. Therefore the sovereignty of God toward His intelligent, free-willed creatures is flexible in its operation. When human hearts change toward God, the sovereignty of God changes toward *them*. When long-ago Nineveh repented of its wickedness, the divine sovereignty relented toward Nineveh, so that instead of immediate judgment there was merciful postponement. When God faithfully forewarned His covenant people, Israel, through Moses 3,500 years ago that if they walked in His statutes He would munificently bless them, but that if they disobeyed He would correspondingly chastise them, He was clearly saying that His sovereignty would act in whatever way Israel's behavior required.

Let no one think that the divine purposes for our human race are thus made to depend on the uncertain will of man, or that the divine sovereignty is dragged in chains behind the chariot wheels of human perversity. There is no incompatibility between divine sovereignty and human free-will. The truth is, that God has superimposed upon our race's history certain far-reaching purposes which He is working out high above all creature interference. Within the big scope of those purposes man is given ample freedom of unfettered choice and conduct, so that at all times individual men and women know that they are acting of their own free choosing. But at the same time, because God foreknows every reaction of the human will, both individual and racial, from the beginning to the end of time, He anticipates and overrules *everything* to the ultimate realization of His ultimate purpose. Thus, in the end, even "the wrath of man" is made to "praise" Him (Ps. 76:10).

Yes, man is free, but God is sovereign. Satan-Diabolos also is free; so are the demons who share in his insurrection against God.

The archfiend and his confederates have rebelled against God's ruling, but even they cannot escape God's *over*ruling. Inside the sovereignty of God there is ample room for fateful opposites. Inside that sovereignty there is a "great white throne" of judgment, and there is a crimson cross of Calvary. Inside that sovereignty there is a moral law which says, "The soul that sinneth, it shall die"; and there is a gospel of free grace which says, "He that believeth shall never perish." Inside that sovereignty there is at present a personal devil who is permitted to tempt and undo men; and there is a dear Savior who "saves to the uttermost" all them that "come unto God by Him." Inside that sovereignty there is at present permitted sin and evil on earth, and there is also a provided salvation which offers "free grace" to free-willed men. Inside that sovereignty there lies, on the other side of the grave, a sinless, fadeless heaven, which may be ours through that crimson Calvary, and there is also a fearful Gehenna to which impenitent men can go by judicial sentence from that "great white throne" of judgment.

[1] That Abram was Terah's youngest son is confirmed by the following considerations. First, in Genesis 11:26, "Terah lived seventy years and begat Abram, Nahor, and Haran." As the three sons were not triplets they could not have been born the same year; therefore the meaning is that they were born successively *after* Terah was seventy. Abram is mentioned first because of his historical preeminence. What, then, was the order of birth? Terah, the father, died at age 205 (Gen. 11:32) at which time Abram was 75 (see 12:4) which means that he had not been born until Terah was 130 years old. So, which of the other two was born when Terah was seventy? The likelihood is that it was Haran, who "died before his father."(11:28) but left a son named Lot who, although he was Abram's nephew, was apparently not much younger than Abram, as he is an "old" man in chapter 19 (see verse 19, and note in verse 14 that already he had "sons in law").

Finally, in chapter 24, Isaac the *son* of Abraham marries the *granddaughter* of his father's brother, Nahor, which again indicates that Nahor (24:15) must have been considerably senior to Abraham. Clearly Abraham was not as old as either of his two brothers. He was the youngest son of Terah.

3

The Sovereignty of God— The New Testament Testimony

We have seen something of the divine sovereignty as exhibited in the first book of Holy Scripture and in the first book of the Hebrew prophets. Let us catch further glimpses of it now as it gleams through the first book of the New Testament.

All who are familiar with the four gospels know that each has its own distinctives in presenting our Lord Jesus. In Matthew's narrative everything is contributory to showing that Jesus is Israel's long-promised Messiah-King. Just as Mark presents Him especially as Jehovah's *Servant*, and Luke presents Him as the ideal *Man*, and John presents Him as incarnate *God*, so Matthew focuses on our Lord's *kingship* as the promised Messiah.

Right away, in the opening genealogy, Matthew connects Him to Abraham and David, i.e., with the Abrahamic covenant He was to fulfill and the Davidic throne He was to occupy. Then comes the Sermon on the Mount, expounding ten first-principles in the *moral code* of the King. Then the next few chapters record ten miracles evincing the *credentials* of the King (8-10). Then the next few chapters report ten responses by different groups showing the varied *attitudes* to the King (11-18). Then, in chapters 19 to 25, everything leads to our Lord's public *offer* of Himself as Messiah-King in Jerusalem. Next, in chapters 26 and 27 there comes the *crucifixion* of the King, with a wooden tablet fixed above His head, "This is Jesus the *King of the Jews.*" Finally comes the titanic climax—the *resurrection* of the King.

Our Lord had said He would "rise again the third day," but His disciples had not grasped it. Their minds were too shocked by His telling them that He was now on His way, not to a throne as they had expected, but to be "condemned," "scourged," "mocked," "killed"

(Mk. 10:33,34). The scribes, chief priests and Pharisees had heard Him say that He would rise, but they pooh-poohed it, especially when His head fell forward in death on the cross. They all thought of death as the once-for-all departure from which there was no return. That cross finished the Nazarene—so they gloated. Both friends and foes assumed that the black deed on craggy Golgotha was the end of Jesus. None ever dreamed that when once He was plainly dead and His corpse was entombed, He would ever be seen on earth again. Nor did even Satan have any advance apprizement of it, or he would never have hounded our Lord to the cross as he did through human dupes. Nor was it known beforehand by any of the angels, either fallen or unfallen; nor to any of the Old Testament prophets, for it is nowhere explicitly predicted in the Old Testament.

Death and the grave were the big, final *test* of our Lord's kingship. If He remained the devil's prisoner in Hades while His body rotted in the tomb, then He was *not* Israel's Messiah-King. He had cleansed the leper, healed the sick, cured the cripple, expelled the demon, given sight to the blind, hearing to the deaf, speech to the dumb, and had even brought the dead back to life; but now He Himself was dead, apparently unable to save Himself. The cross had made Him seem eventually helpless. As He hung there, firmly transfixed to that beam and transom, the chief priests and scribes had taunted Him for His forlornness, "If He be the *king* of Israel, let Him now come down from the cross, and we will believe on Him" (Matt. 27:42).

Yes, that grave was the big, final test. It would prove, once for all, whether He was victim or victor, whether He was Messiah or mistaken, whether He was merely "son of man" or Son of God. Could He come back from the vaults of Sheol or Hades into which He had passed as a disembodied being? Could He overpower that clever monster of evil, Satan, who until then had held "the power of death" (Heb. 2:14)? Could He wrest "the keys of Hades and death" (Rev. 1:18) from the evil jailer, swing back the "gates of Hades," come out from there, re-enter the sepulchre, see His own corpse lying inside there on that rocky ledge, re-occupy it, re-animate it, resurrect it, and re-emerge on earth in that very same body, with a new bodily life which death could never touch again? Could He do all that, and then ascend in that immortal body above all spirit-powers, both friendly and hostile, to the throne of God, to present that ageless, deathless human body there as His proof to God and the universe that He had indeed broken the power of sin and Satan and death forever? If He could do that, then not only is He King; He is King over *all* kings, and Lord over *all* lords. Well, *did* He do it? Did He turn that blood-drained corpse into a living organism again? Yes! Has He really risen in that crucified body? Yes! Is He now alive in that very same though now deathless body? Yes! Has He ascended up to heaven in that radiant, imperishable manhood as the file-leader of a new humanity called "the sons of God"? Yes! Then He *is* the King! In eternal unobliterable capitals, He is THE KING!

But that is not all. Matthew's record has one more thing to add. Turn to his last chapter and the last paragraph. Read it again. If we had not grown so familiar with it, would it not startle and thrill us beyond words?

> And Jesus came and spake unto them, saying: All power is given unto Me in heaven and on earth. Go ye therefore and disciple all nations, baptizing them in the name of the Father, and of the Son, and of the Holy Spirit: teaching them to observe all things whatsoever I have commanded you; and, lo, I am with you every day, even to the end of the age. Amen (28:18-20).

Think of it: "All power is given unto Me, in heaven and on earth"! That word "power" in the Greek is *exousia* which means power, not in the sense of energy but as administrative *authority.* So our Lord's announcement is, "All authority is given unto Me, in heaven and on earth." See the all-encircling *inclusiveness* of it: "All authority...in *heaven* and on *earth.*" See the *limitlessness* of it: "*All* authority." See the *concentratedness* of it: "All authority is given unto *Me...*"—to the exclusion of all others. It means that the control of all issues is in His hands, including the destinies of all nations and of all human individuals. Stars, orbs, angels, demons, all creature-intelligences, even the exquisite seraphs, are subordinated now to *His* determinative governance.

This may well be called the *grand surprise.* Old Testament prediction had made plain that the coming Christ should be the "son of David," and that as such He should reign not only over a regathered Israel but over all the Gentile nations as well. The inspired psalmist had sung that the royal Messiah should have "dominion from sea to sea, and from the river to the ends of the earth," that "all kings" should "fall down before him, and all nations serve him" (Ps. 72:8). But nowhere does Old Testament prophecy fore-disclose that His regal administration, besides being global, would include the *heavens,* and that all the "principalities and powers" of the spirit-spheres should be swept into subservience to His behest.

Note carefully *when* this boundless imperial jurisdiction became His. He says, "All authority *was* given unto Me." The Greek verb is in the aorist tense, referring to a past point of time. What point of time was it? It was when our Lord emerged from that garden sepulchre and walked on earth again in that resurrected body which had been interred as a crucified corpse. At that point the administration of the universe passed into the hands which bore the nail-prints!

Did I say this was the grand surprise? So it was, but it was even more. It marked a startling new turn in the exercise of the divine sovereignty. Can we ever get over the wonder of it? The sovereignty of God is now wielded through and by one who, both in form and nature, is *man*! The prophets Isaiah and Ezekiel, in their visions of the heavenly throne, saw one reigning there in "the likeness and appearance of a man." That Man in the throne is no longer merely a prophetic vision; it is an astounding reality! *Jesus* is there!

I call it "astounding" with good reason. At some point before God refashioned our planet to become the abode of mankind, Lucifer, that super-star among the angels, vaingloriously aspired to sit upon that divine throne, and to wield "all authority in heaven and on earth." His surpassing brilliance of intellect, power and beauty was the very thing which he allowed to betray him into his inane covetousness toward God. He knew that he was not God, but he said, "I will be *like* the Most High" (Isa. 14:14). Self-intoxicated with power-consciousness he thought himself able to manage things equally well as God did. On being denied occupancy of the throne, he rebelled and was stripped of his vice-regency over this earth. There then flamed up in his conceited mind the first hatred ever known in the universe. The alpha star became the archfiend and the instigator of anti-Godism.

As soon as God put this earth under the overlordship of man, Satan contrived to cheat man of his crown and scepter, and succeeded; from which time Satan has been the usurper "prince of this world." Eventually, in the simple-hearted, guileless, self-denying Jesus, Satan met his match, and Calvary was his Waterloo. The little Lamb proved stronger than the "great red dragon"! The stripling David laid low the bragging Goliath! Jesus defeated Satan, not by His inherent power as the incarnate Son of God, but by His invincible moral purity as *man*. Even as man, Jesus is mentally and morally stronger than Satan. Not even Satan's cleverest wiles or most frightening assaults could deflect Jesus one inch from utter obedience to the Father's will. Satan was thus beaten on his own ground. He is still maliciously active, but he is a beaten foe—just as Hitler was a beaten foe for eighteen months before he committed suicide and the Second World War was over. Satan's anti-God campaign continues, but the decisive battle has been fought. He struggles on, but his zero hour is now near. Armageddon will crumple him, and he who has made cruel chains for so many human beings will himself be bound in chains, in the "abyss," that is, in the deepest dungeon of Hades (Isa. 14:15, Rev. 20:3).

Can you imagine Satan's humiliating mortification when Jesus, in the glow of His resurrection mastery, said, "All authority is given unto *Me*, in heaven and on earth"? Can you conceive Satan's tantalizing frustration as he sees Jesus now in that throne, "far above all"? Man, whom Satan dragged as low as only Satan could drag him, God has now lifted as high as only God can lift him! That indeed is now the super-fact in the drama of God, man, and Satan. Man, in the person of the crucified, risen and glorified Lord Jesus, now sits on the very throne of "the Majesty on high." Our dear Savior, of course, has always belonged in that throne as the eternal Son of God, but the thrill of all Christian hearts is that He is now there as "Son of *Man*." Therein lies the startling new turn in the operation of the divine sovereignty. That sovereignty is now exercised by one who looks at us through human eyes, and listens to us with human ears, and loves us with a love which has a human heart-beat in it, and feels for us with human susceptibilities, and beckons to us with human hands. Oh, this new wonder of the divine sovereignty! Oh, this wonderful new guarantee that the God of the sin-troubled earth may be trusted, despite the permitted havoc wrought by Satan! Oh, what gladdening relief of mind, to know that humanity and history and the total future are in those dear, pierced hands! The whole universe seems safer and kinder. The green earth and the starry skies are redolent with suggestions of a gracious, all-pervading presence; and my heart breaks into singing again,

Heaven above is softer blue,
Earth around is sweeter green,
Something lives in every hue
Christless eyes have never seen;
Birds with gladder songs o'erflow,
Flow'rs with deeper beauty shine,
Since I know, as now I know,
I am His, and He is mine.

THE LAST BOOK OF THE BIBLE

We turn now to the last book of Holy Scripture, the Patmos Apocalypse, or "Book of the Revelation," as we call it. Hundreds of treatises have been written ostensibly elucidating its supposedly esoteric symbols and enigmas. Some of those treatises would give one the impression that the Book of Revelation is the "curiosity shop" of the Bible. It has been a playground for fanciful imagination. I have sometimes marvelled at the facility with which certain authors can see what is not there, yet miss seeing what really *is* there. The biggest thing of all in it is the way it objectifies the divine sovereignty. There it is, right at the end of the Bible, with a final completive insistence that in the outright sense of absolute monarchy, *God is sovereign.*

In line with that, let me draw attention to a significant peculiarity in the book. There is a Greek adjectival noun repeatedly used in it which does not occur anywhere else in the New Testament except once in a quotation from the Old Testament. It is the compound word, *pantokrator.* In our standard English versions of the New Testament *pantokrator* is generally translated as our word, "almighty." It certainly does mean almighty, but it is almightiness with a distinctive complexion. Look at that Greek word for a moment—*pantokrator.* The prefix, *pan,* means "all." The remainder, *krator,* means power, but especially power in the sense that the word, *krator,* is united with *pan* in the adjective, *pantokrator.* The special meaning is all-dominion. The nearest English translation of it is "all-sovereign." With that in mind let us quickly look up the passages where *pantokrator* occurs in the Apocalypse.

Chapter 1:8 "I am Alpha and Omega, the
beginning and the ending, saith
the Lord, which is, and which was,
and which is to come, the
ALL-SOVEREIGN."

Chapter 4:8 "And the four living ones had each
of them six wings about Him; and
they are full of eyes around and
within: and they rest not day or
night, saying, Holy, holy, holy,
Lord God *ALL-SOVEREIGN*, which
was, and is and is to come."

Chapter 11:17 "We give thee thanks, O Lord God
ALL-SOVEREIGN, which art, and
wast, and art to come; because Thou
hast taken to Thee Thy great power,
and hast reigned."

Chapter 15:3 "And they sing the song of Moses
the servant of God, and the song of

the Lamb, saying: Great and mar-
vellous are thy works, Lord God
ALL-SOVEREIGN; just and true
are Thy ways, thou King of the
ages."

Chapter 16:7 "And I heard another out of the
altar say: Even so, Lord God, the
ALL-SOVEREIGN, true and righteous
are Thy judgments."

Chapter 16:14 "They are the spirits of demons
working miracles, which go forth
unto the kings of the earth and of
the whole world, to gather them to
the battle of that great day of God
the *ALL-SOVEREIGN.*"

Chapter 19:6 "And I heard as it were the voice
of a great multitude, and as the
voice of many waters, and as the
voice of mighty thunderings,
saying, Hallelujah; for the Lord
our God, the *ALL-SOVEREIGN,*
reigneth."

Chapter 19:15 "And out of His mouth goeth a sharp
sword, that with it He should smite
the nations: and He treadeth the
winepress of the fierceness and
wrath of God the *ALL-SOVEREIGN.*"

Chapter 21:22 "And I saw no temple therein (i.e.,
in the New Jerusalem); for the Lord
God the *ALL-SOVEREIGN,* and the
Lamb, are the temple thereof."

The adjective, *pantokrator*, is never used of any being other than
God Himself. He alone is all-sovereign. But do you observe how
clearly, now, in the Apocalypse, that all-sovereignty is equally pre-
dicated of our Lord Jesus? It is noticeable right from the beginning.
See chapter one, verses 5 and 6.

"Grace be unto you, and peace...from Jesus Christ, who is the faithful witness, and the first-begotten of the dead, and the Ruler of the kings of the earth. Unto Him that loved us, and washed us from our sins in His own blood, and hath made us kings and priests unto God and His Father; to Him be the glory and the *sovereignty* unto the ages of the ages. Amen."

Such sovereignty "unto the ages of the ages" means nothing less than that our Lord's sovereignty is a coequal sovereignty with that of the eternal Father. Again and again this coequal sovereignty of Christ with the Father flashes out in these pictorial revealings of the Apocalypse, until, when we come to the last chapter, we find it climaxed in the New Jerusalem, amid the fadeless glories of the coming new order which will yet transform our earth into a planet paradise. What are the two most important things in any capital city? They are the *temple* and the *throne*, for those two represent worship and government—which more than all else determine the moral quality and collective well-being of any society. What, then, about the temple and the throne in the New Jerusalem? As for the temple, in chapter 21:22 we read,

The Lord God all-sovereign, and the Lamb, are the temple of it.

As for the throne, chapter 22:3-5 tells us,

The throne of God and the Lamb shall be in it, and His servants shall serve Him...and they shall reign unto the ages of the ages.

That is the ultimate, endless glory which the "all- sovereignty" of God holds in its determination for the future of this earth. As certainly as Jesus rose from the grave, Jerusalem shall yet "shake herself free from the dust" and put on her "beautiful garments." The earth itself, also, shall be loosed from the iron bands of sin and the curse, and shall go singing in its orbit around the sun—singing praise to its sovereign Savior-God through millions and millions of enraptured, unsinning human hearts.

Such, then, in brief outline, is the Bible picture of the divine sovereignty. How grateful for it we may well be! In Genesis we see that sovereignty in physical creation, in human probation, in historical retribution, in racial distribution and in individual election. In Isaiah we see that sovereignty stepping down in vast self-abasement from that highest of thrones in heaven to that deepest of woes on Calvary for the sake of earth's perishing sinners. In Matthew we see the administration of that all-sovereignty committed to the risen Savior, the God-Man. In the Apocalypse we see that sovereignty finally emphasized as the joint all-sovereignty of God and the Lamb.

MEANINGS FOR TODAY

How does it all speak to us today? Well, first, should it not the more convince us that this sovereignty superintends the whole of human history? We could refer to many happenings during the centuries which convergently indicate this super-guidance of all earthly events by a watchful heaven. I mention just one—the preservation of the nation Israel. Of all the stories ever written the two most wonderful are the story of the Jewish race and that of the Christian church. Both are true. Both are yet unfinished. Both are filled with alternating triumph and tragedy. Both are to have a final chapter of glorious consummation.

The Nation Israel

In all the records of kings and nations is there anything to match the history of the covenant people from Abraham, Isaac and Jacob onward? Never was there any other such high calling with such deep sinning; never such divine covenant with such human violation; never such a theocracy dishonored by such apostasy; never such unique privilege with such big responsibility. Never was there such a heaven-ordained national ministry and destiny, seemingly frustrated yet persevering through unfolding millenniums, and sovereignly predetermined to issue even yet in a golden age of final realization.

Never has any race or nation suffered such recurrent slaughterings and scatterings without becoming eventually disintegrated into extinction. If the Jewish people could have retained at least some small territorial foothold somewhere on earth, there might have been some semblance of an answer for their continual survival. But for over two thousand years they have had no throne, no kingdom, no colony, no land, no city, no laws of their own. *Yet they are still here!* They have been hated, deprived, peeled, persecuted, suppressed, massacred, driven as helpless fugitives to the four winds. *Yet they are still here!* From the time of Xerxes (Ahasuerus) about 500 B.C., down to the demon-possessed Adolph Hitler of recent date, they have been hounded, tortured, burned together or buried alive together in hundreds or thousands by maddened Jew-haters determined to stamp them out completely. (Hitler slew millions of them!) *Yet they are still here!*

They are back in their own land—"Eretz Yizrael"—with their own government, their own laws, their own legal system, their own coins, their own language and their own preserved institutions. They have had no king of their own, nor have they had any independent self-government since the long-ago days of the Maccabees. Yet now, after an historical hiatus of 2,300 years, they are again acknowledged by the other nations as a self-governing Jewish state! There has never been anything like it in all history.

What does this say to you and me? It says that God is sovereign in history. It says that whatever God may allow to happen in His present, *permissive* will, He overrules all permitted happenings so as ultimately to fulfill His *purposive* will. It says that God does not violate the free-will of men and nations, but allows them to learn through self-incurred suffering, while at the same time He overrules all to a final, righteous outcome. Nothing can ultimately defeat God. His purpose always triumphs in the end.

No philosophy of history is true which does not take into account the sovereign hand of God controlling all permitted developments. God is still God. He has not abdicated. Neither has He changed. Nor has He slackened His control over the nations. He is yet just as truly God though millions of people are still self-blinded to His sovereign activity.

> When statesmen have had their last parley,
> And despots have made their last threat;
> When prophets are dumb with misgiving,
> And forces of conflict are set;
> When factions misleading and treacherous
> Bring chaos where order prevailed;
> When freedom long-cherished is vanquished,
> And leaders long trusted have failed,
> When God and His Word are derided,
> And men call it useless to pray;
> Remember that God is still sovereign,
> And *HE* has the last word to say.

Divine Sovereignty and the Christian

Let our final word be to those of us who are Christian believers. The biblical doctrine of the divine sovereignty should be both challenging and solidly comforting to us. Let me mention four ways in which we should relate ourselves to it.

First, let us thoroughly believe it and speak of it. Some of us have voices which travel further than average: We can be heard in influential circles. Others of us may think that we can scarcely be heard at all. Whichever way it is with us, some reference to the sovereignty of God should often be on our lips, whatever kind of company we are in. Perhaps more than we suspect in these days when things seem to have gone badly askew, people want to be reminded that the reins are in higher hands than those of human governments. Others who may not *want* to hear it are all the more in *need* of hearing somebody say it. It is the missing note which we Christians must keep sounding.

Second, let us not be swept off our feet by the lengths to which anti-God powers may be permitted to go during this closing stretch of the present age. The Bible has forewarned us; yet somehow, when frightening developments actually occur, they too easily over-shock or alarm us. It will be much conducive to our inward stability and composure if we practice a continual mindfulness of our heavenly Keeper's all-control.

Third, if God is still sovereign (and He is), then there is still the possibility of a big-scale spiritual revival. So long as God abides sovereign, and promises like 2 Chronicles 7:14, John 14:13, Ephesians 3:20, 21, and others are in the Bible, mighty visitations may come from our prayer-answering God. Are we not seeing such today in different parts of the world? Be the world-situation what it may, so long as that throne in heaven is the "throne of grace" big answers may be expected by way of soul-saving spiritual awakenings. Look at that throne again—the "throne of grace." It is a "*throne*," for God is sovereign; but it is a throne of "*grace*" because that sovereignty delights to honor the pleadings of the saints.

Fourth, more than ever, let us Christians *rest* in the sovereignty of God. It is thinkable that before many more moons have waxed and waned we may have to suffer for our faith. The words of James 4:14 seem more tremulously true today than ever before: "Ye know not what shall be on the morrow." This we do know, that godless communism now covers half the earth, and godless communism is the ugly, cruel, ultimate denial of God's sovereignty. Already, in recent days, millions have suffered and died for "conscience' sake," and countless victims this very day are having to endure bonds and imprisonment for their Christian faith. If such fierce testing should come our way, let us remember that God is sovereign even when His presence seems least real and the agents of Satan seem unrestrained. If we have to go through the lions' den our God will bring us out at last without a claw-mark on us. If we must go through the seven-times-heated furnace, we shall meet the risen Lord there, and He will bring us out at last without even the smell of the fire upon us.

For the unbeliever and the wicked, the sovereignty of God may well be terrifying, but to the yielded, trusting Christian it is "joy unspeakable." Christian, rest in it. Commit everything to God even though your world seems shaken to its foundations (as my own has been lately). Lie still on His bosom, and listen to the heart-beat of that boundless love from which all the demons either inside or outside of Hades can never pluck you. Do you wish the sovereignty of God to pledge this to you in black and white? Then here it is, in Romans 8:37-39:

> We are more than conquerors through Him that loved us. For...neither death, nor life, nor angels, nor principalities, nor powers, nor things present, nor things to come, nor height, nor depth, nor any other created being, shall ever be able to separate us from the love of God which is in Christ Jesus our Lord.

God is still on the throne,
And He will take care of His own;
Though trials distress us,
And burdens oppress us,
He never will leave us alone:
God is still on the throne,
And He will take care of His own;
His promise is true,
He will see us right through;
God is still on the throne.

4

Triunity in the Old Testament

For most people, the triunity of God is harder to grasp than any other Christian doctrine. It seems an insoluble puzzle that God can be one yet three, or three yet one. Mysterious beyond our comprehension it assuredly is, but the mystery of it no more disproves the reality of it than mystery ever disproves what is actually true.

Moreover, it is well to reflect that this triunity is not the biggest problem in our thinking about God. The most baffling mystery is the *eternality* of God. It seems impossible for these finite minds of ours to imagine a being who never began, but always was, or rather, eternally is—absolutely unbeginning and never-ending. Yet if we do not believe that, what is the alternative? If God had a beginning, then what or who was before Him? He could not have come from nothing. Yet if someone created Him, where did that earlier creator come from?—and who created *him*?—and *his* predecessor? And so we might go further and further back *ad infinitum*, never solving but only compounding the difficulty.

However hard it is to grasp that God never began, it is even more so to believe that He ever *did* begin. Least credible of all is atheism; for if God is *not*, where did all other beings come from? Where did the whole stupendous, organized universe of mind and matter come from? The alternative offered by atheism is absurd.

Involved in the eternality of God is the *infinity* of God, and that again is a staggering mystery beyond our comprehension. It is well nigh impossible for us to apprehend a being who is absolutely boundless; never-never-never-ending in every direction—upward, downward, rightward, leftward—continually filling all conceivable space. Yet if God *has* any boundaries, what is outside Him? And if space ends in any direction, what is outside it? If there *is* anything outside God and space, where does *that* end? And if there is nothing outside God and space, what is nothing? And where does *that* end?

If infinity is boundlessness absolute, then it has no center. Lucretius (first century B.C.), whose treatise, *On the Nature of the Universe*, lately became the cornerstone of Einstein's theory of relativity, said, "There is no center in infinity." Heraclitus, away back in the fifth or sixth century B.C., put the same in different words: "The way up and the way down are one and the same." Quite so: If infinity is sheer boundlessness, it has no dimensions; there is no up or down or sideways. To which we may add that, if eternity is beginningless and endless, it has no middle. Time has a middle because it began and will end, but eternity knows neither past nor future. The universe has a center because it had a beginning and has bounds, but infinity has neither center nor circumference. We are in the realm of utter inconceivables, but what alternative does atheism offer? It offers none but the preposterous.

No, the triunity of God is not the hardest problem in our thinking about the divine being. It is only one of the mysteries enveloping Him; an inexpressibly wonderful mystery, and indeed an exceedingly precious mystery, as we soon shall be reflecting.

There are those who complain that the Christian doctrine of the triunity makes faith too complicated. But when one looks round at some of the more recently disseminated ideas of God, as for instance in the varied forms of Hegelianism and neo-Hegelianism, pluralism, rationalistic existentialism, or when one examines the divinity vagaries of Hinduism and Buddhism, the Bible doctrine of the triune God is simple by comparison.

First, then, how do we know that God is triune? Well, obviously it is one of those realities which, if we are to learn of it at all, must be divinely revealed. It is not something which has been discovered by human investigation, or deduced from the logic of facts, or inferred from converging data. Nor can it be found in any of the non-biblical religions. It can be known only within the sphere of Christian revelation. We Christians have never pretended that the triunity of God can be arrived at philosophically, or demonstrated mathematically or ascertained scientifically. It is exclusively a truth divinely disclosed to us. That revelation comes to us in the Bible and supremely through the Lord Jesus Christ. Therefore its validity stands or falls with the inspiration of the Bible and especially with the witness of the Lord Jesus. In fact, the Christian doctrine of the triunity never could have come into being apart from the revelation of the eternal which was wrought on the earth in the person, life, teaching, death and resurrection of our Lord Jesus Christ.

This revelation of God as a triunity must be sharply distinguished from every form of *tritheism*, the concept of three Gods. It is far removed from the Indian trinity of Brahma, Siva and Vishnu; also from the Egyptian divine family of Osiris, Isis and Horus; and from the neo-Platonic trinity of Reason, Creator, World. The God of the New Testament is not a triad of three separable divinities. Triunity is not merely triplicity. Let it be said over and over again: We Christians are not tritheists, believers in three Gods; we are monotheists, believers in one God eternally existing as a triunity.

Down through the *anno Domini* centuries, the Christian church alone has held and taught this doctrine of the one and only true God existing in the triunity of Father, Son, and Holy Spirit, and has maintained it against the fecund polytheism of heathenism, the rigid monotheism of Jewry, the fiery unitarianism of Mohammedanism, the sterile vagaries of dialectic atheism and the persuasive but disruptive aberrations of heretics.

When we say, for convenience, that there are three "persons" in the Godhead, even that can give a wrong impression; for all other persons known to us are separate entities living within the confines of their own intellect, free will, emotion and self-awareness, having no connection in essence with any other individual. The Father, the Son, and the Holy Spirit are not three persons in that way. Yet neither are they three *non*-personal modes of expression in the one God, as some have thought. They are three real distinctions within the Godhead, each having distinct consciousness, will, feeling, personalness, yet all coalescing in the one essential being of the only true God. We use the expression "three persons" as being approximately useful, and to avoid employing theologically technical phraseology such as "one divine hypostasis in three subsistencies." To the average person, this certainly would leave God distant, frigid, enigmatical, unattractive. Actually, when we rightly understand it, the threefold personalness of God is the most magnetic doctrine in the Bible.

How then did the Christian doctrine of the divine triunity originate? Was it stated in so many words by our Lord Jesus? No. Was it formulated by the apostles? No. Did it develop by a syncretistic process during the first centuries of Christendom? No. When and how, then, did it emerge? That question is sharpened into acuteness by the circumstance that the word "trinity" occurs nowhere in the Bible; nor does sacred Scripture anywhere actually say that God is a triunity. At first that may seem detrimental to the doctrine, but on further inquiry it is found to be otherwise. In a law court, which is the more decisive: a statement or evidence? Not only in law but also in all other connections a statement depends for its validity upon corroborative evidence. Similarly, as regards the triunity of

God, the decisive factor is the total biblical evidence. We may safely say that, although the divine threefoldness is not didactically stated in Scripture, it is plainly and amply revealed. In the Old Testament it is recurrently *foreshadowed*. In the Gospels it is clearly *implied*. In the Acts of the Apostles it is humanly *experienced*. In the New Testament Epistles it is everywhere *assumed*. In the Apocalypse it is completively *endorsed*.

Genesis, chapter one, has been called the "Grand Portico" of written revelation. As many have noted, it is remarkable that the very first sentence in the Bible indicates plurality in the Godhead. It says, "In the beginning God created the heavens and the earth." The Hebrew word for God there is *Elohim*, which is plural. Every Jew should take note of that. All Jews who have been educated in their yeshibahs (rabbinical schools) or have dutifully attended synagogue have been taught that *Elohim* means God (singular) yet their rabbis know that the word is plural. The ending, *im*, is uniformly the Hebrew plural. Just as Baal*im* is the plural of Baal, and seraph*im* the plural of seraph, and cherub*im* the plural of cherub, so *Elohim* is the plural of *Eloah*. Why do not our Jewish rabbis admit and teach so? Is their first loyalty to rigid tradition, or to Tenach (Scripture)?

In the first of the Ten Commandments Jehovah says to Israel, "Thou shalt have no other gods before Me." There the word "gods" is plural, as every rabbi will agree. What is the Hebrew word there for the plural "gods"? It is *elohim*, exactly as in Genesis 1:1. Why, then, should it be correctly read as plural in Exodus 20:3 yet wrongly as singular in Genesis 1:1? As a matter of fact, *elohim* is a plural *always*—as for instance Deuteronomy 13:2 (verse 6 in Hebrew Tenach): "If there arise among you a prophet...saying, 'Let us go after other gods [*elohim*],' thou shalt not hearken."

So, strictly, Genesis 1:1 says, "In the beginning Gods created..." Yet although *Elohim* is plural, the verb "created" (*barah*), which goes with it, is singular—a strange grammatical irregularity inasmuch as Hebrew grammar requires that a plural subject must always have a plural verb. In Genesis 1:1 the plural subject with a singular verb at once suggests a divine plurality acting as a unity.

Jewish and other scholars have tried to negate the force of that significant grammatical feature in the first verse of Holy Writ by arguing that *Elohim* is there used as merely the so-called "plural of majesty," i.e., like the plural sometimes used in royal edicts, ascribing majesty fulsomely to one who nevertheless is a single royal personage. But there are decisive objections to that. Here is one: The purpose of the Mosaic literature and legislation was above all else the restoration of belief in the one and only true God. Would Moses (or, rather, the divine inspiration which spoke through him) have jeopardized that vital truth of the one true God for the sake of a needless grammatical device? Either of the singular forms, *El* or *Eloah*, could have been used, and then there could have been no possible doubt as to the solely monotheistic meaning. Would that plural form, *Elohim*, have been used unless there was a truth at stake which required the risk? As H.P. Liddon asks, would that plural have been used unless it was necessary to express "some complex mystery in God's inner life until that mystery should be more clearly unveiled by the explicit revelation of a later day"?

But there are three other considerations that completely do away with that plural of majesty suggestion. First, no such plural of majesty is found anywhere else in the Bible. Second, wherever it is used outside the Bible, the verb used with it (so far as I know) is plural too. Third, in that same first chapter of Genesis, verse 26, we find God actually speaking of the divine being and activity in the personal plural: "Let *Us* make man in *Our* image, after *Our* likeness." That same divine plural occurs again in chapter 3:22, "And Jehovah God said, Behold the man is become as one of *Us*, to know good and evil." We find it again in chapter 11:6,7, "And Jehovah said...Let *Us* go down and there confound their language."

Some have submitted that when God said, "Let *Us* make man in *Our* image," either He was holding a dramatic colloquy with Himself (surely an artificial idea) or He was conferring with angels as participants. But how can angels participate in an act of creation? The angels themselves are created beings, and no created being can create another creature. Besides, what fundamental community of being and nature is there between created angels and uncreated God, that God should say, "Let *Us* make man in *Our* image, after *Our* likeness"? It has been asked with good reason: Why should created entities such as angels be invited to take part in a creative act at all? No, scarcely can God be addressing angels, for the "us" and "our" assume equality of rank between the speaker and those addressed.

Moreover, in certain distinguishing particulars man is *not* made in the "image and likeness" of angels. The angels are sexless and non-reproductive. They are not a race, with a unity in one common father, nor are they a family through transmitted life and heredity. There are no mother angels; therefore God could never have become incarnated as an angel. The angels do not have flesh and blood, so there never could have been an incarnation of God into the life of the angels such as there was in that wonderful birth at Bethlehem.

It will be objected, of course, that just as the angels do not have sex or bodies or raciality or heredity, so neither does God—and how then can man be made in God's image any more than in the image of the angels? Admittedly we are skirting deep mystery, yet this clearly flashes out, that man is so made after the "image" and "likeness" of God that through incarnation God can take into the deity a real human nature, and do so with such perfect harmony that in "the man Christ Jesus" man's divine "image" and "likeness" can be seen in exquisite and everlasting perfection. In all the various biblical references to man's origin, nowhere is there the faintest suggestion that he was made in the image of the angels. We are meant to understand that man is a unique mirror of the divine *mind*. In some supremely distinctive way, man's spiritual, mental, moral, intellectual, volitional, emotional nature is a finite facsimile of the divine.

Be that as it may, the words, "Let *Us* make man in *Our* image," certainly seem to indicate a conference of beings within a plural Godhead. And what we are here inferring finds varied confirmation elsewhere in the Old Testament, a notable instance being Isaiah 6 which records the prophet's transforming vision of God. First Isaiah sees "the Lord" (*Adonai*: a proper name used for God only). Then, in verses 3 and 5, that "Lord" is identified as "Jehovah of Hosts." In verse 8 that same Adonai-Jehovah asks from the throne, "Whom shall *I* [singular] send, and who will go for *Us* [plural]?" That certainly cannot be any "plural of majesty," for there are both the "I" and the "We" used of God by God Himself in the one sentence. Nor can we make it mean God and the angels without importing something utterly alien to the wording. Clearly there seems to be indicated a plurality in the deity; and (we may cautiously ask) is the threefold plurality of God indicated in the thrice-uttered "Holy, holy, holy" of the seraphim?

There are some who would tell us that the plural, *Elohim*, and God's saying, "Let *Us* make man in *Our* likeness," are remnants of ancient polytheism, the primitive belief in many gods. They base this on the idea that the Genesis account of creation is derived from the Babylonian creation myths, and that, although Moses purified them, bits of polytheism accidentally lingered. The answer to that is definite and final. All of us who happen to have compared the Babylonian stories with Genesis know well enough that the stately, sober, never-yet-refuted Genesis account could *never* have been a revised version of the Babylonian medley. But, besides that, the spade of the archeologist has now completely overturned that idea of a primitive polytheism. Archeological discovery has shown that the further back we go to the beginning of things, the more we find a primal monotheism, and that polytheism was a later deterioration as the original truth concerning God became blurred.

Without claiming too much, I think it is fair to say that those opening chapters of Genesis do seem to indicate a reciprocal plurality in God. They do not state it or conclusively imply it, but they at once take us by surprise and prepare for further disclosures on the subject. Every time we read, "And God said," "God saw," "God made," "God created," it is the plural *Elohim* with a singular verb. What is even more arresting is that each time we have the compound name, *Jehovah Elohim*, Jehovah is singular yet is linked with the plural, *Elohim*, surely suggesting a divine plurality in unity. And, perhaps most strikingly of all, that uni-plurality is again expressed in connection with man's expulsion from Eden. See chapter 3:22-24: "And Jehovah [singular] Gods [plural] said, Behold the man is become as one of Us [plural]...So He [God: singular pronoun] drove out the man, and He [God: singular] placed...cherubim to guard the way to the tree of life." To say the least, it seems persuasively indicative that God is somehow a plurality in unity.

Testimony of Shema

Weighty confirmation of this comes in the declaration of Deuteronomy 6:4,5, which the Jews have always taken as their prime proof-text that God is an absolute numerical one.

> Hear, O Israel: The LORD our God is one LORD; and thou shalt love the LORD thy God with all thy heart, and with all thy soul and with all thy might.

That is the wording as in our King James Version and in other standard versions, except that some give the name, *Jehovah*, instead of "LORD" in capitals.

This is the great Jewish *Shema*, or "Hear..." with which the Jewish synagogue starts the daily liturgy morning and evening, and which every Jew is supposed to repeat at least once daily. It comes second in the *Thirteen Principles of Jewish Faith* as drawn up by Maimonides in the twelfth century. Our Lord Jesus Himself has set His seal that this is the foundation pronouncement and "first commandment" of the Mosaic law (Mk. 12:29,30). It is the basis of both Jewish and Christian monotheism; and by both Jewish and Gentile unitarians it has been seized upon as being supposedly fatal to our Christian doctrine of the divine triunity. "There, now," they say, "nothing could be plainer. God is a moneity, not a plurality. He is one, not three, for Deuteronomy 6:4 says, 'Jehovah our God is *one* Jehovah.' " Yet the stubborn fact is that the Hebrew wording of this bedrock statement gives us one of the clearest pointers to the triunity of God anywhere in the Bible. Few Jews (and perhaps far too few Christians) know the exact meaning of the original Hebrew word, for it is partly lost in translation. A literal translation of verse 4 would read:

> Hear, O Israel: Jehovah [singular] our Gods [plural] is Jehovah *echad* [*echad*—a unity].

Does the Hebrew really say "our Gods" (plural)? It does. The Hebrew for "our Gods" is *elohenu*, from *elohim* which is the plural of *eloah*. Just as *im* is the Hebrew plural in words like seraph*im* and cherub*im*, so is *enu* the plural possessive pronoun-suffix denoting things which belong to us, as for instance *abbothenu* (our fathers) in Numbers 20:15, and *pesha'enu* (our transgressions) and *avonothenu* (our iniquities) in Isaiah 53:5. So Deuteronomy 6:4 does indeed say, "Jehovah our Gods."

But now look at that Hebrew word, *echad*: "Jehovah our Gods is Jehovah *echad*." Admittedly it is right to translate it as "Jehovah our Gods is *one* Jehovah," so long as we understand that *echad* means "one" collectively or unitedly, not one as an absolute digit. That adjective, *echad*, derives from *achad* which means to unify or to collect together. On looking it up in the Old Testament, I find that it occurs well over six hundred times, so we easily can ascertain its common use and intended meaning. The Hebrew language has an alternative word for "one," i.e., *yachid* (feminine, yachida) which does not often occur in our Old Testament but is the word used whenever an only one is meant, or a single unit, as when Isaac is called Abraham's "only son," and Jephthah's daughter his "only daughter." Even that word can and sometimes does mean a kind of group one, though more loosely than *echad*. Its main emphasis is that of a single entity; and presumably that is the word which would have been used in Deuteronomy 6:4 if a mathematical oneness of God had been meant.

We come back, then, to that word, *echad*. Those who insist it always means a uni-plurality (so it seems to me) are over-stretching, for again and again it is used of a single thing or person; but this is certainly true, that when a compound "one" is meant to be emphasized, *echad* is the word used. It is used to express the dual oneness of evening and morning in one day, as in Genesis 1:5, "There was evening and there was morning, *one* day"; also the dual oneness of wedlock, as in Genesis 2:24, "They two shall be *one* flesh." It denotes a multi-unit in Genesis 11:6, "Behold, they are *one* people," as it does also several times in Exodus 26, "And thou shalt make fifty clasps of brass and put the clasps into the loops and couple the tent together that it may be *one.*" It is the word used in such phrases as "one cluster of grapes" (Num. 13:23), "one company" (1 Sam. 13:17), "one troop" (2 Sam. 2:25), "one network" (1 Kgs. 7:42), "one tribe" (1 Kgs. 11:13), "one nation" (1 Chron. 17.21).

That is how it must be taken in Deuteronomy 6:4, after the plural *Elohenu* ("our Gods"). What that great, basic Shema says is

Hear, O Israel, Jehovah our Gods is Jehovah a Unity.

We may well appeal to the millions of Jews who still believe in the authentic inspiration of Tenach (our Old Testament) to take careful note of *echad* and the plural *Elohenu* (our Gods) in Deuteronomy 6:4. In the *Thirteen Principles of Jewish Faith*, which is meant to be the standard guide for all Jews, why have the Jewish scholars who framed it changed that *echad* in Deuteronomy 6 to that other word, *yachid*? They were Hebrew specialists. They well knew the difference between *echad* (a plural unity) and the other word, which denotes a single unity. As already mentioned, *echad* is from the root *achad* which means to collect together; and to this day *achad* retains that meaning; for a Hebrew dictionary recently published (1949) in the new State of Israel gives the English equivalent of *mu'achad* as "collective." Why then was *echad* changed to *yachid* in the *Thirteen Principles of Jewish Faith*? Undoubtedly that switch has much influenced general Jewish thinking as to the being of Jehovah.

In the "Authorized Daily Prayer Book of the United Hebrew Congregations of the British Empire," sanctioned by the late Chief Rabbi, Dr. N. M. Adler, *yachid* is used of the eternal one, whereas Tenach (the Old Testament) never uses that word of Jehovah. Strikingly enough, though, there is one instance in which it is used of the Messiah, and where it remarkably confirms what we are saying here. The passage is Zechariah 12:10-14. We Christians believe that the "pierced" one in verse 12 is our Lord Jesus Christ. As we here quote that verse, note the word "only," which we put in capitals, for it is the Hebrew *yachid.*

> And I will pour upon the house of David, and upon the inhabitants of Jerusalem, the spirit of grace and of supplications: and they shall look upon Me whom they have pierced, and they shall mourn for *Him* as one mourneth for His ONLY Son, and shall be in bitterness for Him as one that is in bitterness for His firstborn.

And on the heels of that see chapter 14:9, where twice in one verse the collective unit, *echad*, is used of Jehovah as being a compound or collective "one."

> And Jehovah shall be King over all the earth. In that day there shall be *ONE* Jehovah, and His Name *ONE*.

In view of such ample evidence, let it be grasped once for all that what Deuteronomy 6:4 really says is "HEAR, O ISRAEL, JEHOVAH OUR GODS IS JEHOVAH A UNITY." Through defective transmission of its meaning, Jewish thought about God has been diverted from trinitarian monotheism to unitarian monotheism. Most Jews think that we Christians are tritheists, worshiping a trinity of deities of whom two are not truly God. What we must keep telling them is that we are just as monotheistic as the most orthodox Jew, that we worship the same eternal Jehovah and that our trinitarian worship of Jehovah we owe originally to their own Jewish Scriptures. I have seen the surprise among Jewish friends when the wording of their great "Shema" (Deuteronomy 6:4,5) has been truly interpreted to them. That solemn word of God through Moses was directed not only against polytheism but against monotheistic unitarianism, i.e., the worship of God as numerically one instead of complexly one.

I do not wish to read more into that bedrock text than is really there, but does it latently suggest that this uni-plurality of Jehovah is a *tri*-unity inasmuch as the name, Jehovah, occurs in it just three times?

> Hear, O Israel, *Jehovah* our Gods is *Jehovah* a unity: and thou shalt love *Jehovah* thy Gods with all thine heart, and with all thy soul, and with all thy strength.

The Priestly Blessing

That triple mention of the sacred name might be inconsequential were it not for significant parallels. Take the God-given, standard form of benediction in Numbers 6:22-27. It is another *tria juncta in uno*, or three joined in one.

> And Jehovah spake unto Moses, saying, Speak unto Aaron and unto his sons, saying, On this wise ye shall bless the children of Israel, saying unto them,
> *Jehovah* bless thee, and keep thee:
> *Jehovah* make His face shine upon thee, and be gracious unto thee:
> *Jehovah* lift up His countenance upon thee, and give thee peace.

And they shall [thus] put *My name* upon the children of Israel;
and I will bless them.

Let it be reflected: God alone actually can confer blessing; that
is why the threefold use of the name in this benediction seems indicative, just as the threefold "Holy" of the seraphs in Isaiah 6. But
it becomes the more so by reason of God's final comment upon it:
"And they shall [thus] put My *name* upon the children of Israel."
As is generally so in the Old Testament, especially with the names
of God, the name is meant to express something pertaining to the
one who hears it. Does the triple pronouncing of the sacred name
in this standard benediction betoken the triunity of God? Would not
a single mention of the name have been more in keeping if God is
a digital one? Was the tri-mention another shadowing forth of God
as three in One? We will not over-press it, but with the light of the
New Testament now thrown upon it, how meaningful it seems! The
benediction runs in three clauses, each complete in itself, each consisting of two members; and we Christians can see in them a correspondence, respectively, with the heavenly Father and the Lord Jesus
Christ and the Holy Spirit.

First comes, "Jehovah bless thee, and keep thee," engaging for
us the sovereign providence and guardianship of the Almighty, and
speaking especially of God the *Father*. Second comes, "Jehovah make
His face shine upon thee, and be gracious unto thee," speaking of
revelation ("face") and redeeming love ("gracious") and foretelling
of our Lord Jesus, God the *Son*, through whom God did indeed come
to look upon us through a human face ("The glory of God in the face
of Jesus Christ"—2 Cor. 4:6). Third comes, "Jehovah lift up His
countenance upon thee, and give thee peace," telling of something
not only revealed but communicated, namely an imparted, inward
peace, and at once suggesting reference to the third member of the
divine triunity, the *Holy Spirit*. With the first pronouncement of the
name we see the divine sovereignty *above* us. With the second pronouncement we see the divine presence drawn *near* to us. With the
third we have the divine blessing of peace *within* us. How captivatingly it anticipates the revelation of the triunity which breaks upon
us in the New Testament!

"They shall [thus] put My *name* upon the children of Israel"—
"Jehovah...Jehovah...Jehovah." We are not suggesting that either
priests or people in Israel suspected the triune nature of God in that
benediction. But the point is: If the Old Testament was written for
our sakes as well as theirs (1 Cor. 9:10 and 10:11), and if the Bible
is progressively all of a piece, then it is scarcely possible to avoid
perceiving in that God-given form of benediction a latent witness to

the threefold being of God, and that we were *meant* to see it, temporarily veiled in measure from the eyes of the elect nation, but clear enough now to the perception of the enlightened Christian.

Alas, just as the true meaning of Shema (Deut. 6:4,5) has been misinterpreted and largely lost among the Jews, so has the *name* in that threefold benediction of Numbers 6:24-27 become lost to them. First, out of an exaggerated, legalistic fear of its ever being profaned, they disobeyed the divine instruction by substituting *Adonai* for it, except inside the sanctuary. Eventually, after the death of Simeon the Just, the priests no longer pronounced that name at all, thereby losing the tradition by which the pronunciation was fixed. As a result, our present way of spelling and pronouncing the name as "Jehovah," although conventional, is probably inaccurate. Indeed, there are those among the devout, even in Israel (so we glean) who believe that the name was forfeited until the time of Israel's eventual regathering.

The Three Annual Feasts

That threefold occurrence of the name in the Shema of Deuteronomy 6 and the priestly benediction in Numbers 6 reminds us that there were three principal Jewish "feasts" which were ordained for annual observance: (1) the Feast of Passover, or Unleavened Bread: see Exodus 12:14-18, Leviticus 23:4-14; (2) the Feast of Pentecost, or Feast of Weeks because it was observed seven weeks after Passover: see Exodus 34:22, Leviticus 23:15-22; (3) the Feast of Tabernacles: see Leviticus 23:34-44.

Three times a year, at these "feasts," all the males in the nation were to congregate before the Lord. "Thrice in the year shall all your men children appear before Jehovah God, the God of Israel" (Ex. 34:23). Why these *three* feasts and assemblings? Once again we do not wish to "read in" what is not there, but in the light of the New Testament how can we help observing that the Passover is specially connected with our Lord Jesus, and the Pentecost with the Holy Spirit? We must also see the connection between the Feast of Tabernacles with God as Israel's great Father-God who Himself tabernacled with them in that threefold tabernacle where shone the supernal light of the Shekinah.

Later and Fuller Evidence

However, the foregoing Old Testament indications of plurality in God are not the only data. They are preliminaries to much more persuasive evidence. There are the *theophanies*, or self-revealings of God to Old Testament personages in such a way that one who is repeatedly called the "Angel of Jehovah" is definitely distinguished *from* Jehovah yet equally identified *as* Jehovah. It is a recurrent peculiarity which simply has no adequate explanation apart from a plural unity in God.

In the Hagar incident (Gen. 16:6-16) it is the Angel of Jehovah who, speaking as God, says, "*I* will multiply thy seed exceedingly." Even more striking is the differentiating yet identifying of God and the "Angel of Jehovah" in Genesis 21:17-19. "And *God* heard the voice of the lad...and the Angel of God called...*I* will make him a great nation." Later, in that tense moment when Abraham lifts the knife to slay his beloved Isaac, it is the Angel of Jehovah who calls to him from heaven, saying, "By Myself have I sworn, saith Jehovah, that because thou hast done this thing...that in blessing *I* will bless thee, and in multiplying *I* will multiply thee" (Gen. 22:15-1). The same identifying of that Angel with Jehovah reappears in Jacob's words, "The Angel of God spake unto me...*I* am the God of Bethel...where thou vowedst a vow unto *Me*" (Gen. 31:11-13).

Most striking of all is its recurrence in Exodus 3: "And the Angel of Jehovah appeared to him [Moses] in a flame of fire out of the midst of a bush....And *Jehovah*...*God* called to him out of the midst of the bush...I am the God of thy father, the God of Abraham, the God of Isaac, and the God of Jacob....I AM THAT I AM." Could any wording make it plainer that the Angel of Jehovah and Jehovah Himself are somehow one and the same?

Is there need for more examples? Then we have them in the following passages (wording in A S V and R S V preferable): Numbers 22:22, 27, 28; Joshua 5:13-15; Judges 2:1-4; and 6:12, 22; and 13:3, 18 with 22; 1 Chronicles 21:16-18. In Isaiah 63:9 that Angel of Jehovah is actually called "the Angel of His *presence*," which means that in a unique way He is the very presence of Jehovah though yet Himself a distinguishable being acting *for* Jehovah. It is the more notable because the Hebrew phrase, literally translated, is "the Angel of His *face*." In various Old Testament instances, "face" is used as a synecdoche representing the whole personal presence (Gen. 16:6; Ex. 2:15; Lev. 17:10; Deut. 31:17; Isa. 16:4; etc.). As used in Isaiah 63:9, "the Angel of His *face*," suggests Jehovah's *looking* on men, and *speaking* to men, and *revealing* Himself to men through this mysterious Angel who is somehow both distinct from Him yet one with Him. Inevitably we are reminded again of Paul's words, "the glory of God in the *face* of Jesus Christ."

There are places, also, where this Angel of Jehovah appears

without being called by that name, as for instance Genesis 32 where the mysterious "Man" from the unseen wrestles with Jacob, and of whom Jacob afterward says, "I have seen *God* face to face." There is Joshua 5:13-15 where Joshua is suddenly confronted by that supernatural Man who calls himself "Captain of Jehovah's host," whom awe-stricken Joshua worships and before whom he is commanded to take off his shoes because the ground whereon he stands has suddenly become "holy."

There are other such instances, to which, however, we need not here refer, for already the question is provoked: Who *was* that mysterious being, distinct from Jehovah yet apparently identical with Him? Is He named in any way which gives us a clue? Desperately clinging to Him at Peniel, Jacob besought him, "Tell me Thy name." Albeit the name was not then divulged. Later, however, when Manoah, the father of Samson, asked, "What is Thy name?" that same "Man" with "countenance very terrible" (Jdgs. 13:6), also called "the Angel of Jehovah" (3), replied, "My name is *Wonderful*" (18).[1] It is the same Hebrew word as in Isaiah 9:6, "His name shall be called *Wonderful*"—and all expositors, whether Jewish or Christian, agree that Isaiah 9:6 refers to the promised Messiah.

So, then, in view of the evidence thus far, even before we consider more specific indicators of triunity in God, how can we Christian believers help seeing in that wondrous Angel of Jehovah the preincarnate Christ who later became incarnate as Emmanuel, *God* with us? And how can our Jewish brethren fail to see that at least plurality-in-unity is indicated in the one true God, even Jehovah? Furthermore, even though a *triunal* plurality may not so far be deducible, are there not clear pointers to a *duality* of personal subsistencies in the one God? Zechariah 2:10,11, comes to mind, in which one Jehovah is represented as sending another Jehovah.

> Sing and rejoice, O daughter of Zion; for, lo, I come and will dwell in the midst of thee, saith *Jehovah*. And many nations shall be joined to Jehovah in that day, and shall be *My* people; and *I* will dwell in the midst of thee, and thou shalt know that Jehovah of hosts hath sent *Me* unto thee.

In that quotation the first speaker is Jehovah, who says, "I will dwell in the midst of thee." The second speaker is the "sent" one who says exactly the same: "*I* will dwell in the midst of thee," adding "And many nations...shall be *My* people." Strange? Yes, but only until we recognize two co-equals, one of whom later became by incarnation Israel's visible Messiah-King and the world's Savior.

An even more specific case of this may be seen in Malachi 3:1, which is plainly interpreted in Matthew 11:10 as forespeaking of John the Baptist and our Lord Jesus.

> Behold, I [Jehovah] will send My messenger [John the Baptist according to Matthew 11:10] and he shall prepare the way before *Me* [so the one prepared for is Jehovah]; and the Lord whom ye seek shall suddenly come to *His* temple [so the "Lord" who comes is the Lord of Jehovah's temple!].

Who can that coming "Lord" be who is prepared for as being Jehovah ("Me") and to whom belongs the very temple where Jehovah is worshiped ("His temple")? Besides being the Lord who comes from Jehovah, must He not somehow be Jehovah Himself in manifestation?

What about Micah 5:2, which, over seven hundred years after it was written, Jewish scribes unanimously affirmed (to Herod the Great) that it predicted their expected Messiah? Orthodox Jews *still* believe it refers to the Messiah, and rightly so.

> But thou, Beth-lehem Ephratah, though thou be little among the thousands of Judah, yet out of thee shall *He* [Messiah] come forth unto *Me* [Jehovah] that is to be Ruler in Israel; whose goings forth have been from of old, *from everlasting*. Therefore will He [Jehovah] give them up [the people of Israel] until the time that she which travaileth hath brought forth [a reference to the Messiah's birth through a human mother].

Can this wonderful one whose "goings forth" are "from everlasting" be less than Jehovah himself in some assumed embodiment? Does that term, "from everlasting," truly transmit the Hebrew original? Well, the Hebrew word, *olam* occurs at least 377 times in our Old Testament, out of which it is rendered as "ever" or "everlasting" or "evermore" or "eternal" or "perpetual" or "since the beginning of the world" or "world without end" no less than 359 times. Among the other 18 places where a different English word is used to translate *olam* in our King James Version, more recent translations change back to "everlasting" or "forever" unless *olam* is used hyperbolically. Undoubtedly, in Micah 5:2 *olam* ascribes to the Messiah not only pre-existence but timeless priority. His "goings forth"[2] have been from before time itself began.

The "Son" and the "Spirit"

Again, there are those Old Testament passages which apprize

us that Jehovah has a "Son." Admittedly, the sons of Seth in Genesis 6 are called "sons of God" in contrast with the carnal men of the Cain line; and either men or angels are called "sons of God" in Job 1:6, 2:1, 38:7. But there is one who apparently is the "Son of God" (Dan. 3:25) in a way which transcends all mere creature-relationships with God; a sonship which is unspeakably sacred, exalted and exclusive. What about Agur's challenge in Proverbs 30:4?

> Who hath ascended up into heaven,
> and descended?
> Who hath gathered the wind
> in His fists?
> Who hath bound the waters
> in His garments?
> Who hath established all the ends
> of the earth?
> What is His name? And what is His
> *Son's* name, if thou knowest?

Who is that Son of the Creator? And who is that Son of Jehovah in Psalm 2, to whom Jehovah says, "Thou art my Son: this day have I begotten Thee"? Far removed from the language of this psalm is any such suggestion as "Thou art *one* of My sons." It is a solitary sonship which lifts this Son above all others. To no other, whether man or angel, does Jehovah say, "Thou art My Son; this day have I begotten Thee," as is vouched for in Hebrews 1:5. Jehovah has "begotten" no other. This Son is in that sense, even in the Old Testament, the "only-begotten Son."

Or, reverting to Genesis 1:2 again, why does that verse say, the *Spirit* of God was moving (or brooding) upon the waters if the "Spirit" is simply another name for God, or merely His influence? Why does God say in Genesis 6:3, "My *Spirit* shall not always strive with man," if it means no more than "*I* will not"? We will not over-argue it. Perhaps, as some aver, the word "spirit" is used in its earliest meaning of "breath" and denotes no more than God's outspreading energy. Yet on the other hand, do not the verbs "brooding" and "striving" suggest distinct will and personalness? What about David's words, "The Spirit of Jehovah spake by me" (2 Sam. 23:2)? What about "His Spirit hath sent me" in Isaiah 48:16? Do not these, as well as others, seem to signify a personal, volitional being?

Foregleams of Triunity

But now we may go further and say that there are Old Testament passages which do indeed seem to denote a trinity of co-equally divine beings in the Godhead. As for plurality in God, many a Jew has been surprised to learn that Koheleth's words in Ecclesiastes 12:1, "Remember now thy Creator in the days of thy youth," when strictly translated are "Remember now thy *Creators*" (plural); yet it need not be so surprising since it simply confirms what we have already found in Genesis 1:1—"In the beginning *Gods* created...." To which we may add that in the closing book of the Old Testament we have the same plural in God's word through Malachi, "And if I be *Masters* [plural]...saith Jehovah of hosts" (Mal. 1:6). Are these just grammatical solecisms? Or do they tie in with all the other clues and pointers to a uni-plurality in God?

Surely there can be no explaining away the triunity of God indicated in Isaiah 48:12-17. Observe carefully that in these verses it is the "sent one," i.e., the Messiah, who speaks and tells us who He really is.

> Hearken unto Me, O Jacob and Israel, My called; I am He; I am the first, I also am the last [i.e., eternal]. Mine hand also hath laid the foundation of the earth, and My right hand hath spread out the heavens [so this sent one is Creator]; when I call unto them they stand up together....I have not spoken in secret from. the beginning: from the time that it [the earth] was, there am I. And now the Lord Jehovah hath sent *Me* and His *Spirit*.

Despite some scholarly attempts to find more than one speaker in the passage, attributing certain sentences either to Cyrus or to Isaiah, the close Hebrew sequence forbids it. The sent one is the speaker all through. He is the "I am," the "First" and the "Last," the Creator, therefore the one true God, even Jehovah. Yet He says, "The Lord Jehovah hath sent *Me*, and His *Spirit*." Any unprejudiced reader, so it seems to me, must see that there are three co-equal beings here named, and that the one who speaks distinguishes Himself personally from the other two. It has been truly said that inspired prophecy could scarcely retain intendedly veiled and mystic character if it spoke more plainly of the trinity than in Isaiah 48:12-17.

The same may be seen in Isaiah 63:9-11, where the heaven-guided pen writes:

> In all their affliction *He* [Jehovah] was afflicted, and the *Angel of His presence* saved them...but they rebelled, and grieved His holy *Spirit*.

Again there are the three distinct persons: (1) Jehovah, (2) the "Angel of His presence," (3) the holy "Spirit." We cannot comfortably maintain that the "Holy Spirit" here is merely an impersonal influence emanating from Jehovah, for personal susceptibilities and activities are ascribed to Him. He was "grieved." Also, in verse 14, "the Spirit of Jehovah *caused* them to rest." As for the Angel of Jehovah, we have already noted that again and again He is spoken of interchangeably with Jehovah Himself although personally distinct. Surely, then, Isaiah 63:9-11 gives further strong implication that the one true God is triune.

We find the same triple differentiation in the Gideon episode (Judges 6) where first the Angel of Jehovah appears as distinct from and yet as *being* Jehovah (14, 16). Then the "Spirit" (34) "comes upon" Gideon. So we have Jehovah, the Angel, and the Spirit. Soon afterward, in the Samson saga we have exactly the same threefold distinction yet oneness, followed by the same autonomous activity of the "Spirit of Jehovah."

The same divine triunity gleams out yet again in Isaiah 59:19,20.

> So shall they fear the name of *Jehovah*....When the enemy shall come in like a flood the *Spirit* of Jehovah shall lift up a standard against him. And the *Redeemer* shall come to Zion....

Who is that coming *Redeemer*? Thirteen times that word, "Redeemer," occurs in the wonderful messianic poem which comprises the last twenty-seven chapters of Isaiah, and each time the Redeemer is said to be Jehovah Himself (41:14; 43:14; 44:6, 24; 47:4; 48:17; 49:7, 26; 54:5, 8; 59:20; 60:16; 63:16). According to those references Jehovah *alone* is Israel's promised Redeemer. Therefore the predicted Redeemer who was yet to come to Zion must be Jehovah Himself in some visible, personal form. To my own mind, it is difficult *not to* see in such prophecies a triunity of God, however much of a mystery it may seem. Incidentally, this text may well remind us that over and over again in the Old Testament the divine Spirit is described as acting with personal distinctness from Jehovah Himself, yet as being no less the "Spirit *of* Jehovah" (Ps. 106:33; 139:7; Isa. 63:10; Ezek. 3:12, 14).

Deity of the Promised Messiah

Finally, this Old Testament witness to a triad of co-equal "persons" in God, intendedly veiled yet growingly clearer, strongly corroborates itself in what we call "messianic prophecy." In the light of predictions such as Isaiah 7:14 and 9:6, can we any longer doubt the eternal deity of the Messiah—that second, mysterious member of the Godhead, the "Angel of Jehovah's presence"?

> Hear ye now, O house of David...the Lord Himself shall give you

a sign: Behold, a virgin shall conceive and bear a son, and shall call His name *Immanuel.*

Every Bible reader knows that Immanuel means "God with us." How then could anyone seriously suggest that such a prediction was fulfilled in King Hezekiah, the son of Ahaz to whom the sign was fore-disclosed? Hezekiah was not born of a virgin; and although he was Judah's godliest king he certainly was not "God with us." Attempts to refer this prediction to Ahaz's queen, or to a suppositionary future wife of Isaiah, or to some purely imaginary ideal personage, have all been so obviously artificial, not to say self-contradictory, that there is no need here to comment on them. There was only *one* who could fulfill that sign, for it foretells the greatest of all marvels, namely, the incarnation of Jehovah Himself by a real human birth of a virgin mother.

There are two components in the sign. The first is the birth of a son by a maiden prior to sex contact. The other is, that the son should be identified by the name Immanuel, or "God with us."

That the Hebrew word *almah* means strictly a virgin is certified, among other evidences, by the fact that three hundred years before our Christian era, i.e., long before Isaiah 7:14 and other prophecies had become clouded by biased controversy, the Septuagint translation of the Hebrew Scriptures into Greek rendered that Hebrew word by the Greek *parthenos*, which means an unmarried virgin, or, in its masculine form, an unmarried youth. That Septuagint Version, remember, was made by *Jewish* scholars who knew their own language expertly, and the accepted means of that particular word well enough.

But there is further confirmation. In its several Old Testament occurrences *almah* is nowhere used of a married woman. By contrast, in Genesis 24 it is used of Rebekah who is explicitly stated there to have been at that time not only pre-nuptial but *virgo intacta* (cf. verse 43 with 16). Furthermore, we find *almah* in its masculine form, *elem*, used in 1 Samuel 17:56 and 20:22, where it is translated as "stripling," "youth," "boy," "lad" (cf. KJV, ASV, RSV). So, can there be any doubt that the feminine form means strictly a *virgin*?

If there still is lingering uncertainty, then the Song of Solomon 6:8 and Proverbs 30:19 should dissipate it. In the first of those verses "virgins" (plural of *almah*) is distinguished so sharply both from concubines and from royal consorts that one wonders how any other meaning could ever have been read into it. Similarly, in Proverbs 30:9, *almah* (translated as "maid") must mean a virgin, not only in contrast to the married female adulterers in the next verse, but because it is her very virginity which the lustful man in the proverb seeks to compromise. The New Testament, also, gives its unanswerable endorsement. That endorsement, that *almah* means strictly a virgin as in Matthew 1:23, actually reproduces Isaiah 7:14 as "Behold, the virgin [*parthenos*, an unmarried daughter]...shall bring forth a Son."

Indeed, when one reflects on it, what special sign could any merely ordinary birth of a baby boy have been to the house of David? Evidently the Lord Himself (emphatic) who gave the sign considered it a super-normal marvel and intended it to be publicized to the whole kingdom. Understandably so, for how could such an all-eclipsing miracle as the incarnation of *Immanuel*, "God with us," take place apart from birth by a virgin? No child with a human father could possibly be God incarnate. That the mother be strictly a pure virgin was an absolute neccooity. As a born son, He *must* have a human mother, but as incarnate God He could *not* have a human father.

Isaiah 9:6

But was He verily "God manifest in flesh," personally distinct from Israel's covenant God, Jehovah, yet co-equally one with Him? Is not that settled once for all by that other prediction in Isaiah 9:6?

> For unto us a Child is born, unto us a Son is given; and the government shall be upon His shoulder; and His name shall be called Wonderful, Counselor, the Mighty God, the Everlasting Father, the Prince of Peace. Of the increase of His government and peace there shall be no end, upon the throne of David, and upon His kingdom, to order it and to establish it with judgment and with justice from henceforth even for ever. The zeal of Jehovah of Hosts will perform this.

Those certainly are astonishing names to be used of a promised baby boy. They would be ridiculous, in fact, if they applied only to Hezekiah, son of Ahaz. Moreover, they are not strictly names (plural) but "name," the one name including all. And, as is uniformly so in special Old Testament names, the name here is meant to express the nature. It is not surprising therefore that all the earliest Jewish rabbis unanimously took this Isaian prophecy as most decidedly describing the promised Messiah. It is during later times only, since polemical prejudice brought bias into exegesis, that alternative interpretations have appeared. All such interpretations are patently fallacious because apart from the Messiah considered as a divine person there is simply no other figure in history to whom the remarkable words can be realistically applied.

The objection that the New Testament nowhere applies this prophecy to our Lord Jesus is not only feeble, it is wrong; for plainly the angel Gabriel in his annunciation to Mary alludes to it. First, Gabriel says that Mary's child was to be "the Son of the Highest," corresponding to "To us a son is given." Second, the babe, Jesus, was to be "great," corresponding to the great name(s) in Isaiah 9:6. Third, He was to reign on the throne of His father, David, which plainly repeats the Isaiahn phrase, "His government...upon the throne of David." Fourth, Gabriel's words, "And of His kingdom there shall be no end," are practically a quotation of the final words in the Isaiahn text. However, without for the moment applying Isaiah's prediction to our Lord Jesus, let us halt at some of the wording.

"His name shall be called *Wonderful*." As already noted, the Hebrew word so translated here is the same as in Judges 13:18, where the Angel of Jehovah, who actually identifies Himself as Jehovah, says His name is "Wonderful."

"The *Mighty God*." Here the Hebrew name for God is not *Elohim* (which occasionally is used in the lower sense of those who are representatives of God); it is *El*, which is never used by Isaiah or any other Old Testament writer in any sense lower than that of absolute deity.

The Hebrew word translated as "mighty" is *gibbor*—derived from *geber* which basically means a "man," and is repeatedly so rendered in our English Bible. That very word *gibbor* is in common use today among the Hebrew-speaking Jews in the new State of Israel, and still means a *man*. Its feminine form is the equally common word for a woman. So, while I am not dissenting from the rendering "Mighty God" in Isaiah 9:6, I would point out that the underlying meaning of *El gibbor* is "God-Man"! The identical phrase, *El gibbor*, reappears in chapter 10:20, 21, where beyond all possible doubt it means Jehovah Himself. This settles it—the Messiah predicted in chapter 9:6, whose name is Wonderful, is none other than Jehovah incarnate who comes to reign on earth in a kingdom without end. Those verses say:

> It shall come to pass in that day that the remnant of Israel...shall stay upon Jehovah, the Holy One of Israel, in truth. The remnant shall return, even the remnant of Jacob, unto the *Mighty God*.

Whether or not we bring out the underlying meaning of God-Man, or God-Mighty-Man, does not detract from this: The predicted Messiah in Isaiah 9:6 is coequally *one* with Jehovah though at the same time distinct from Him and sent by Him.

Yes, coequally one with Jehovah, for He is also named here the "Everlasting Father," or as the English Revised and ASV marginal renderings and other translations have it, "Father of Eternity." Let there be no beating around the bush: Whether we are orthodox Jews or Gentile unitarians or evangelical Christians, must we not all sincerely agree that in this Isaian pre-depicting of the coming Messiah (whether we understand it or not) such titles as "God-Man," or "Mighty El," and "Father of Eternity," or "Father of Futurity" or "Father of Coming Ages" (see Septuagint), cannot be truly applied to any mortal man or to any other creature, but only to one who is indeed "very God of very God"? Those titles are no mere exaggerations of prophetical afflatus; they are divinely revealed designations of Messiah in the Book which never lies.

That He, the eternal, the almighty *El*, should take manhood into Himself by a human birth is the marvel of all marvels, at which can we ever cease to be astonished? Yet surely it is foretold with a perspicuity which only a needless spiritual blindness can miss seeing. The prophet Micah, who was Isaiah's rustic contemporary, similarly fore-heralds the birth of Immanuel through a human mother's travail, and describes Him as the coming Ruler whose "goings forth have been from of old, even from everlasting" (5:2, 3). Amazing? Yes, yet had not God fore-revealed this super-wonder right from the time that humanity's first parents were ejected from Eden? Away back then it was pre-announced that the "seed of the woman" should "crush the head" of the deceiver—and we need to remember that the account in Genesis is obviously a condensation, and that God then may have said much more in amplification which is *not* recorded. How, for instance, did Enoch, the seventh from Adam, know and foresee our Lord's still-future coming "with ten thousand of His saints"? We are not saying that he knew all the evangelical truth wrapped up in what he foresaw, but evidently he was given to foresee it.

According to our Authorized Version, when Eve's first son was born she exclaimed, "I have gotten a man from the Lord." The American Standard Version and the Revised Standard Version alter it to "I have gotten a man with the help of the Lord." But if, as Ellicott says, we allow the Hebrew construction to speak normally instead of our throwing the emphasis on "gotten," what Eve actually said was, "I have gotten the man—Jehovah." I do not suggest for a moment that Eve knew the meaning of that name Jehovah, as we ourselves now do, or that she had any such information about the incarnation of God the Son as we now have. But evidently God had told her that the "seed of the woman" should be a divine one who would be born into this world. Eve, therefore, joyfully but mistakenly presumed that the birth of her first son was the speedy fulfillment of the promise. The later theophanies, or self-revealings of Jehovah as the Angel of Jehovah, distinct from God yet Himself divine, all prepared the way for that matchless wonder, the incarnation of Immanuel.

In all this, however, the one aspect which directly concerns our present subject is that, along with all the other adduced evidence, it shows, through the Old Testament, that there are indications of *plurality* in the Godhead. We especially see a *duality*, with strong suggestions later of a threeness, all of which blend into a pre-Christian revelation of *triunity* in God. There can be only one Mighty God, only one Father of Eternity, yet two are so named. And if the Spirit of Jehovah is merely an influence from Him, how does that impersonal influence have a distinct will of its own, speaking and acting of itself? The Spirit of Jehovah is given what seems to be a disinct personalness, and in such a way as distinguishes Him from both Jehovah and the equally divine Angel of Jehovah, while yet being one with them.

Yes, before ever we reach the clear New Testament doctrine of the Father and the Son and the Holy Spirit, the Old Testament has prepared us for the transcendent manifestation that the one true God is the glorious, gracious Creator-Redeemer *Triunity*.

¹ Not "secret" as in King James Version.
² Not his "origin," as the R S V regrettably mis-renders it. The Hebrew word rendered "goings forth" is *motssa ah*. It is basically the same Hebrew word as is translated in the earlier part of the verse, "Out of thee [Bethlehem] shall He *come forth....*" In fact, some expositors render it "comings forth" instead of "goings forth" in the latter part of the verse.

5

Triunity in the New Testament

One of the most engrossing pursuits is to travel through the Bible tracing the progressive unfolding of those divine truths and spiritual realities which it reveals. Its supremo object, of course, is God, and, as with other subjects, its presentation of God is progressive. In particular, that is true of the way it releases to our intelligence the triunity of God.

It is when we pass from the Old Testament to the New that we find the biblical disclosure of threeness in God emerging into full-flowered amplitude. As already remarked, in the Old Testament that triunity is recurrently *foreshadowed*; in the Gospels it is plainly *implied*; in the Book of Acts it is humanly *experienced*; in the Epistles it is everywhere *assumed*; and in the Apocalypse it is completely *endorsed*. By the time we reach the end of the New Testament we have begun to appreciate how precious indeed this revelation of the divine triunity is.

THE FOUR GOSPELS

Right at the threshold of the New Testament we see this triunity manifested in the profound miracle of the virgin birth (Matt. 1:20-23, Lk. 1:35). The angel Gabriel announces to Mary: "The *Holy Spirit* shall come upon thee [i.e., God the Spirit], and the power of *The Highest* [i.e., God the Father] shall overshadow thee: therefore that holy one which shall be born of thee shall be called the *Son of God* [i.e., God the Son]." In those expressions, "the Holy Spirit," "the Highest" and "the Son of God," do we not see an intended indication of three persons, each distinct yet each divine? Some may take the liberty of objecting that we are seeing more than actually is implied, but even they will acknowledge a triune participation indicated in what took place. And, in the light of what follows, this becomes at least a significant pointer.

The same is evident at our Lord's baptism in the Jordan (Matt. 3:16, 17). The *Father's* voice speaks from heaven, "This is my beloved Son." The *Holy Spirit* descends in visual and symbolic form as a dove. The incarnate *Son* stands bodily there in sinless manhood. Surely that, too, seems at least *intended* to exhibit an external three-ness yet an internal oneness—especially so along with the many other contributory factors yet to be considered.

The same suggestion meets us again at our Lord's temptation in the wilderness (Matt. 4). Jesus is "led up of *the Spirit* into the wilderness." The tempter begins, "If Thou be the *Son of God*...." Our Lord replies, "Man shall not live by bread alone but by every word which proceedeth out of the mouth of *God*."

So does this seemingly significant threeness appear in other such instances; but it is in what our Lord Jesus actually taught that we find the mysterious threeness-in-oneness becoming unmistakably articulate. If we are fair to the full data must we not agree that our Lord Jesus both assumed and affirmed that He was God the Son, that He revealed the fatherhood of God as no other did or could, and that He claimed a relationship with God the Father altogether above that of either humans or angels? We think of His "Before Abraham was, I am" (not merely "Before Abraham was, I *was*," but "I *am*") indicating not only pre-existence but eternality, for He appropriates to Himself the very phrase by which Jehovah named Himself to Moses. We think again of His words, "I and My Father are one" (John 10:30), in which He not only expresses the oneness of equality (see context) but gives Himself priority mention: not "the Father and I," but "I and the Father." We recall His words in John 5:23, "All men shall honor the Son, even as they honor the Father," wherein He claims equal homage and worship with the Father.

He used of Himself the Jehovistic "I AM." In John 4:26 He says, "I that speak unto thee am He." In John 8:24 He says, "If ye believe not that *I am He*, ye shall die in your sins," and again in verse 28, "When ye have lifted up the Son of Man, then ye shall know that I am He," and again in verse 58 the already quoted, "Before Abraham was, *I AM*." His Jewish hearers rightly took Him to be claiming full deity (see verses 53 and 59). Again, in chapter 10:33, His hostile hearers say, "For a good work we stone thee not, but for blasphemy; and because Thou, being a man, *makest Thyself God*."

Nor is it His direct claims only which declare His deity, but His continuous *assuming* of it. We think, for instance, of His saying, "If a man love Me, he will keep My words: and My Father will love him; and *WE* [i.e., the Father and the Son] will come unto him, and make our abode with him" (John 14:23). In that utterance not only does He claim closest oneness and equality with the Father, but the divine attribute of *omnipresence*, i.e., in His promised indwelling of His people's hearts the world over. Such assuming of omnipresence is absurd if Christ is not God incarnate. See also Matthew 18:20 and 28:20 for similar assuming of omnipresence. Equally, He evinces the divine attribute of *omniscience* (see John 11:11, Matt. 24:5-44), and *omnipotence* (see John 5:21, 28, etc.).

There is no need here to spread out the whole data, for in many an able treatise they have been marshalled, assessed and shown to be conclusive. In fact, so multiple and cumulative is the evidence, we begin to feel a sickly suspicion that those who explain it all away are victims of peculiar, self-inflicted blindness.

Yet, although Jesus so perspicuously affirmed and implied His coequal oneness with the Father, He just as unambiguously indicated His personal distinction from the Father. Again and again He did so in memorable pronouncements such as:

I am the way, the truth, and the life: no man cometh unto the *Father* but by *Me* (John 14:6).

No man knoweth the *Son*, but the Father; neither knoweth any man the *Father*, save the Son, and he to whomever the Son will reveal him (Matt 11:27).

The *Father* judgeth no man, but hath committed all judgment to the *Son*; that all men should honor the *Son* even as they honor the *Father* (John 5:22, 23).

If I judge, my judgment is true: for I am not alone, but *I* and the *Father* that sent Me (John 8:16).

He that hath seen *Me* hath seen the *Father* (John 14:9).

Everywhere there is essential oneness with the Father, yet distinction personally from the Father. Mystery? Yes, deep beyond our understanding, yet as clear in its expression as it is fathomless in its meaning.

The twelve apostles who continually companied with Jesus in public and in private, watching Him on all occasions and under all circumstances, observing His reactions, hearing His wisdom, perceiving His character through close-up confidentiality, were more and more driven by the sheer force of it all. Recognize in Him sinless manhood expressing incarnate Godhead, until amid the glowing mystery of His resurrection Thomas found speech for all of them when he fell at Jesus' feet exclaiming, "My Lord and my *God!*" (John

20:28).

Moreover, our Lord Jesus not only made it indubitably clear that He and the Father were one yet distinct, He expressed equally lucidly the relationship of the Holy Spirit to the Son and the Father. Especially in His later teaching of the twelve apostles did He repeatedly emphasize the *personalness* of the Holy Spirit. See, for instance, John 15:26, "But when the Comforter is come, *whom* [Greek masculine] I will send unto you from the Father, even the Spirit of truth, which proceedeth from the Father, *He* [masculine pronoun] shall testify of Me." Or again, "If *I* depart, I will send *Him* to you. And when He is come, *He* will reprove the world...."

Yes, our dear Lord certainly emphasizes the personalness of the Holy Spirit by that masculine pronoun, but we are not dependent solely on that. Even where He uses the usual Greek neuter noun for the Spirit (Pneuma), He does so in ways which surely indicate personalness (e.g., Matt.10:20; Lk. 4:18; 11:13; John 3:5-8; 7:39).

A young Christian student was accosted by a self-sure, modern skeptic who sneered at the idea that the Holy Spirit is personal. Said the skeptic, with fancied intellectual superiority, "Surely it is credulity for you to think that the Spirit is a person. Why, in the Greek the very word which is translated into English as spirit simply means the *wind*."

The young Christian replied, "If that is so, will you be good enough to tell me the meaning of these words in John 3? 'Except a man be born of water and of the "wind," he cannot enter into the kingdom of God. That which is born of the flesh is flesh; and that which is born of the "wind" is "wind"....The wind bloweth where it listeth, and thou hearest the sound thereof, but canst not tell whence it cometh, and whither it goeth; so is every one that is born of the "wind." ' " The skeptic was visibly jolted, and while he fumbled for something to say in return the Christian youth slyly aded, "Verily, verily, it is thy words which are born of the wind, for they certainly are not of the Spirit!"

Furthermore, our Lord ascribes divine attributes to the Holy Spirit. Being omnipresent like the Father and the Son, He would indwell the hearts of all true believers everywhere (John 16:8). Being also omniscient, He would "show them things to come" (16:13). Moreover, our Lord Jesus repeatedly speaks of Himself and the Father and the Holy Spirit as acting together in a triune oneness indicating a triunity of personal beings coequally divine. See the threeness in oneness in the following excerpts.

> And *I* will pray the *Father*, and He shall give you another *Comforter*, that He may abide with you for ever (John 14:16).

He [the Holy Spirit] shall be in you....I will come to you....Ye shall know that *I* am in the *Father*....and I in you (14:17-20).

But the *Comforter*, which is the Holy Spirit, whom the *Father* will send in *My* name... (26).

When the *Comforter* is come, whom *I* will send unto you from the *Father*, He shall testify of *Me* (15:26).

Four features stand out sharply by the time our Lord Jesus has given His parting words on the Holy Spirit: (1) The Holy Spirit is a Person. (2) He has the divine attributes. (3) He is neither the Father nor the Son. (4) He is "sent" by both the Father and the Son yet is coequal with them, and of His own will He "comes." Surely (so it seems to me) they are dull eyes which cannot see in such teachings an intrinsic triunity of essentially equal beings; so completely a three-in-one that the Holy Spirit's indwelling of believers *is* the indwelling Lord Jesus (14:18,20) and *is* the indwelling Father (14:23)!

As already noted, at the outset of our Lord's public ministry the three persons of the Godhead are objectively distinguished in the Jordan baptism: the "beloved Son" in the water, the heavenly Spirit descending "like a dove," and the Father's attesting "voice from heaven." Corresponding to that, right at the end, after Jesus' resurrection from the dead, comes His final testimony as the great revealer: "Go ye therefore, and teach all nations, baptizing them in the *name* [singular] of the *Father*, and of the *Son*, and of the *Holy Spirit*." What clearer, final declaration could there be? By the "name," remember, our Lord did not mean merely an appellation in our modern way of giving names, but in the way the name of God is used always in Israel's Scriptures, that is, to denote the divine nature. He was now solemnly confirming that the being of God is triune; one name, three persons. That baptismal formula is fundamental. It is textually authentic, being found in all the Matthew manuscripts and ancient versions without exception and without variation. Our Lord's repeated "and of the" (conjunction and definite article) i.e., "and of *the* Son, and of *the* Holy Spirit" indicates a deliberately expressed tripartition of persons, yet all three are equally one as the object of faith for those who are baptized into the name.

Clearly, the apostles were not to call upon men to believe in one God and two subordinate gods, which would have been a form of tritheism, and therefore only a novel modification of polytheism. Nor were men to believe in God plus a mediator and an impersonal influence, for the titles "Son" and "Holy Spirit" are not merely titles of office or modes of divine activity. Just as the word "Father" here implies personalness and relationship, so does the word "Son" and so does the equal close-coupling of the name "Holy Spirit" with "Father" and "Son."

By "the Father" our Lord obviously meant the eternal "I AM" (Exod. 3:14), and "JEHOVAH" (6:3) and the great "FATHER" (Mal. 2:10) of Israel, the one of whom the scribes and Pharisees had said, "We have one Father, even God" (John 8:41). All who heard our Savior's teachings knew that by "the Father" He meant the one and only true God, Jehovah, God of Israel. They soon knew, also, that in His continual reference to Himself as "the Son" He was betokening a union with the Father which was unique, unshared by any other. Now, therefore, as He utters the commanding baptismal formula, His uniting of Himself as the Son with the Father, and then His uniting of the Holy Spirit (the paraclete whose divine nature He had so tenderly expounded) with both the Father and the Son, can mean no less than coequality of Father, Son, and Holy Spirit, and their oneness in essence as the Triune God.

Yes, by the time we reach the end of the four Gospels the triunity of God has been more than amply confirmed. Our Lord's post-resurrection baptismal formula at last gives open speech to that recurrent Old Testament undertone of allusion to a plurality of persons in the Godhead. It marks a dividing line between the incomplete Old Testament revelation and the completive manifestation given in the incarnated Emmanuel, or Lord Jesus Christ. Suddenly the veiled and shadowy is brought out into the open, and with good reason, for the New Testament is now going to show us the eternal three together operating as one—in creation, in redemption, and in the sanctification of believers.

THE ACTS OF THE APOSTLES

If the Old Testament is full of God as Elohim-Jehovah, the great Father-God, and if the four Gospels are full of our Lord Jesus as the now-incarnate God the Son, the further revelation given to us in the Acts of the Apostles is full of the Holy Spirit. He is referred to by name no less than fifty-five times, and most of the narrative concerns either His direct or His indirect activity through the apostles. Everywhere now, also, He is referred to as speaking, acting, guiding and controlling as a person. For instance:

The Spirit *gave* them utterance (2:4).
The Spirit *said* unto Philip (8:29).

The Spirit of the Lord *caught away* Philip (8:39).
The Spirit *said...I* have *sent* them (10:19,20).
The Spirit *bade* me go with them (11:12).
The Holy Spirit *said:* "Separate me Barnabas and Saul" (13:2).
They, being *sent forth* by the Holy Spirit (13:4).
It *seemed good* to the Holy Spirit (13:4).
They were *forbidden* of the Holy Spirit (16:6).
The Spirit *suffered* them not (16:7).
The Holy Spirit *witnesseth*... (20:23).
The Holy Spirit hath *made* you overseers (20:28).
Thus *saith* the Holy Spirit (21:11).
Well *spake* the Holy Spirit... (28:25).

The Holy Spirit, then, is distinctly a person. He is not God the Father, nor is He God the Son, yet He is everywhere regarded just as truly personal, and as being coequally one with them, and as expressing them. He is the "Spirit of the Lord" (5:9, 8:39). It was the Spirit who sent Peter to the household of Cornelius (10:19,20), yet later Peter says it was God (28). All the way through it is taken for granted that the Holy Spirit is God; that His activities are those of God the Father and of God the Son through Him. Continually, now, the narrative recognizes the three, but brooks no other; and the three have become one in the spiritual apprehension of those Spirit-filled first believers. They knew that the Father had sent the Son, for they had seen and companied with the Son who had said, "He that hath seen Me hath seen the Father"; and they knew that the promised Holy Spirit had now filled them as, so to speak, our Lord's other self. They knew that it was the Spirit of God and of Christ who filled them, and that in having the Spirit they had the Father and the Son as well. In other words, they had now learned the triunity of God in vivid experience.

Yes, the Above and the Beyond had now become the Within, lifting those first believers to a new level of life and a new understanding of God. Their experience of the Holy Spirit's moving and working in and through them, purifying and empowering, was such that they knew it must be God who was doing it (Phil. 2:13). Not that the Christian doctrine of the divine triunity grew out of Christian experience only—the experience by itself could not have given them a clear mental concept of the triunity—but it was the culminating verification of it. Along with the known facts (the virgin birth, the Jordan baptism, the miracles, the resurrection, etc.) and the teaching of Jesus, the Pentecostal experience vividly confirmed that Christ and the Holy Spirit were indeed coequally God with the Father.

In all this we see at once a correspondence to the threefold, overall revelation of God in history and Scripture: (1) In the Old

Testament, God is the sovereign Creator-Governor of the world; (2) in the Person and teaching of the Lord Jesus Christ, God is the gracious Father-Savior of mankind; (3) in the Pentecostal experience, God is our Regenerator-Indweller by the Holy Spirit. At the same time we see more clearly how the Christian doctrine of the triunity emerged. First came the outward *facts* gathering around our Lord and His teaching. Next came the inward *experience* which corroborated and illumined those facts. Then came attempted *definition*, gradually solidifying into apostolic doctrine.

THE NEW TESTAMENT EPISTLES

Just as truly we may now say that in the New Testament Epistles the triunity of God is everywhere assumed. How natural that it should be so when we reflect on what had now happened in the minds of those first disciples! They had seen Jesus die on that cross, had seen the corpse taken down, and the sepulchre where it was deposited. Then, with awed minds, and scarcely able at first to grasp it, they had seen Him actually alive again with the crucifixion marks still in His body. They had conversed and companied with Him for forty days after that, watching Him now with a wondering intensity beyond description. It was really the same Jesus, still human, yet now, in that supernalized body and amid that post-resurrection mystery-glow, more movingly and unmistakably superhuman than ever. Awed and thrilled, and now utterly convinced, they had seen Him actually ascend visibly from the earth into space until distance covered Him from further view. And now, ten days later, Pentecost had happened, supernaturally confirming and illuminating it all within them. They were now men possessed by the Holy Spirit! This wonderful envelopment of them was exactly what Jesus had said He would do on returning to the Father! So He now *was* with the Father! He had done what only God can do, that is, He had poured out on them the very Spirit of God!

That finally settled it for them: He *is* God. Yet He is not the Father. He and the Father had sent the Holy Spirit—as He had said would happen. But, most wonderful of all, Jesus Himself had now come back to them. They needed no one to tell them. They knew it by the Spirit's inward witness, and they remembered the word of Jesus that He would come back to them and actually dwell within them by the Spirit. So, also, they knew now by inward reality that although Jesus and the Holy Spirit were distinct from each other they were somehow *one*! In having the Holy Spirit they inwardly had their ascended Savior too! Not by reason and deduction merely (though they had their part) but by luminous evidential experience they knew, they felt, they inwardly saw and grasped that the Father, the Son, the Holy Spirit were distinctly three yet were coequally God, and were somehow triunely one!

We must not forget that by Jewish upbringing and tuition and conviction those first disciples were still strict, even bigoted monotheists. They were the last men on earth who could have been turned into Trinitarians by some philosophical school or religious theorizers even if such had existed—which they did not. Nor did any of those first disciples immediately start trying to formulate the newly realized triunity of God into a systematized theology of it. They simply began transmitting what they knew from proven facts and corroborative experience. That is how the truth of the divine triunity emerged. It was never announced or argued or formalized. Rather, it was gradually *recognized* as being inescapably involved in that most wonderful being who ever trod this earth—Jesus. What Jesus demonstratedly was in Himself, along with what He revealed of the heavenly Father and of the Holy Spirit, settled it once for all, to those first Christians. God is one in three and three in one.

Nevertheless, this Christian doctrine of the divine triunity as it comes to us through the testimony of those first Christians, all of them Jews, does not nullify the *unity* of God, it amplifies and sublimates it. Those inspired Scriptures, which we now call the Old Testament, restored to men the original, true monotheism. It is monotheistic Jews who now, in New Testament times, gave us the trinitarian finality of that monotheism. In doing so they betray not the slightest awareness of any inconsistency. They were *still* monotheists: and so are we who, like them, worship the "God and Father of our Lord Jesus Christ," the God who, in Pauline phrase, is "our Savior-God" (Titus 1:3). By the three divine "persons" we mean three real distinctions within the Godhead, yet all three expressing one single divine life. They are distinguishable, indeed unmistakable, but absolutely and eternally inseparable. That doctrine arises solely and wholly out of the revelation which has come to us in and through our wonderful Lord Jesus Christ. It is not an attempt to solve a metaphysical problem, but a natural corollary from proven facts and confirmatory experience.

As examples of how this triunity is everywhere assumed in the New Testament Epistles we pick out the following. Note the italic capitals in our quotations.

> But ye are not in the flesh, but in the *SPIRIT*, if so be that the
> Spirit of *GOD* dwell in you. Now if any man have not the Spirit

of *CHRIST* he is none of His (Rom. 8:9).

Observe not only that all three members of the triunity are there named, but that the Holy Spirit is both the "Spirit of *God*" (i.e., of the Father) and the "Spirit of *Christ*" (i.e., of God the Son).

> Now there are diversities of gifts but the same *SPIRIT*. And there are diversities of administrations, but the same *LORD*. And there are diversities of operations, but it is the same *GOD* who worketh all in all (1 Cor. 12:4-6).

> Now He which establisheth us with you in *CHRIST* and hath anointed us in *GOD*; who hath also sealed us, and given the earnest of the *SPIRIT* in our hearts (2 Cor. 1:21,22).

> The grace of the *LORD JESUS CHRIST*, and the love of *GOD*, and the communion of the *HOLY SPIRIT*, be with you all (2 Cor. 13:14).

> That the God of our *LORD* Jesus Christ, the *FATHER* of glory, may give unto you the *SPIRIT* of wisdom and revelation in the knowledge of Him (Eph. 1:17).

> For through *HIM* (Christ) we both have access by one *SPIRIT* unto the *FATHER* (Eph. 2:18).

> In *WHOM* [Christ] ye also are builded together for an habitation of *GOD* through the *SPIRIT* (Eph. 2:22).

> For this cause I bow my knees unto the *FATHER* of our *LORD* Jesus Christ...that He would grant you...to be strengthened with might by His *SPIRIT*... (Eph. 3:14-16).

> There is one body and one *SPIRIT*...one *LORD*, one faith, one baptism, one God and *FATHER*... (Eph. 4:4-6).

> Elect according to the foreknowledge of God the *FATHER*, through sanctification of the *SPIRIT*, unto the obedience and sprinkling of the blood of *JESUS CHRIST* (1 Pet. 1:2).

> We have confidence toward *GOD*....And this is His commandment, that we should believe on the name of His *SON* Jesus Christ....And hereby we know that He abideth in us, by the *SPIRIT* (1 John 3:21-24).

> Hereby know ye the *SPIRIT* of God: every spirit that confesseth that *JESUS CHRIST* is come in the flesh is of *GOD* [i.e., of the Father] (1 John 4:3).

> But ye, beloved, building up yourselves on your most holy faith, praying in the *HOLY SPIRIT*, keep yourselves in the love of *GOD*, looking for the mercy of our *LORD* Jesus Christ unto eternal life (Jude 20, 21).

The foregoing, of course, are but a few from the continuous recurrences of this trio-mention, taken from the three main penmen of the Epistles. (See for further instances Rom. 15:16; 1 Cor. 2:2-5; 2 Cor. 5:5,6; Gal. 4:6; Phil. 4:3; Col. 1:6-8; 2 Thess. 2:13; Titus 3:4-6; Heb. 6:4-6 and 9:14 and 10:29; 1 Peter 4:14). It is so prominent and pervasive as to be characteristic of apostolic teaching and of the original Christian faith.

The one big question remaining is: In this characteristic trisecting yet uniting of Father, Son, and Holy Spirit in the deity, are the divine triad really considered as being co-eternally and co-equally one triune God? The answer is yes, as we may see from most of the foregoing texts if tied in with their context. Take, for example, 1 Peter 1:1,2, where our salvation is ascribed to all three in distinctness yet oneness, and read it in the light of the following context (verses 11-13) where we find that the Holy Spirit in the Old Testament prophets was the "Spirit of Christ." Or take Ephesians 3:16-19, where the Father, the Son, and the Holy Spirit are said to be indwelling the Christian believer. But let me pick out just one, at least, of the foregoing texts for particular consideration. It is the Pauline benediction at the end of his second letter to the Corinthians. I refer to it the more gratefully perhaps because it is the familiar benediction with which our sanctuary services are usually concluded.

> The grace of the Lord Jesus Christ, and the love of God, and the communion of the Holy Spirit, be with you all, Amen (2 Cor. 13:14).

Surely beyond all cavil three distinct *personal* entities are differentiated in the phraseology. All will agree that "the Lord Jesus Christ" is a real person, and that here, as elsewhere, He is personally distinguished from the one who is here called "God." All will agree that the one who is called "God" is also meant to be understood as personal, and is called "the Father" in corresponding passages. All must agree that the "Holy Spirit" is here mentioned in exactly the same way, as though similarly personal and similarly distinguishable. If this be not the intended meaning here, are not these interlinked phrases blameworthily misleading?

But does not this benediction also imply that these three are *equal*? If not, then again the grammatical form is strangely deceiving. If, as the various unitarian sects say, Christ is but a creature, and the Holy Spirit only an impersonal emanation, then does it not border on blasphemous confusion for this benediction to associate them so closely, so co-actively, so supremely, with the one who alone is God? And if, as even some trinitarians hold, the Son and the Holy Spirit are essentially subordinate to the Father, why, in such a formal, measured benediction, is the Son mentioned before the Father? Would not the Father most certainly have been given priority of mention here if there were eternal priority of status? In various other passages the Father *is* given priority of mention; but the very inversion of that order here, in this benediction, shows that there is no rigid uniformity, and that the order of mention is determined simply by sequence of thought.

That there is functional subordination of the Son and the Holy Spirit to the Father, in the economy of creation and redemption, we do not deny: but the trinity considered economically must be distinguished from the trinity considered essentially. Any such subordination is volitional and operational, not fundamental. It is functional only, not essential. Taken at its face value, and read without any pre-formed bias, this Pauline benediction surely implies that the Father, the Son, and the Holy Spirit are coequal.

Again, this benediction implies that the Father, the Son, and the Holy Spirit, besides being three and being equal, are one. They are not only a trinity, they are a tri*unity*; for if, as we have seen, the phrasing implies that the three are equally divine, then although we ourselves cannot grasp the mystery of it, they simply must somehow be one. There cannot possibly be three separate infinities; even infinity itself can hold only one infinite. If the Scriptures assign divine attributes to each of the three (and they do), then the three *must* be one in essence, for there can be only one absolute God.

But the finalizing proof of all this lies in the fact that this benediction is in reality a prayer. The words, "I pray that," are to be understood at the beginning of it just as really as if Paul had written them before your eyes. Who would deny that? Who would say that this benediction was a mere optative wish? Its supreme attractiveness lies in the fact that it is a prayer with an expected answer. But is not prayer to be offered to God alone? Why then is it offered to the Lord Jesus Christ and the Holy Spirit equally with God the Father? If they are not equally God, why are they also and equally invoked in such a prayer? How strange for an inspired apostle to pray to a mere creature and an impersonal influence along with the one true God!

If Christ be but an exalted man or angel, how strange for Paul to solicit the grace of that man or angel on the same level with the love of God Himself! How strange that in such a considered and deliberate farewell prayer Paul should place the name of a mere man or even an angel *before* that of the eternal God! And how strange, if Christ be a mere creature, that Paul should pray to Him as having the God-like prerogative of conferring spiritual qualities! Yes, it is indeed strange, if Christ be not "very God of very God!"

Further, if the Holy Spirit is merely an effluence or attribute, how strange that Paul should pray to such an impersonal concept in abstraction from the living deity Himself, in and of whom are *all* such attributes and emanations! How *could* prayer be prayed to an attribute or influence? Yet here, in this benediction, the Holy Spirit is not only prayed to, but presumably is expected as an intelligent, self-acting agent, to impart blessing distinct from that which the Father and the Lord Jesus confer. There is the same distinction here indicated as that which exists between Christ and the Father.

Surely then this parting pen-prayer furnishes clear proofs of personal tripartition in the Godhead—proofs which, so far as we know, have never been satisfactorily countered by unitarian spokesmen, and which, so far as we can see, cannot be overthrown. As the colors of light are broken up by the prism and exhibited separately on the spectrum, so undoubtedly, seen through the prism of the New Testament, the deity becomes distinguished into the Father, the Son, and the Holy Spirit. Such is the God of Paul's threefold benediction and of the New Testament Epistles as a whole; and such is our meaning when we speak of trinitarian theology. The New Testament is trinitarian but not tritheistic. Paul was not a tritheist—a believer in three Gods. He was a trinitarian—a believer in *one* God subsisting as one in three and three in one.

Perhaps I ought just to add that the doctrine of the divine triunity is not derivable *only* from those passages where the Father and the Son and the Holy Spirit are mentioned together in clear threeness yet seeming oneness. All through the New Testament Epistles the deity of Christ and of the Holy Spirit is recurrently affirmed or implied, until we simply have to recognize, unless we water down the wording, that there are three (but no other) personal beings who are regarded as being triunely the one God.

Even apart from mighty expositions of our Lord's deity such as John 1:1-14, Colossians 1:14-20,[1] and Hebrews 1:1-14, there is the fact that He is everywhere so coupled with the Father as to imply coequal oneness. For example, in the first apostolic letter which Paul ever wrote (so far as we know) he begins, "Unto the church of the Thessalonians which is *in God the Father and in the Lord Jesus*

Christ." Could the strictly monotheistic Pharisee-Jew, Paul, have thus spoken of all those believers as being "in" both the Father and Christ if he did not believe that both the Father and the Son were coequally *omnipresent* and therefore coequally divine? He goes on to salute those Thessalonians: "Grace be unto you, and peace, from God our Father, and the Lord Jesus Christ."[2] Would Paul have bracketed our Lord with the infinite Father as being thus equally one with the Father as the source and imparter of divine grace and peace if Christ were not coequally God?

It is the same with the Holy Spirit. As we have seen in the Gospels and again in the Epistles, His personalness is both taught and shown. Throughout the apostolic letters that wonderful person is equally the Spirit of God the Father (Rom. 8:11; 1 Cor. 6:11; 2 Cor. 3:3) and the Spirit of our Lord Jesus (1 Peter 1:11; Gal. 4:6). Indeed, Romans 8:9 brings both aspects together in one verse:

> But ye are not in the flesh, but in the Spirit, if so be that the *Spirit of God* dwell in you. Now if any man have not the *Spirit of Christ* he is none of His.

But not only is the Holy Spirit thus *statedly* the Spirit of both the Father and the Son, as in that ninth verse, but verses 10 and 11 also add that now, through His indwelling us, both God the Father and Christ abide within us.

> And if *Christ* be in you....But if the Spirit of Him that raised up Jesus from the dead [God the *Father*] dwell in you....

If such close interchange and blending of phrases do not intendedly indicate a personal three who are essentially one, what language could, except a direct, dogmatic statement? In 2 Corinthians 3:17 and 18, the Holy Spirit is not only called "the Spirit of the Lord," but there is the didactic statement, "Now the Lord *is* the Spirit."

And so we might go on, but we refrain, for the evidence is abundant. As the receding tide leaves sparkling crystals on a sandy beach, so these significant blendings of the Father and the Son and the Holy Spirit scintillate everywhere up and down the New Testament Epistles. We see also that a stage is now reached in the biblical revelation of the divine triunity where that triunity is continually *assumed* and everywhere propagated as a basic truth of the Christian faith.

LAST BOOK OF THE BIBLE

As we have said, that which is recurrently *foretokened* in the

Old Testament, and then firmly *implied* in the four Gospels, and then humanly *experienced* in the Acts, and then everywhere *assumed* in the Epistles, is completively *endorsed* in Revelation, the last book of the Holy Writ.

Looking back now over the biblical revelation as a whole, we see that it moves in five distinct stages as it progressively communicates to us the triunity of God. First, the Old Testament is distinctively the revelation of the first person of the Godhead, with emphasis on the divine sovereignty, power, wisdom, holiness, righteousness. Then, second, the four Gospels bring forth the second member of the Godhead as the only begotten Son of the Father in the profound mystery of the incarnation and the atonement. In the Acts of the Apostles it is peculiarly the Holy Spirit who speaks and acts as the third member of the threefold Godhead, the Spirit of the Father and of the Son; the inward revealer, regenerator, enduer, sanctifier. Fourth, in the New Testament Epistles the whole Godhead—Father, Son, and Holy Spirit—is expressed in threefold unification as the eternal triunity, the one true God. Then, fifth, in the Apocalypse we find this triunity finally confirmed in vivid vision and symbol.

To begin with, this closing book of Scripture is notable for its finalizing testimony to the Holy Spirit. At the outset it attributes the whole Apocalypse to Him. John says, "I was *in the Spirit* on the Lord's day" (1:10). That does not mean merely that John was in some ecstatic state of mind, it means a controlling envelopment by the personal Holy Spirit Himself. That is at once confirmed by the seven re-occurrences of the same expression ("the Spirit") in the letters to the seven churches. Seven times, it comes as the signature, so to speak, at the end of those seven letters respectively: "He that hath an ear, let him hear what *the Spirit* saith unto the churches."

Yet the Apocalypse is equally from God the Father and God the Son, as the introductory words to it indicate:

> The revelation of *Jesus Christ* [i.e., given by Him] which *God* gave to him (1:1).

So the unveiling was given from God (the Father) through Jesus Christ (the Son), and then in the Spirit (the Holy Spirit). If any book of the Bible is trinitarian, this last one is. But see now the testimony of the Apocalypse to the deity of our Lord Jesus Christ. In chapter 1:7, 8, we read:

> Behold, He cometh with clouds; and every eye shall see Him, and they that pierced Him: and all kindreds of the earth shall wail because of Him. Even so, Amen. I am the Alpha and the Omega, the beginning and the ending, saith the Lord God, which

is, and which was, and which is to come, the Almighty.

To most of us it seems pretty clear that it is our Lord Jesus who there says, "I am the Alpha and the Omega," a title which makes Him none less than God. However, unitarian sects, e.g., the so-called Jehovah's Witnesses, deny this, claiming that the speaker in verse 8 is not our Lord Jesus. They maintain that the "Amen" after verse 7 marks a division, so that now in verse 8 the speaker is "the Almighty"—so named at the end of the verse. Well, I have looked up the ablest commentators at my command, and *they* confirm that *Jesus* is the speaker. Nevertheless, for argument's sake we will concede the point for the moment, because we have the same in verse 11 where it surely seems certain that the "great voice" (cf. 10 and 12) is that of our Lord Jesus. I quote from the King James Version:

> A great voice, as of a trumpet, saying, I am Alpha and Omega,
> the First and the Last; and, what thou seest, write in a book....

What can our modern unitarians say to that? They have a ready reply, namely, that there is insufficient manuscript evidence to authenticate the words, "I am Alpha and Omega, the First and the Last." It is true that in English translations *since* the Authorized (or King James) Version of A.D. 1611 those words *are* omitted, but that is because those translations are not based on the *Textus Receptus*—a matter into which we cannot go here. Like many others, I myself believe the words to be authentic. However, again, for argument's sake we will momentarily concede that point too. But what then about verses 17 and 18? John writes,

> And when I saw Him I fell at His feet as dead. And He laid His
> right hand upon me, saying to me, "Fear not; I am the First and
> the Last; I am He that liveth, and was dead; and behold, I am
> alive for evermore, Amen; and have the keys of Hades and of
> death."

All must agree that our Lord Jesus is there the speaker. Also the manuscript evidence is undeniably valid. Our Lord says, "I am the First and the Last, the Living One." If that is not the assumption of eternal deity what could be? How lame and shuffling is it for unitarians to tell us that the title, "the First and the Last," is not really equal to "Alpha and Omega" which, they say, belongs to God alone! We would respectfully remind them that three times in Isaiah this very title, "the First and the Last," is used of Jehovah Himself.

> Thus saith Jehovah the King of Israel, and His Redeemer
> Jehovah of Hosts; I AM THE FIRST, AND I AM THE LAST;

and beside Me there is no God (Is. 44:6, see also 41:4 and 48:12).

Would even our risen Lord Jesus appropriate to Himself that exclusive title of God if He were anything less than God? Would it not be unthinkable blasphemy? (That is not putting it too strongly.)

However, there is no need to argue the matter further, as it is finally resolved for us in the very last paragraph of the Bible. See Revelation 22:12,13, where the speaker, beyond the faintest fleck of doubt, is our dear Lord, and about which there can be no question as to manuscript unanimity.

> Behold, I come quickly; and my reward is with Me, to give every man according as his work shall be. I AM ALPHA AND OMEGA, THE BEGINNING AND THE END, THE FIRST AND THE LAST.

So there, right at the end of the Apocalypse, is the climactic testimony of the Bible to the eternal deity of our wonderful Savior. All three couplet-titles are brought together in one unanswerable triad. All in one He is

THE ALPHA AND THE OMEGA,
THE FIRST AND THE LAST,
THE BEGINNING AND THE END.

Such are the very titles used of God the Father in chapter 21:6,

> And He that sat on the throne said; Behold, I make all things new....I am Alpha and Omega, the Beginning and the End. I will give unto him that is athirst of the fountain of the water of life freely.

That promise, "I will give unto him that is athirst of the fountain of *the water of life* freely," connects us at once with the last mention of the Holy Spirit in the Bible, i.e., chapter 22:17,

> And the *Spirit* and the bride say, Come. And let him that heareth say, Come. And let him that is athirst come. And whosoever will, let him take *the water of life* freely.

Yes, just five verses from the end of the Bible, the Holy Spirit speaks His final word, and it is that gracious invitation, "Come...take *the water of life* freely." As the Apocalypse *begins* with "what the Spirit saith to the churches," so it *ends* with what the Spirit says to the thirsting soul: "take the water of life freely." And therein, if we have eyes to see and ears to hear, the written Word of God gives us its final, wonderful picture of the threefoldness which eternally inheres in the deity. It is that "water of life" which finally exhibits it.

What *is* the "water of life"? For the answer to that we turn back to John 7:37-39 (in quoting which kindly allow me to put some words in capitals and to alter slightly our English punctuation so as to emphasize the true meaning).

> In the last day, the great day of the feast, Jesus stood and cried, saying, "If any man thirst, let him come unto *ME*, and drink. He that believeth on *ME*; even as the Scriptures hath said, out of *Him* [the Christ] shall flow rivers of *living water*."

It is out of Christ,the promised Savior, that the "rivers of living water" flow, not out of the one who drinks by believing (as well-known translations seem wrongly to imply). Nowhere does the Old Testament predict that such "living waters" would flow out of the thirsting human who believes, but it *does* say that the coming Messiah-Savior would be the source of those living streams. And we know what that "living water" is because of the explanatory comment which follows our Lord's invitation on that "great day of the feast." John adds,

> But this spake He of the *SPIRIT*, which they that believe on Him should receive: for the *HOLY SPIRIT* was not yet given; because that Jesus was not yet glorified.

So the "living water" is the Holy Spirit. "This spake He of the Spirit." But what meaning there is in that further comment, "the Holy Spirit was not yet given; because Jesus was *not yet glorified!*" With that in mind turn back again to the Apocalypse and see Jesus glorified. See His oneness with God the Father successively displayed.

> One with the Father in titles and ascriptions: "The Alpha and Omega, the First and the Last, the Beginning and the End" (1:8, 18; 21:6; 22:12,13).

> One with the Father in the worship of heaven; they "fell down before the Lamb" (5:8). "Blessing, and honor, and glory, and power, be unto Him that sitteth on the throne, and unto the Lamb for ever and ever"(13).

> One with the Father in the throne of eternal glory: "I also overcame, and am set down with My Father in His throne" (3:21). "The throne of God and of the Lamb" (22:1 and 3).

Think of it: He is one with the Father in titles of deity; one with Him in the worship of all creatures; one with Him in the throne of the universe. That is the ultimate picture of Jesus glorified. He is in the very throne of God. He has always belonged there as the second person of the eternal Triunity, but now He is there also as the Lamb-Lion, Messiah-Redeemer, God-*Man*! And when Jesus is thus supremely glorified then the Holy Spirit flows forth in fullest freeness. That is why we read in chapter 22:1,

> And he showed me a pure river of *water of life*, clear as crystal, proceeding out of the throne of *God* and of the *Lamb*....

It is the last and in some ways perhaps the most remarkable biblical picture of the eternal triunity. God the Father, all-supreme, is now visibly expressed in the throne as Redeemer-God by the God-Man Lord Jesus; and from that joint throne emanates the Holy Spirit as the water of life, given in such endless, copious fullness that "whosoever will" may take the water of life freely! The Holy Spirit at last, and now forever, is thus given because Jesus is now finally glorified!

Is not that crystal river flowing from "the throne of God and of the Lamb" indeed a beautiful picture of the eternal triunity self-communicated for the continuous renewal of grateful and adoring creatures in blissful immortality? And is not this last book of the Bible indeed a remarkable endorsement of the whole biblical testimony to the eternal one in three and three in one?

[1] For comment on these passages and their testimony to our Lord's deity I refer any interested reader to my book, *The Master Theme of the Bible*, chapter 11, published by Tyndale House Publishers, Wheaton, Illinois.

[2] Some manuscripts omit these words in 1 Thess. 1:1, but the identical greeting occurs in 1 Cor. 1:3; 2 Cor. 1:2; Gal. 1:3; Eph. 1:2; Phil. 1:2; 2 Thess. 1:2; 1 Tim. 1:2; 2 Tim. 1:2; Titus 1:4; Philem. 3.

6

Triunity in the Universe

T he triunity of God is everywhere stamped on the universe. Both the outer universe of matter and the inner universe of mind reflect and express God's triunity by the most remarkable correspondences to it.

Recently, as never before, we have come to know the staggering immensity of the universe. When scientists tell us that by means of sound wave photography starry systems have been discovered twenty million light years away, we can only gasp at such vastness. Or when we learn that inside an atom the electron orbits around the proton a quadrillion times a second, we can only marvel in dumb inability to comprehend such infinitesimally concentrated intensity. But as we now know, these things *are*, and they make the riddle of the universe more absorbing than ever.

Is the universe rationally understandable? Is the totality of things actually a *universe*, i.e., an all-comprehending unity? Is there a discoverable and understandable reason why the structure and functioning of it are what they are?

To begin with: What are the basics of the universe? What are those realites which lie behind and exist within it and which include all other things? There are three. We call them (1) space, (2) matter, (3) time. The whole investigable universe is a basic trinity of those three.

Space

Take the first of that trinity: *space*. It is basic because it underlies everything else. Whether we think of space as an outward reality or only as our way of seeing the universe, it still remains that the universe that we know is a universe of space.

What is space? It consists of three directions: (1) length, (2) breadth, (3) height. Any other dimension is mere theory. Time is not a dimension of space, as Einstein postulated, for it cannot be demonstrated that space either includes time or produces it. Space, as we know it, is these three: length, breadth, height.

Matter

Take the second of the three basics in the structure of the universe: *matter*. We know now that what we call matter is not a static fabric but is primarily energy. This energy issues in motion. Then, as motion assumes those myriad forms which come to us as light, sound, color, heat, tangible shapes, and so on, it becomes what we call phenomena. So, then just as space is three, i.e., length, breadth, height, so matter is three, i.e., energy, motion, phenomena.

Time

Take the third of the three basic realities of the physical universe: *time*. Whether we regard time as an outer reality or as our inner concept of things, it is threefold. It consists of (1) past, (2) present, (3) future. Time does not belong to eternity· it belongs to created things. So the universe, including our own world, is a universe of time; and time registers itself as that inseparable trinity: past, present, and future. There are no more than those three. There are no less than those three. There are always those three. Time cannot have being at all without those three; they are an absolute threeness, yet the threeness is an inseparable threeness in oneness. It is a fundamental triunity.

The Basic Three

Here, then, is a remarkable fact. The physical universe consists of three basic realities: space, matter, time. Each is so distinct from the other two that the three are a real threeness. Yet the three are so one that they are a triune oneness. There simply has to be space if there is matter, for matter cannot exist without space to hold it. There simply has to be time if there is matter, for matter is energy in motion, continually producing phenomena, which means succession; and succession means time.

It is even more remarkable that each of those three universal basics, i.e., space, matter, time, is itself a further triunity. Space is length, breadth, height. Matter is energy, motion, phenomena. Time is past, present, future. So the universe is one vast, mysterious triunity of space, matter, time, and each of those is itself a triunity. In each case, the threeness is oneness. Space, matter, time are one universe. Length, breadth, height are one space. Energy, motion, phenomena are one matter. Past, present, future are one time. It is a universal oneness-in-threeness and threeness-in-oneness. Indeed, we may say that the universe is a *tri*-universe.

Is This The Key?

That suggests a further question. Since the basic threefoldness of the physical universe so obviously corresponds with the threefoldness of God in the Bible, could it be that both the universe and the Bible express the same divine triunity in different terms? I believe the answer to that is "Yes." I have believed it all the more since I read a book published over fifty years ago by the late Dr. Nathan R. Wood, *The Secret of the Universe.* Let me here pay my tribute to it and gladly acknowledge my indebtedness to Dr. Wood for the main ideas in this chapter. I wish it were possible to include large quotations from his book, but I can only summarize his thoughts and offer what I hope may be some helpful observations of my own.

Think how extraordinary the scriptural revelation of the divine Triunity is. As we have already seen, all that is claimed for the Father is equally claimed for the only begotten Son and again equally for the Holy Spirit and for those three only. It is an absolute threeness. No one member can possibly be either of the other two. Yet the threeness is nonetheless an absolute oneness, for the three are not three parts of God, but each *is* God. The Father is in the Son; the Son is in the Father; the Spirit is in them both; and they are both in the Spirit. It is such a mysterious doctrine that it simply could not have been invented. Yet even after being clearly revealed it is the most puzzling of all the teachings in Scripture. Yet it is just as necessary as it is mysterious if we are to do full justice to the biblical testimony. God is progressively disclosed as being undoubtedly three, yet nonetheless one. Gradually, the unveiling proceeds until Father, Son, and Holy Spirit are recognized by us as three modes of *personal consciousness* in one infinite being. They are definitely distinguishable, yet inasmuch as God is personal, the three are inseparably one; personality is not divisible.

Nor is that all. The New Testament seems to present the Father as first, the Son as second, and the Holy Spirit as third. That, however, cannot mean first, second, third, in order of greatness, for all three are infinite. Nor does it mean first, second, third, in order of time, for all three are eternal. But it does seem to indicate an order of self-expression or activity. The Father is the *source*. The Son is the *begotten* of the Father. And the Holy Spirit *proceeds* from the Father through the Son. Furthermore, the Father is unseen. The Son embodies and reveals Him. The Holy Spirit then makes the revelation real to creature intelligences. It is indeed a written and historical revelation of divine triunity, as fascinating as it is mysterious.

What, then, about the triunities in the physical universe? Do they really and exactly correspond to that biblical triunity of God? Well, take first the three absolute basics of the physical universe, i.e., space, matter, time. Space must come first because as we have remarked, there is no room outside of it where matter can exist. Just as obviously, matter must come second, for it is matter that as energy, motion, and phenomena becomes successive continuity from which proceeds time. Yes, space first, matter second, time third. Yet that is not the order of priority, but only the order of operation. As is now well-known, space is not empty nothingness. Somehow, it is energy as well as the sphere of energy. As long as there has been matter (energy, motion, phenomena), there have been space and time. All three are equal in duration. It is a most arresting parallel with the biblical doctrine of the Father, the Son, and the Holy Spirit—in that same sequence, yet coequal in duration.

Furthermore, think about the subsidiary triunity inside each of those three basics that we call space, matter, time. Observe the triunity inside space, namely, length, breadth, height. We usually think of length as forward, and breadth as sideward, and height as upward. And we always think of them in that order: first length, then breadth, then height. I suppose that we always think of length (or forward) as being first because man's eyes are set in his head in a forward direction. Breadth comes second because, though man's eyes must turn left or right to it, breadth is still horizontal, like length. So, height comes third. It includes up and down, neither of which is level with man's eyes, but requires either the lifting or lowering of the head. Subtle? Yes, but there it is. Yet, though there is that subtle sequence of first and second and third, it is not the order of succession but of simultaneous existence. Length simply could not exist before breadth, for length can only go forward when there is breadth through which to go. And what applies to length equally applies to the other two. All three are interdependent and coexistent. It is an intriguing parallel to the triunity of the Father, the Son, and the Holy Spirit.

Next think of matter and its three constituents: energy, motion, phenomena. Energy necessarily comes first. Then comes energy in motion-waves, electrons, atoms. Then as energy through motion breaks on our senses in its varying velocities as light or sound or heat, and as tangible textures, we have phenomena. Verily, that is the order: first energy, then motion, then phenomena. Yet again, it is not the order of either precedence or importance but strictly of procedure or coexistent function. Energy causes. Motion expresses. Phenomena communicate. But motion and phenomena do not only express and communicate energy; they are energy. All three are equally and indivisibly one. It is another astonishing correspondence to the biblical doctrine of the coequal divine Triunity—the Father, the Son, and the Holy Spirit.

Furthermore, think of that third subsidiary triunity that comprises what we call time: past, present, future. Where does time come from? Perhaps it may surprise some, but time comes to us from the future. The common assumption is that time comes to us from the past, but that is because the past is the only part of time that we can see and because so much comes to us from the past by way of history, memory, records, and influences. Time itself does not come to us from the past; it comes to us a day, an hour, or a minute at a time from that which has not yet been. A moment's reflection will convince anyone that time simply cannot come to us from the past, i.e., from that which has already come and gone. Select any date or piece of time that you will, and then trace its course. It never moves from the past into the present and then into the future. No, all time comes to us from the future, moves into the present, then passes into the past. So the causal order of time is: (1) future, (2) present, (3) past.

Thus, as with space and matter, the order of the three aspects of time is not according to importance. No, for each of the three is all of the three. Reflect: All of time past or present has been future. In the very beginning, all time was future. But again, all time has been, now is, or will be present. From the very beginning, time has been becoming the present. And eventually, all time is or will be past. From the very beginning, time has been becoming the past. At the beginning, the whole of time was future. Intermediately, the whole of time is present. At the end, the whole of time is the past. Each one is the whole. Past, present, future are not something that time *does*. They are what time *is*. All three are equally time. It seems to be nothing less than another amazing mirror of the biblically revealed triunity in the Godhead: the Father, the Son, the Holy Spirit.

The Crowning Correspondence

But the crowning correspondence of the universe with the triunity of God is seen in man, for man is not only matter but also mind. Therefore, he reflects the triunity of the Godhead in a personal way which inanimate matter cannot do. Man's threefold reflection of God, however, does not lie in the fact that man is spirit, soul, and body, as is generally supposed, for in the triune deity, the Father, Son, and the Holy Spirit are all the one God, whereas in man the spirit, soul, and body are not all the one man. The soul is the real man. The body is not the man, though the man lives in it. Nor is the spirit the man. It is the highest attribute of the soul. The three are truly three, but they are not one. Besides, in the New Testament presentation of the divine triunity, the Father, Son, and Holy Spirit are three distinct centers of personal consciousness in one being. But in the human trio of spirit, soul, and body, those three are not three distinct centers of consciousness, for the body does not think or have self-awareness at all, and the spirit does not think apart from the soul, of which it is an attribute.

Nor does the likeness of man to the triunity of God inhere in the fact that the human mind is apparently threefold: (1)intellect, (2)volition, (3)emotion. Those three may be the main components of the human mind, but are they the only three? What about memory, imagination, and intuition? And even if we include those in intellect, volition, and emotion, do those three really parallel the triunity of the Godhead? I think not. They are not three modes of being, such as we see in the triune Godhead, but only three capacities of the soul. They are three areas of activity ("I think," "I act," "I feel") in and by which the mind, or soul, does something. Nor are they three-in-one in a way that corresponds to the triunity in God. Intellect is not emotion. Emotion is not will. Will is neither intellect nor emotion, though it may act for the one and seek to control the other. Therefore, intellect, volition, and emotion are no more than a superficial parallel to the three-in-one mystery of God.

The fact is that man is a triunity in a much deeper way. In the very basis of his being, man is triune. What is the very inmost aspect of man to which we can penetrate? The philosopher Descartes told us. To get at the ultimate reality of man, Descartes discarded everything that could be explained away, until he came to one fact that nothing could dislodge, namely, "I think." From that arose his famous philosophical statement, *Cogito ergo sum*, "I think, therefore I am." In any conscious being, that is the first basic. In the rising scale of conscious creatures on this earth, from the lowest up to man, self-consciousness and the feeling-capacity parrallel each other exactly at each level of the ascending scale. The capacity for feeling, whether of joy or pain, corresponds to the level of consciousness. (That is why our Lord's sufferings on Calvary are beyond our human comprehension. In His sinless manhood and boundless deity, He had the capacity for an infinite suffering which gave an infinite value and significance to His atoning death.) All the many forms of being which are without thought are also without consciousness. There cannot be thinking without conscious being. Thinking is not in itself the conscious being, but it is the most basic evidence of it. There simply can be no thinking without self-conscious being, nor can there be self-conscious being without thinking. So, then, the first thing about man is that he is a thinking, self-aware ego.

What is the second basic in man? It is the kind of "I think" that is true of him. Human thinking includes perceiving, knowing, reasoning, grasping, desiring, resenting, hoping, fearing, deciding, choosing, willing, and acting. These, and especially the power of self-determination, make not only a self-aware ego, but also a human person. In this, he is above all other earthly creatures. The animals may have individuality, but they are not persons. One of the main dictionary definitions of "person" is "a human being as distinguished from things or animals." There is another distinguishing ingredient in man's "I think" which lifts him above all other earthly creatures. We call it moral consciousness, or conscience. Who can explain it? Neither the biologist nor the psychologist can; but it is there, providing a sense of responsibility that is as ineradicable as it is unique. That, then, is the second thing. Man's inmost being says not only "I think, therefore I am" but also "I think, know, feel, and act as a separate entity." In other words, man is not only a self-aware ego, but he is also a self-recognized person.

What is the third basic in man? It is what we call personality. All of us sense that person and personality are not identical. Person is what I am in myself. Personality is what I am in expression. Person is the self as known by itself. Personality is the person as known to others.

These are the three real basics, the three things every human being is in the ultimate analysis. We are: (1) ego, (2) person, (3) personality. Essentially, those three are self-awareness, self-recognition, and self-communication. Are they distinctly three? Yes, they are. Are they equally one? Yes, they are. Can any of the three exist without the other two? No. Are they all of the same duration? Yes. Is each of the three, therefore, the whole man? Yes. The three are utterly a trinity in unity, the closest of all resemblances on earth to the triunity of the Godhead as set forth in the Scriptures. Of course, .there can be no perfect parallel to the divine triunity, for God is infinite, and all creatures are only finite. Ego, person, and personality in man are not three persons in one being, as in the Deity, but they are three modes of consciousness, activity, and communication that correspond to the Father, the Son, and the Holy Spirit.

Triunities Everywhere

Thus, both in the outer world of phenomena and in the inner world of the human mind, we find triunity stamped on the elemental facts of the creation, a triunity that reflects the God who is the originator and ground of the universe. Yet, that is not all. We find triunity everywhere in the fundamentals of human thought and activity.

Take logic, or the science of reason, for example. Logic has been called the first and most basic of all the sciences because it is the science of thought itself. Without logical thought, there can be no valid reasoning. At the very center of logic or valid reasoning is the syllogism. And what is the syllogism? It is another trinity in unity. It consists of major premise, minor premise, and conclusion. We see this in the following simple illustration.

> Major premise: All human beings are mortal.
> Minor premise: All men are human beings.
> Conclusion: Therefore, all men are mortal.

Of course, we do not always have the two premises and conclusions arranged in that simple and regular order. Sometimes, the conclusion is stated first, or the two premises are inverted, or one of the premises or the conclusion is left unexpressed (in which case the argument is called an enthymeme). But however an argument is arranged, or however complex and elaborate our reasoning may be, it must move in true syllogisms or else it is fallacious. Many of us may never have studied logic. But whether we are conscious of it or not, we continually make syllogisms. We are so created that thought has to be that way. Glance back at our simple illustration. Those three statements are definitely three, yet they are just as definitely three-in-one because they are interdependent. The conclusion is implicit in the two premises, and the united meaning of the two premises becomes explicit in the conclusion. Thus, the syllogism is a most remarkable reflection of the divine triunity as taught in Holy Writ. As such, it lies at the very foundation of all valid thought.

It is the same in human art and, indeed, in all the creative works of man—painting, sculpture, poetry, music, building, mechanics, and industry. Everywhere, we find triunity. Take that captivating work of art in your local art gallery, for example. What is the principle that it expresses? It is threefold. First, there is the original *idea* in the artist's mind. Second, there is the visible *embodiment* of that idea in the picture. Third, there is the self-transmitting *effect* of the idea on other persons. In other words, the idea must first live in the mind. Then it must assume a visible form, and then it must speak to other minds. In all art there are always those three, and they are always three-in-one. Each of the three is necessary to the other two. First comes inspiration, then incarnation, and then communication.

It is the same everywhere in nature. Look at the garden, the orchard, and the harvest field. First comes the seed, then the plant, and then its use or communication to others.

It is the same in aesthetics. The Platonist says that beauty lies solely in the abstract ideal. The realist says that beauty lies mainly in the concrete expression—the statue, the flower, the symphony, the sunset, the edifice. The pragmatist says that beauty lies solely in the mind of the beholder; it is purely subjective, he says. What is beautiful to one is not so to another. The sunset that charms the poet may be perceived as a lurid glare to a cannibal. The truth, however, is that beauty resides in all three, but all three must be taken together. The abstract concept, its expression to the senses, and the ability to appreciate it are a trinity-in-unity.

Perhaps the most fascinating peculiarity about all these basic triunities of the universe is the subtle way in which their threeness is always a oneness corresponding to the biblical threeness-in-oneness of the triune Godhead. How God can be three and yet one has not only been a puzzle to many, but also has been treated as absurd by unitarian writers. They argue that if God the Father is one distinct person and the Lord Jesus another distinct person and the Holy Spirit yet another distinct person, then they are so definitely three that they cannot possibly be one. One plus one plus one equals three, they say. But they are wrong. The heavenly Father, the beloved Son, and the Holy Spirit are not one plus one plus one. Let me explain.

Think again about space, one of the three fundamental realities of the physical universe. Space is length, breadth, height. But it is not length plus breadth plus height. As anyone knows, when you have three dimensions, you never add them to get their area or content. For instance, if you have an oblong ten feet in length by five feet in width, you do not add the length to the breadth to find the space or area inside the oblong. That would give you only fifteen feet, whereas the enclosed area is fifty. If you want cubic footage, you do not add length, breadth, and height. It is never length plus breadth plus height. It is always length multiplied by breadth multiplied by height. So it is with the divine triunity. God is not one plus one plus one, which equals three. God is one multiplied by one multiplied by one, which equals *one!*

The triune God is not three Gods, nor is God in three parts. In one plus one plus one, each one is only a part. But in one multiplied by one multiplied by one, each is the whole, for the whole is in each. One multiplied by one multiplied by one produces a multiplied, intensified unity—a *tri*unity. Such is God.

As it is with space, so is it with matter. As we have seen, matter is energy, motion, phenomena. It is wrong to say that matter is energy plus motion plus phenomena, for that would make them separate from each other, whereas all three are matter. They so interpenetrate and express each other that we may truly say that energy multiplied by motion multiplied by phenomena equals matter. It is another case of one multiplied by one multiplied by one equals one, as in the Deity.

It is the same with time. Although time consists of the future, the present, and the past, it is not true to say that the future plus the present plus the past equals time. All time was at first future, and all the past was once the present, and all the present was once future and will be past. It is another case of one multiplied by one multiplied by one equals one, as in the biblical triunity of the Father, Son, and Holy Spirit.

I will not elaborate further. The fact is that this trinity in unity, this one multiplied by one multiplied by one equals one, is found everywhere throughout the basic features of the universe. To summarize, we see it in the three basics—space, matter, time. Then we see it in each of those three. Space is length, breadth, height; matter is energy, motion, phenomena; and time is future, present, past. Then we see it in man—not only as spirit, soul, body, or as intellect, volition, emotion, but as nature, person, personality. We see it in human logic, art, painting, sculpture, poetry, music, building, mechanics, industry, aesthetics and in plant life throughout nature. To modern science, the universe of so-called matter has become a whole universe of electrical charges, and those electrical charges operate in the all-comprehending, all-penetrating categories that we have briefly considered.

A Crop of Questions

This at once raises a crop of questions. (1) This vast, all-inclusive, super triunity embracing lesser triunities which everywhere characterize the structure and function of the universe—what can it mean? (2) Does not the tremendous logic of the universal facts point us through the triunities of the creation to the triunity of the Creator? (3) Assuming that the Bible is truly the inspired Word of God and that its message of the triune God is therefore true, is there not strong likelihood that such triunity would register itself in the created universe? (4) Also, conversely, is not the presence of such constitunional triunities throughout the universe a powerful corroboration of the Bible in its revelation of the supreme three-in-one and one-in-three? (5) Although some of us might not agree that the force of the facts demands triunity in God, do those facts not at least suggest it by seeming to reflect it? (6) Since there must be a cause and explanation of this triunity throughout the universe, is it not reasonable to think that it must be in the nature of the great Architect? (7) If we ask why there are these all-controlling triunities which condition the structure and functioning of the universe, is it not true to say that the only answer that fits the facts is the biblical doctrine of the triunity?

That brings us to the last question. (8) Do the triunities of the universe and the revelation of the triunity of God in the Bible correspond so closely that they validate each other and thus become a double witness to the triune nature of the Godhead? I believe that the answer to that question is yes. Reflect on it for a moment or two.

First, the threeness in each of the triunities found in the universe is an absolute threeness; no one of the three can be either of the other two. Space, matter, time are an absolute three. So are length, breadth, height. So are energy, motion, phenomena. So are future, present, past. Yet each of those threes is also an absolute oneness, for each is the whole of the three, and the whole of the three is each. Corresponding exactly to that is the biblical doctrine of God the Father, God the Son, God the Holy Spirit—absolutely three. No one of the eternal three is either of the other two. Yet each of the is one with the other two; each of the three is infinite God, not just a third or a part.

Again, the triunities of the universe are always in trinitarian progression. None of them is either statically one or statically three. They are a moving oneness, continuously expressed in threeness. Nothing is inactive in the universe, as science now knows it, not even space. No longer is space thought of as emptiness. There could be neither energy nor motion in nothingness! Space consists of invisible electromagnetic power that is the source and continuum of everything. Consider the first, vast, and most inclusive of all the universe's triunities: space, matter, time. Those three include all the others, and they are a continual progression. Space becomes matter, and matter in turn causes succession, or time. So it is, also, with the sub-triunity of matter: energy, motion, phenomena. Energy becomes motion, and motion in turn becomes phenomena. So it is, again, with the triunity of dimension: length, breadth, height. Length becomes recognizable direction only through breadth, and then both length and breadth become so through height. So it is with the triunity of time: future, present, past. The future becomes the present, and the present becomes the past. So it is, furthermore, in the constitution of mankind. The basic nature assumes individual form in the human person, which in turn becomes self-communicating as personality. So it is with all the universe's triunities.

Paralleling this, as we have noted, is the divine triunity as progressively presented in the Bible. The Father is first; the Son is second; the Holy Spirit is third. It is a oneness expressed in trinitarian progress. The sovereign, holy Creator revealed in the Old Testament becomes the gracious heavenly Father revealed through the incarnate Son in the four Gospels. The Father and the Son are savingly communicated to us through the Holy Spirit.

Most remarkably, in the triunities of the universe, it is always the second member of the three that acts or activates. It is so in that first and most basic triunity of space, matter, time. It is matter, the in-between member, that activates space into movement, thereby causing succession, or time. So is it with that further triunity of matter—energy, motion, phenomena—where again it is the middle member that acts, i.e., motion. It is equally so with the triunity of time: future, present, past. It is the middle member, i.e., the present, that activates time into observable, historical movement. So it is with the subtriunity of space: length, breadth, height. A straight line is the shortest distance between two points. But between which two points? There cannot be a straight line forward, either seen or even merely conceived, without breadth going crosswise to provide that in which the two points occur. There simply cannot be length without breadth, but as soon as you have breadth, length is revealed thereby. So it is with all the triunities.

Although it is always the second member that acts, that member does not do so independently of the other two. No, in reality the second member acts only because the first member moves through it. That is so with the space-matter-time trinity, for it is the ever prior space-power that becomes an active force through matter. It is so with the energy-motion-phenomena trinity, for what is motion but the ever prior energy released in action? It is so in the future-present-past trinity, for it is the ever prior future from which the active present is begotten. So it is with all the universe's triunities.

All this corresponds in an amazing way to the triunity of God as revealed to us in the Bible. It is the eternal second member of the divine three-in-one who always acts, yet He never acts independently of the other two. The eternal first person becomes active will and power through Him, as a few quotations will exemplify.

> In the beginning was the Word, and the Word was with God, and the Word was God. The same was in the beginning with God. All things were made by Him; and without Him was not anything made that was made (John 1:1-3).

The Word, or Logos, is both distinguished from and identified with God, for He was both with God, and He was God. Taken without bias and in terms of other didactic statements in the New Testament, the Greek cannot mean other than that. In verse 18, that same being, the Word, which was with God, is called "the only begotten Son, which is in the bosom of the Father." Those two metaphors, the Word and the Son, supplement and protect each other. To think of the second person of the divine Triunity only as the Word might suggest merely an impersonal quality or faculty in God. To think of Him only as the Son might falsely limit us to the concept of a personal, yet created, being. But the combination of the two terms protects both aspects of the Bible's teaching. Our Lord and Savior, the second member of the Triunity, is both personal and eternal. As with all the triunities of the universe, it is the second member who acts. As the Word, He creates, and "without Him was not anything made that was made." As the Son, He redeems, for He "was made flesh, and dwelt among us...full of grace and truth" (v.14). Yet He does not act with independent volition, for the text says "all things were made by Him." He is the eternal agent in and through whom the whole Deity acts.

> For by Him were all things created, that are in heaven, and that are in earth, visible and invisible, whether they be thrones, or dominions, or principalities, or powers: all things were created by Him, and for Him (Colossians 1:16).

> God, who at sundry times and in divers manners spake in time past unto the fathers by the prophets, hath in these last days spoken unto us by His Son, whom He hath appointed heir of all things, by whom also He made the worlds (Heb. 1:1-2).

In all the triunities of the universe it is the second member which expresses. We see this in the first and most fundamental triunity of space-matter-time, for space-power is invisible, but matter expresses it visibly. We see it in the triunity of energy-motion-phenomena, for energy is invisible, but motion expresses it in action. We see it in the triunity of future-present-past, for the future is unknown and invisible to us, but present time is visible and knowable. We see it in the triunity of length-breadth-height, for length is impossible even to conceive of or to imagine until breadth gives it expression in measurable direction. So is it with all the universe's triunities. And so it is, again, with the triunity of God as set forth in the holy Scriptures. See it in the following, well-known quotations.

> Neither knoweth any man the Father, save the Son, and he to whomsoever the Son will reveal Him (Matt. 11:27).

> He that hath seen Me hath seen the Father (John 14:9).

> The glory of God in the face of Jesus Christ... (2 Cor. 4:6).

> Who [Christ] is the image of the invisible God... (Col. 1:15).

> Who [Christ] being the brightness of His (God's) glory, and the express image of His person... (Heb. 1:3).

> The life [eternal] was manifested, and we have seen it, and bear witness (1 John 1:2).

As the prologue to John's Gospel states, our Lord Jesus Christ is the Word, the expression of God, not only toward man, not only from premundane antiquity, but prior to all the creation (vv. 2-3)—fundamentally, eternally, indivisibly. He was so not merely from the beginning; He already was in the beginning (v. 1). The Greek word *Logos*, translated as "Word," is richly useful to convey the meaning in large degree. As a word may be distinguished from the thought that it expresses (for the two are not identical) so can the second person of the Godhead be distinguished from the first. Yet as there simply cannot be a word apart from the thought that it expresses, so also God and the Word simply cannot be conceived of as ever having existed without each other. They are distinguishable but inseparable. But our Lord is not only the Word, He is also the Son—which brings a wonderful warmth into the relationship. And just as the eternal wisdom and the eternal Word eternally require each other, so does the eternal fatherhood require the eternal sonship. Thus, our Lord Jesus Christ, the eternal second member of the divine Triunity, is the eternal expression of the Godhead. As the Word, He expresses the divine wisdom. As the Son, He expresses the divine love. As the Word, He is the executive of all creation. As the Son, He is especially the mediator of redemption. Yes, the second member of the Triunity is the one who expresses the Deity.

Finally, the triunities of the physical universe all indicate a threefold process of existence. Without exception, the first member of the three-in-one begets and becomes the second, and the first and the second issue in the third. That, apparently, is the universal threefold law of existence—a continual becoming through the triune operation of origination, manifestation, and communication. To us human beings, that is how the universe comes to us.

See it in the space-time-matter, the most basic of the vast, physical triunities. As we have seen, space is an invisible but all-pervasive power. As such, it originates all else. Then it becomes dynamically or visibly manifested as matter. Then, through time, it is communicated to us. Time is nonphysical; it belongs to the mind. Time, indeed, is the link between the physical universe and the nonphysical mind. Space and matter are physical; they do not themselves enter the mind. But matter-as-motion begets a consecutive succession which creates time, and so physical existences become perceptual to the mind. Our minds must think in terms of succession. Time enters our human consciousness and becomes a part of our life.

Such, we repeat, is the continuous triune becoming which is the universal process of existence. We see it not only in the basic space-matter-time triunity but in all the other triunities of the universe. And so it is with the biblical revelation of the triune God. Corresponding, for example, to the space-matter-time triunity, we see God the Father, God the Son, and God the Holy Spirit in exactly the same relationship. Corresponding to originating space-power is the Father. Corresponding to matter, which manifests, is the Son. Corresponding to time, which communicates universal realities intelligibly to the mind, is the Holy Spirit who communicates spiritual realities so that they come alive in our human experience.

Much more might be added, but have we not now said enough to show that the biblical doctrine of the eternal Triunity has its vast endorsement throughout the physical universe?

So, the universe is a vast circuit out from the infinite mind of God through space-power, matter, and phenomenal time back to the infinite mind that conceived it. And this vast cycle of becoming and expressing and fulfilling perfectly parallels in its nature and functioning the glorious, divine three-in-one God who is revealed in the Bible. In the physical universe, space (i.e., outspreading power) is the source, just as the Father is in the biblical Triunity. Matter (motion) is the space-power activity that parallels the biblical revelation of God the Son. Time (which comes to us from space through matter), that which registers phenomenal realities in our human apprehension, corresponds to the biblical revelation of the activity of the Holy Spirt. Furthermore, just as everything first proceeds from space-power, then takes active form in matter, and then reaches fulfillment in time, and just as the fullness of time is the return of all matter to the Godhead, so it is in the activity of the biblical Triunity. The creative life of the Father goes out through the revelatory and redeeming work of the Son and reaches human experience in the regenerative work of the Holy Spirit, from which it all returns in the "fullness of time" (Eph. 1:10). It returns to the infinite, gracious Godhead in the worship, praise, adoration, and gratitude of "a multitude which no man can number," and from worlds which ten million telescopes could never bring into our vision, "that God may be all in all" (1 Cor. 15:28). The whole magnificent splendor of it flashes out through one concentrated, inspired statement in Romans 11:36,

> For of Him, and through Him, and unto Him, are all things: to whom be glory for ever. Amen.

Practical Values

Do we sufficiently realize, I wonder, the preciousness and practical value of the divine triunity as revealed in the Bible? To begin with, that doctrine gives us the most intelligible concept of God. Consider that a God without distinctions such as Father, Son, and Holy Spirit, an absolutely single, solitary unit, would have no inherent, basic relationship with any other conscious being, either within or outside of Himself. We cannot conceive that such a unit could sustain in His essence a personal relationship with any created, finite being, for a personal relationship would contradict His absoluteness. Such a monistic understanding of God is bleak and emotionless, and portrays Him as absolutely and coldly separated from all finite forms of being and consciousness. Such a concept of God prohibits any thought of possible communion with Him. But to think biblically of God as triune, who by this very nature is a threefold, reciprocal fellowship of Father and Son and Holy Spirit makes God seem wonderfully warm and close.

To that we may add that the Christian revelation of the divine Triunity brings God to us in the dearest of thinkable relationships. In an unspeakably precious way, the biblical revelation of God portrays Him as personal and paternal. Think of it. *God* is our *Father*! That fatherhood is not only didactically stated in the Holy Scripture, but it is also visibly demonstrated to us in the incarnate Son. We could never have known the real fatherhood of God apart from its manifestation in the life of Christ. Through the coming of the eternal Son to mankind, we see God's fatherhood written across the strange course of permitted human history.

In the revelation of God in the Bible, we see the sonship-fatherhood relationship manifested in sublime perfection. At the same time, we learn that human fatherhood corresponds with something inherent in the God who breathed life into us, though of course human fatherhood, even at its noblest, is no more than a dim reflection of the divine. But the most captivating significance of God's fatherhood is that the way in which He relates as Father to the eternal Son is, in most respects, the same way that He relates to us as His sons. Never did our Lord Jesus reveal a more thrilling teaching than when He said in prayer to the Father, "Thou hast loved them, as Thou hast loved Me" (John 17:23), to which He added, "That the love wherewith Thou hast loved Me may be in them" (v. 26). When once we really understand God's fatherhood, life is never the same again. In fact, the whole universe has a different feel about it. What is more, we are even called to a fellowship with the Father which corresponds to that between the Father and the Son (John 17:21; 1 John 1:3).

Through the revelation of the triunity of God, we learn of the divine capacity of sacrifice. If God were an eternal monad, what could He have given for our redemption that would have cost Him anything? Would it have hurt Him in the least to offer on our behalf a mere creature, even the most resplendent being He had ever created? And what significance would it have had for us if a being less than God had made atonement for us? But when the Father gave up His eternal Son, who is "in the bosom of the Father" (John 1:18), it tore the very heartstrings of the Deity! It hurt the father-nature of our Creator beyond our comprehension. That is why it could be written, "God so loved the world, that He gave [in the sense of 'gave up,' i.e., to the cross] His only begotten Son...." There is an elastic capacity in the *so* that transcends all four boundless dimensions of the whole created universe. Apart from the eternal sonship of Christ and the triunity of the Godhead, there never could have been such a manifestation of divine love and self-sacrifice as there was at Calvary! Never must we forget that the Father suffered in the sufferings of the Son and that in the sufferings of the Son, the Father suffered for us.

Moreover, the Christian doctrine of the divine triunity seems necessary to the truth of the profound teaching that "God is love." Some have argued that God, considered as eternal Mind, requires an eternal object of thought that cannot be found anywhere outside Him (because all that is outside Him is not eternal). Others have argued that God, considered as eternal Will, must have a corresponding object of action, which (so it is said) implies the eternal Son and the Holy Spirit. But such arguments seem dubious and abstruse. It is true that God, considered as eternal love, seems to imply an eternal object of that love. Perfect love is the supreme moral glory of the divine being. But if there are no such personal distinctions as Father, Son, and Holy Spirit within the Godhead, then there was no object for that love until God willed the universe into existence. If that is the case, then God's love is something subsequent to His being and to the act of creation. If someone argued that love could have been present, though dormant, in God before the universe began, it is still very difficult to think that love could exist apart from an object to love. Love (unlike holiness, wisdom, or other moral qualities) is by its very nature outgoing and is called into existence by an object that already exists. Only the biblical disclosure of the divine triunity explains the superwonder that God is love.

But the most wonderful of all the practical values in the triunity of God is that it wonderfully meets the deepest need of our creaturehood. It means something so inexpressibly dear that words are poor vehicles to use to thank God for it. Yes, for it answers a threefold outreach of my deepest being to the God who made me. Let me explain. There is something deep within me that needs a God who is transcendently high and in sovereign control of all things. Unless He is "up there," high above all and in absolute control of the world, He is not really God at all. Unless I have a God like that, I cannot feel safe. So, before all else, the insistent cry of my inmost consciousness is for that all-supreme, sovereign, omnipresent God. And that need of my heart is answered in the person of God the Father who rules in the throne of the universe.

But there is also within me that which cries out and says, "Yes, I must have an almighty God up there, but oh, I wish He were not so distant in His impenetrable, governmental magnitude. I wish that somehow, without any diminution of His sovereignty, He could come close to me and walk with me along the dusty road of my earthly life, with its ups and downs and troublous windings." Indeed, it is so. My being longs for that, too, and that need of my heart is answered in the second person of the divine Triunity, who, as God the Son incarnate, born of a human mother into our human race, comes to me as my "kinsman redeemer," "in all things...made like unto his brethren" (Heb. 2:17), and "touched with the feelings of our infirmities" (4:15). As my risen Savior, He links His arm through mine and says, "Lo, I am with you alway, even unto the end of the world" (Matt. 28:20).

But there is yet another heartfelt cry within me. I find myself saying, "It is indeed wonderful to have such a sovereign, righteous God who overrules everything in heaven and on earth. It is the loveliest flood of sunshine that ever swept over me to know that in the person of His eternal Son, He took human flesh and blood to become my Savior, companion, and brother during my years of pilgrimage here. But, oh, how completely satisfying it would be if, when I cannot be in the sanctuary, and cannot be bowed in prayer, and cannot be reading the Scriptures, that same Savior-God could somehow be within me, talking to me, listening to me, answering me, communing with me, while I am in the thick of daily business, problems, temptations, and weaknesses!" Yes, such is the further, sensitive longing that wells up from deep within us. That wistful outreach to heaven is answered in the third person of the divine Triunity, the Holy Spirit, who comes not only to abide with me for ever but to be in me as the ever indwelling heavenly paraclete, comforter, guide, teacher, consoler, and strengthener (John 14:16,17)!

How truly and sympathetically the triunity of God answers that deep, threefold need of my humanity! And the loveliest wonder of all is that because the Father, Son, and Holy Spirit are not only three but three-in-one, to have the Holy Spirit in me is to have the Father and Son, too! So, my regenerated personality becomes a living temple of my triune Creator. The triune God continually and lovingly, with divine sufficiency, meets all my needs. He envelops me in fatherly care, brotherly sympathy, and motherlike comfort. What provision! The heavenly Father cares for me all my life; the sympathetic Savior bears with all my trials; and the indwelling Spirit shares all my human experiences! Is there any wonder more precious than that? To my own mind, God's triunity seems like an equilateral triangle. God the Father is the apex, and God the Son and God the Holy Spirit are the earthward angles. At the apex, God the Father controls all things. On the earthly plane, the Lord Jesus enfolds, and the Holy Spirit indwells. That analogy beautifully corresponds to the only trinitarian benediction in the New Testament. "The grace of the Lord Jesus Christ, and the love of God, and the communion of the Holy Spirit, be with you all" (2 Cor. 13:14).

The love of the Father becomes saving grace through the Son, and then both become the fellowship, or communion, in the Holy Spirit. That is the order of divine operation in the economy of redemption. The love of God is the active source. The grace of the Lord

Jesus is the outward movement. The communion of the Holy Spirit is the realized objective.

In that Corinthian benediction, however, the "grace of the Lord Jesus" is placed first. That is because Paul's order follows the order of human experience. First, we receive forgiveness and restoration to God through the riches of His grace. Then, as one of the first results, we come to know the infinite love behind that grace. Then, we begin to cry, "Abba Father," and to know the "communion of the Holy Spirit."

How deeply thrilling the divine Triunity is to the ransomed, reborn, Christian believer! Our experience of the Triunity bathes its mystery in beauty. What is mysterious to the intellect has become heavenly sunshine to the heart. Our experience of salvation in Christ more and more confirms the reality of the triunitarian nature of God. We know that the all-sovereign God the Father has spoken in Christ the Son, and we have accepted His revelation as such. We have believed on God the Son as our Savior. As a direct consequence of that, we know experientially that the Lord Jesus has done within us what only God can do. But how has the invisible Lord Jesus changed us from within? He has done it by the Holy Spirit, whom He promised to send to believers, as the New Testament clearly teaches. What the sacred Scriptures teach and what we now have experienced fit together like hand and glove to settle once and for all that our wonderful Savior-God is God the Father, God the Son, and God the Holy Spirit—the eternal Creator-Triunity, to whom be glory and adoring worship unto the ages of the ages. Amen.

7

The Holiness of God, Part One

In the biblical revelation of God nothing is accentuated more frequently or solemnly than the divine holiness. Let none of us who call ourselves Christians ever presume either to think or to speak loosely of God, for in His sin-abhorring holiness "our God is a consuming fire" (Heb. 12:29). One of Moses' parting reminders to Israel was the same, "Jehovah thy God is a consuming fire" (Deut. 4:24). Almost on the heels of that he added, "Jehovah thy God is a merciful God" (31), but he would have us to understand reverently that God's mercy must never be banked on in any way which ignores His awesome holiness.

Forty times in the Old Testament Scriptures God is called "the *Holy* One," or "the *Holy One* of Israel." Twenty-two times we read about His "*holy name*." Again and again He calls His covenant people to holiness because He Himself is holy. Leviticus 19:2 is representative: "Ye shall be holy: for I Jehovah your God am holy." Nearly one hundred times in the New Testament the Spirit of God is designated, "the *Holy* Spirit." Both in Old Testament prediction and in New Testament description our Lord Jesus is called, "the *Holy* One," or "the *Holy One* of God." On recognizing Him demon spirits cowered and cried out, "I know Thee who Thou art, the *Holy One* of God" (Mark 1:24). May we Christians never forget the utter holiness of our triune God! At every remembrance of it may our hearts deeply revere.

Everything associated with this ineffably holy deity is correspondingly holy. If He speaks through a burning bush the place becomes "holy ground" (Ex. 3:5). The articles used in worshiping Him are "holy things" (Num. 4:19). The weekly sabbath is His "holy day." The place where He is worshiped is His "holy house" (1 Chron. 29:3). That house is His "holy temple" (Ps. 5:7). The high priest's golden crown, engraved with the words, "Holiness to Jehovah," is "the holy crown" (Ex. 29:6). The ark of the covenant is "the holy ark" (2 Chron.

35:3). Because of His sanctifying presence Zion is His "holy hill," and Jerusalem is "the holy city." The whole of His tabernacle is sacred, but the inner sanctuary is "the holy of holies." Heaven above is His "holy habitation" (Deut. 26:15). His throne in the heavens is inconceivably holy, even as Psalm 47:8 proclaims: "God reigneth over the heathen: God sitteth upon the throne of His holiness." Before that throne the flame-like seraphim continually cry, "Holy! Holy! Holy!" Such is its white-heat moral splendor that even the flashings of seraphim wings are as flitting shadows. Against that sheer glory-light even "the heavens are not clean in His sight," and "the stars are not pure" beforeHim! (Job 15:15, 25:5).

Such is the divine holiness that when Moses wistfully pleaded, "I beseech Thee, show me Thy glory," God replied, "Thou canst not see My face: for no man can see Me, and live." When Isaiah beheld that holiness in his vision of the heavenly temple he cried out in prostrating awe, "Woe is me! For I am undone!" When Job, the best man on earth (Job 1:8), came into the presence of that holiness he groaned, "I abhor myself, and repent in dust and ashes." When Ezekiel caught a glimpse of it he "fell on his face" in speechless subduement. When John saw that holiness blazing out through the person of the risen Christ on lonely Patmos, he "fell at His feet as dead!"

Oh, the holiness of God! It is altogether beyond our most penetrating or sensitized comprehension, for there is nothing else which can be compared with it. How could *any* human sinner ever stand amid the devouring flame of *His* presence who, as Paul says, is "the blessed and only Potentate, the King of kings and Lord of lords; who alone hath immortality, dwelling in the light which no man can approach unto; whom no man hath seen nor can see: to whom be honor and power everlasting. Amen" (1 Tim. 6:15, 16)?

In the "so great salvation" which God has wrought for us in Christ, nothing is more graciously astounding than this: that when our salvation through Christ is eventually consummated, we shall live amid the eradiating glory-light of that sheer holiness, and find our heaven there. With sinless hearts and immortal bodies and minds interpenetrated by exquisite rapture, we shall be "partakers in the inheritance of the saints *in light*" (Col. 1:12). That which would blind us now will be bliss to us then!

Fifty or sixty years ago three Christian leaders in England were discussing hymns. They were members of a select committee compiling a new denominational hymnbook. All three were musicians. All three were experts in adjudging the literary and spiritual merits of hymns. They decided that they would try to reach unanimity as to which was the greatest hymn ever written in the English language. They reached agreement gradually down to five, which were: (1) Henry F. Lyte's "Abide With Me," (2) Samual Stone's "The Church's One Foundation," (3) Isaac Watts's "When I Survey the Wondrous Cross," (4) Charles Wesley's, "O Thou Who Camest From Above," (5) Thomas Binney's "Eternal Light, Eternal Light."

　　　Bit by bit, carefully appraising the merits of each; the poetry of every verse, the depth of thought, the spiritual value and literary purity, the progress of idea from verse to verse, they reduced the five hymns to three, then to two, then to one. All three men finally agreed that one was the greatest—it was Thomas Binney's hymn about the divine holiness. Read it carefully, with a worshiping mind. Note especially the progress from verse to verse, until in the last stanza the Eternal Light and the Eternal Love come together in sublime union.

> Eternal Light! Eternal Light!
> How pure the soul must be
> When, placed within Thy searching sight,
> It shrinks not, but with calm delight
> Can live, and look on Thee!
>
> The spirits that surround Thy throne
> May bear the burning bliss;
> But that is surely theirs alone,
> For they have never, never known
> A fallen world like this.
>
> Oh, how shall I, whose native sphere
> Is dark, whose mind is dim,
> Before the Ineffable appear,
> And on my naked spirit bear
> That uncreated Beam?
>
> There is a way for man to rise
> To that sublime abode:
> An offering and a sacrifice,
> A Holy Spirit's energies,
> An Advocate with God.
>
> These, these prepare us for the sight
> Of Majesty above;
> The sons of ignorance and night

May dwell in that Eternal Light
Through the Eternal Love!

With such preparatory reflections in mind, let us now thought-fully contemplate the holiness of God.

To begin with, we should realize that if God is holy, then God must be personal. We cannot conceive of holiness without thinking of a person. As an abstract idea, holiness has no real conceptuality to our minds. It can be known to us only as we see it expressed to us through some personal being. Some of us who have traveled in non-Christian areas of the world have been required to take our shoes off before entering certain Mohammedan mosques or Hindu temples because the building has been regarded as holy. Yet Moham-medans and Hindus know, just as well as we do, that no such building is holy in itself. That which gives it holiness is its dedication to, or imagined occupation by, some supposed deity. If that same building were used as a warehouse such holiness would be non-existent. Its holiness consists entirely in its sacred association with the god wor-shiped in it. The utensils and other attachments are all holy, not of themselves, but in connection with the god-person worshiped there.

Even in nature-worship, the sun and the moon and other phys-ical objects or forces are worshiped because they are imaginatively personified. We simply cannot think of holiness apart from some personal being. Neither can we think of the supreme holiness without thinking of the one and only true God as being personal.

The holiness of God is a necessity to any true concept of *worship*. We cannot truly worship that which is not truly holy. Worship, remember, is primarily adoration. In the strict meaning of the word, we cannot adore that which is not morally perfect. Our deepest human intuition requires that God must be all-holy. It may be asked: "What about the gods of the Greeks and Romans? Were not they worshiped even though far from holy?" The answer is, that if we use the word worship in a lower, looser way, then yes, they were wor-shiped after a sort. But in the stricter meaning they were not wor-shiped at all; they were dreaded. The inner compulsion to bow before those fictitious semi-human gods was not genuine godly fear—the fear to offend divine righteousness—but the fear of spiteful reprisal if the required offerings or payments were not made. It is a cringing rather than a communing. If we want factual proof that it was not real worship, we only need reminding that by the time Jesus was born nearly all the better-educated had abandoned faith in all those gods and goddesses.

The same is true today of so-called "worship" in Hinduism and other non-Christian religions. Who can really worship the all-pervading, cold, soul-less *IT* known as Brahma? The very idea of a loving adoration toward such a bleak, non-personal, pantheistic abstraction is absurd. Putting it at its very best, the so-called worship in Hinduism is no more than misguided—though pathetically sincere—contemplation. Whoever could think of such a merely speculative concept of totality as *holy*?

No, we cannot truly worship that which is not personally and perfectly holy, for anything less cannot be truly GOD. The God of the Bible is not only absolutely sinless (the negative aspect), and absolutely righteous (the positive aspect), He is all-holy, the essence and origin and expression of shadowless love (the crowning aspect). That is why the holiness of God, although terrible to evildoers in its burning intolerance of sin, is the joy and rejoicing of godly hearts. In Psalm 30:4, the psalmist exclaims, "Sing unto Jehovah, O ye saints of Him, and give thanks at the remembrance of His holiness." We might rather have expected, "Give thanks at the remembrance of His tender mercies." But no, David's gratitude is for Jehovah's *holiness*—for that is the infinite, out-flaming light which guarantees the safety of the universe, and of all the godly on this tiny planet of ours.

It is because God is holy that sin, which is not only disobedience but uncleanness, requires *atonement*. To say, as some opponents of Christianity do, that the God of the Bible demands blood before He will forgive is cruelly wrong. They quote Hebrews 9:22 which says, "Without the shedding of blood there is no forgiveness"; but why do they always quote it incompletely? What it actually says is, "And almost all things, *are by the law* purged with blood; and without shedding of blood is no forgiveness." That verse states what was peculiar to the Mosaic law, not what is fundamental to the universe. The basic truth is, not that God "demands blood" (repulsive thought) but that sin requires atonement—for the safeguarding of the universe.

The transcendent wonder of the biblical message is that the God whose holy governorship *demands* atonement is the very God whose holy fatherhood *provides* it. We find this partly forepictured back in Genesis 3:21. "Unto Adam and to his wife did Jehovah God make coats of skins, and clothed them." At that time flesh-meat had not been included in man's diet; so those coats of skins were not from animals eaten as food. They were from some animal sacrificed for the specific purpose of providing bodily covering. It was Jehovah Himself who provided that covering, even as He has provided for *us* the covering of "justification by faith" through the sacrifice of Christ on Calvary.

But now let us get right into the biblical revelation of the divine holiness. That holiness is made known to us by four main modes of communication: *symbols*, of which the most frequent is fire; *similies*, of which the most striking is light; *visions* given to selected individuals and recorded for our enlightenment; *incarnation*, in the person of our Lord Jesus Christ.

The Symbol of Fire

That the most common symbol of the divine holiness is *fire* perhaps is not surprising, for fire is purity in maximum intensity, and at the same time is the most intense of all purifiers. Impurities which can withstand other cleansing agents cannot survive fire. Whereas other means of purifying may be useful for dealing with *external* defilements, fire burns right through all dross, and penetrates all *internal* alloys, refining through and through with its scorching heat and searching flame. It is both life-giving by the light it sheds, and life-destroying by its concentrated blaze. It is both comforting in the warmth it communicates, and terrifying in the devouring destruction it can bring. Among the Greeks, Hephaistos was a god of fire. So was Vulcan among the Romans. Almost all the well-known religions of history have had some form of fire worship. Whether seen in the sun, or in the lightning or in other natural phenomena, fire seems to have frightened men more than. nearly anything else.

For all these reasons it is not surprising that Jehovah, the self-existent, thrice-holy I AM, should reveal Himself as wrapped in fire, and express His glorious yet awesome holiness in the white-heat flame. Back in Genesis, immediately after the expulsion of fallen man from His paradise in Eden, we see the outflashing of that holiness in the fiery cherubs and the flaming sword which "turned every way," debarring access to the tree of life (Gen. 3:24). Those two fiery beings *symbolized* the divine holiness; the flaming sword *guarded* it. That sword was not scabbarded; for the Hebrew, literally translated, is, "the flame of a sword turning itself." It was self-suspended, and in continuous rotary motion. It was neither sheathed nor a sword at rest, it was a drawn sword of annihilating flame. The unholy dare not draw nigh!

That same holiness flashes out again in Exodus 3, from the flaming bush of Horeb. As Moses drew near to investigate it, a warning voice called, "Moses, Moses [the name uttered twice to express urgency]...draw not nigh hither; put off thy shoes from off thy feet; for the place whereon thou standest is holy ground" (Exod. 3:4,5). Moses not only took off his shoes, he "fell on his face"; for as the narrative says, he was "afraid to look upon God."

Much more spectacularly, the inviolable holiness of God is expressed by fire from Mount Sinai when God welds the twelve Hebrew tribes into one nation, Israel (Ex. 19). As the trumpet from the skies "waxed louder and louder" amid thunders and lightnings, until the gathered thousands of Israel trembled, Mount Sinai became "altogether in a smoke, because Jehovah descended upon it in *fire...*" (18); and "the sight of the glory of Jehovah was like *devouring fire* on the top of the mount in the eyes of the children of Israel" (24:17).

Later, after Jehovah had come to "dwell among" His covenant people, and the shekinah flame of His presence burned in the holy-of-holies, those Israelite people were to learn again and again how awful was that fire of the divine holiness. When the priests commenced their ministry in the newly erected tabernacle, there suddenly came "a fire out from before Jehovah" and consumed the burnt offering upon the altar, at which "all the people shouted and fell on their faces" (Lev. 9:24).

That same day, when Nadab and Abihu presumptuously offered incense independently of divine direction, a blast of that same fire which had swept the brazen altar struck them dead on the spot! None must presume (Lev. 10:2)!

When the people complained at Taberah the same fire "burned among them and consumed them" (Num. 11:1-3). A still more frightening manifestation of that awesome fire occurred when it suddenly leapt out and "consumed the two hundred and fifty men" who offered competitive incense in the jealous rebellion of Korah (Num. 16:35).

Certainly, to old-time Israel, Jehovah was a God of fire. And that fire, as they well knew, was a symbol of His inviolable *holiness*. In his wise and weighty farewell teachings to Israel, the venerable Moses well said,

> Did ever people hear the voice of God speaking out of the midst of the fire, as thou hast heard, and live?... Unto thee it was showed, that thou mightest know that Jehovah He is God; there is none else beside Him. Out of heaven He made thee to hear His voice, that He might instruct thee: and upon earth He showed thee His great fire; and thou heardest His words out of the midst of the fire....Jehovah talked with you face to face in the mount out of the midst of the fire" (Deut. 4:33-36, 5:4).

That same fire appeared in intervals all through Israel's history, in incident, psalmody and prophecy. Jehovah is the God who answered by fire on Mount Carmel. Elijah was swept skyward in a chariot of fire. The psalmist said, "Jehovah reigneth....Fire goeth before Him" (Ps. 97:1, 3). Ezekiel's vision of the heavenly sovereignty was of a throne enswathed with fire; the cherubim were like "burning coals of fire"; and the One who sat in the throne was completely enwrapped by "the appearance of fire." Isaiah said, "The Light of Israel [i.e., Jehovah] shall be for a fire, and his [Israel's] Holy One for a flame: it shall burn and devour his thorns and his briers in one day" (Isa. 10:17). That same prophet had the "sinners in Zion" fearfully asking, as they dreaded Jehovah's vengeance, "Who among us shall dwell with the devouring fire? Who among us shall dwell with everlasting burnings?"(33:14).

Oh, this holiness of God! As the wisdom of God is His mental perfection, and the love of God is His emotive perfection, and the righteousness of God is His judicial perfection, and the will of God His administrative perfection, so the holiness of God is His moral perfection. As Jehovah will yet be a wall of fire round about Jerusalem in the age-end "day of Jacob's trouble" (Zech. 2:5), so is the glorious, sin-abhorring holiness of God now and forever a wall of fire around all the other divine attributes. To the hosts of unfallen angels, and to all the myriads of God's other unsinning creatures, the divine holiness is a glorious sun which fills the universe with light. But to the sinner, whether angel, demon, or human, that holiness is a scorching fire which tortures the eyes, is intolerable to the conscience, devours hypocrisy, and is hell to endure.

In this age of grace, this gospel dispensation, and especially in these latter days of Christendom's permissive society, the easiest blunder is to forget the holiness of God. The fashion in public evangelism is to play up the welcomes and soft-pedal the warnings; to preach the love of God almost to the obscuring of His holiness. It is wrong. The awesome fire of that ineffable purity still enwraps the throne of the Majesty on High, and its lightning flashes are as threatening as ever to earth's evil-doers. Over against the lax presumptions about God which are prevalent today, we Christian believers should live and worship more reverently than ever in the light of that glory-blaze which encircles the throne of the Almighty.

Biblical Similitudes

See now the holiness of God in *similitude*. One vivid illustration of it is the sun. See, for instance, the striking parallel in James 1:17.

> Every good gift and every perfect gift is from above, and cometh down from the Father of lights, with whom is no variableness,

neither shadow of turning.

There is much more in James's metaphor than meets a casual glance. Do you know what parallax is? You certainly know at least one aspect of it if you are interested in photography. It is our faulty sighting of an object when we are going to take a close-up picture of it. If you are going to take a snapshot of a friend just a few feet away, you look at him or her through the view. When you have the positioning seemingly right, you click the camera, only to find later, when you develop the negative, that your snapshot has cut the top half of your friend's head off. The partial decapitation is because you did not allow for the fact that the camera lens which takes the photo is an inch or so lower than the view through which you looked at your friend. That slight space between the view and the lens causes parallax. Or, more exactly, if you imagine a straight line from the view to the person being photographed, and also a line from the lens to him or her, the space between those two lines is parallax.

Now when James speaks of God as "the Father of lights with whom is no variableness," the Greek word which he uses is *parallage*, which in English is "parallax"; and to say the least, it is arresting. It is an astronomical allusion to parallax caused by transmutation of phase or orbit. Imagine yourself standing upright at 12 o'clock noon, with the sun exactly above you. A straight line from the sun to you, and on through you, would go right to the center of the earth. And because of your being in the direct line from the sun to the center of the earth, you would cast no shadow. But when the sun rotates westward to any point between zenith and sunset, a direct line from the sun to the center of the earth would not pass through you; and that would cause a shadow of you on the earth's surface. The space between the sun's line to the earth's center at noon, and the sun's line to you on the earth's surface past noon, is parallax; and (note it well) wherever there is parallax there is always shadow.

And now read James 1:17 again. See how precisely it keeps to its astronomical metaphor. God is "the Father of lights," that is, the originating Light from which all other luminaries in the universe derive. Next, God is the Father of lights "with whom there is no parallax," that is, there is no orbital circuit or rotation, no slantwise shining which causes shadows.

The implications are tremendous. First, this sun knows no parallax and is always at meridian or noon. Could any other figure more remarkably express the superlative holiness of God than that of a super-sun, or "Father of lights," always at shadowless zenith? Second, here is a sun without either sunrise or sunset—without beginning or ending. Could any other figure more strikingly express the eternality of God? Third, this Sun does not revolve around any center; it is itself the center. Could any figure more captivatingly express the centrality and supremacy of God, or the theocentricity of the unverse?

Indeed, this sun which is supreme and central to all else, may well illustrate to us the holy triunity of the Godhead. Analysis of sunlight separates its chemical rays into different sorts, mainly three. There are rays which are *invisible*: they can be neither seen nor physically sensed. There are the light rays, which can be *seen*, yet not felt. There are other rays which can be *felt* but not seen. In that threeness yet oneness do we not see a parallel with the divine triunity? God the Father is the *invisible*; He can be neither seen nor touched. God the Son is the divinity *revealed*. God the Holy Spirit is not seen, but He is *felt*: He is God in human *experience*.

"God is Light"

Another eloquent simile of the divine holiness is *light*. The First Epistle of John, chapter 1:5, says, "God is Light." That statement, of course, is not to be taken literally. God is not actually physical light, but in His holiness He is to the moral and spiritual realm what natural light is in the physical world. It is definition by parallel. Only in light can we see, yet light itself cannot be seen. It is manifestant yet in itself transparent. It may be prismatically broken up into its primary and secondary spectra, but light itself is invisible, even as the omnipresent God is.

The full statement of 1 John 1:5 is, "God is light, and in Him is *no* darkness at all." Think what that means by way of parallel. Light in which there is no darkness at all means light sheer and shadeless; light of such translucent transparency that it represents in God a holiness which is purity exquisite.

Today, there is an unresolved discussion as to what is the nature of light. Until well into our twentieth century, light was believed to be radiation in the form of waves in an all-pervading massless medium. That theory then became supplemented (rather than supplanted) by evidence that light seems rather to be streams of exceedingly minute particles.[1] But whichever view we take, it remains that light is energy radiated from self-luminous bodies such as the stars or the sun or lamps, or even the firefly and the glowworm. The energy-vibrations which make light are emitted from luminous bodies at a terrific velocity of over 186,300 miles per second.

The more we think of light, the more salutary it becomes as a similitude of God. Light is that which alone enables the eye to see. Without it, the best eyes can see nothing. So is God the originating emitter of all spiritual light in which we really "seek" spiritual truth. Apparently the psalmist has that parallel in mind when he says, "In *Thy* light we shall *see* light" (Ps. 36:9).

Again, light, or electro-magnetic radiation, is the most outgoing of all conceivable phenomena. Light never lights itself, it sheds itself entirely for others. You simply cannot think of a light which does not light others. So is God the infinite eradiator of enlightening truth; the "true Light which lighteth every man" (John 1:9). The psalmist perceives the similitude when he prays, "Send out (radiate) Thy light and Thy truth" (Ps. 43:3). Yes, of all physical consistencies light is the most outgoing; and of all minds God is the most outgoing, especially so as the redemptive self-revealer, enlightener, Savior.

Suppose John 1:5, instead of saying, "God is light," had said, "God is sound." What a different concept of God it would have given! Both light and sound are energy waves, but sound waves will not travel through a vacuum, whereas light travels through it easily. That is why, although we receive light from the sun and the stars, we never receive sound from them. Sound can neither go beyond earth's atmosphere nor come from beyond it; but light travels through the whole universe, reaching us from immense distances which can be measured only as light years. What a picture then does the pictorial statement of 1 John 1:5 give us: "God is *light!*"

But look at another aspect of the words: "God is light." Consider those waves, or quanta, or photons, which register on the eye as light. When they are passed through a prism, they break up into seven different wave-lengths, or colors—three primary and four secondary. So is it with the mysterious being God. In His nature and attributes He is the sevenfold deity; the three primaries being the three essentials which He *is*, and the four secondaries being the four attributes which *belong* to His essence. The three constituents which God *is* are: (1) God is spirit, (2) God is light, (3) God is love. The four attributes which belong to God are: (1) He is *personal*, (2) He is *triune*, (3) He is *infinite*—which includes omnipotence, omniscience, omnipresence, eternality, (4) He is *immutable*, i.e., eternally unchangeable.

The three qualities which God "is" are the *essence* of His being. The four attributes which inhere are the *dimensions* of His being. They are, so to speak, the boundless "breadth and length and depth and height" (Eph. 3:18) of His deity. We may say that the breadth is His infinity, and the length His eternity, and the depth His mysterious triunity, and the height His sublime personalness.

Now it is remarkable that it takes *triunity* to give us breadth and length and depth and height. For example, take two sticks or poles, and cross them horizontally at right angles as in a weather vane. This gives us north, south, east, west—breadth and length, but not height and depth. There must always be a third, or perpendicular pole as well (so that we have right and left and up and down) if there is to be breadth, length, and depth and height. That triunity of God, expressing itself in breadth, length, and depth and height, is fundamental to the structure of the universe.

In alliance with that, the three things which God *is* (i.e., spirit and light and love) have each a special relationship to this four-dimensioned universe. Think about this for a moment. First: "God is spirit"; and, as such, God is the outspreading energy which fills so-called "space" everywhere. Science knows now that space is not emptiness. Science also knows now that space is not filled with ether—not at least in the earlier meaning of that word (the rarified element formerly believed to fill the upper regions of space). Almost without knowing it (so it seems to me) science is on the eve of discovering that the ether of space is not merely ether at all, nor even electrical energy, but the invisible omnipresence of *God*, who is "spirit." It is from God as the life-giving Spirit that there continually flows the energy which fills all space, transmuting itself into motion, phenomena, and time.

That energy is the link between the spiritual and the physical: and in consonance with that, "God is light"—both natural light (through ever-emanating energy-waves) and spiritual light (through the omnipresent Holy Spirit, as is magnificently expressed in Psalm 139:7-12).

Crowningly, "God is *love*"—an outreaching fatherhood and saviorhood bigger than all the universe; bigger than all the measurements of men; and bigger than the whole totality of sin. Mark well: It is not merely that God has love, or that He feels love, or that He expresses love. Let the emphasis be on that little but tremendous copula, "God IS love." His love is not even merely the greatest of His attributes: It is His very *being*. That all-eclipsing reality floods both the moral and the physical universe with radiant meaning and purpose. Let us appreciate, then, these three supreme wonders:

1. God is spirit—the great Renewer, universally renewing,
2. God is light—the great Revealer, continually revealing,
3. God is love—the great Redeemer, graciously redeeming.

Outflashing Facets

"God is light." As from a flashing diamond the statement radiates the holiness of God in a variety of facets. Light is *unstainable*, incorruptible. It cannot be defiled by any medium through which it passes. To the natural eye, fresh-fallen snow is pure whiteness, and often is brilliantly so. Yet how soon snow is soiled by human tread, or stained by intermixing influences! Similarly, water, fresh-flowing from some crystal mountain spring, is sparklingly pure; yet how soon is it polluted by muddy terrain, or by industrial spillage! In contrast, the purity of light is never made any less pure either by what it passes through or by what passes through it. Light is not susceptible to contamination either by infection or contagion. Whether it is sunlight, moonlight, starlight, lamplight; whether it is more intense or more pale, light is always nothing but light. See those pencils of light streaming through the none-too-clean window? Not one speck of impurity is picked up on the way through. See those dust-particles glistening in the long, rectilinear sunbeams? The dust-particles are lit up and exposed, but not one speck is absorbed. No matter which avenue light sweeps through and illumines, it remains always and everywhere pure. Such is the holiness of God, both eternally and universally, both naturally and spiritually: it is the perfect light in which there is "no darkness at all."

Again, light, when unimpeded by obstructions or intervening shadows, is always *bright*. The clear beaming of the sun is not only sunlight, it is sunshine. The whole day is "bright" when no cloudiness veils the sun. Even the night is beautiful with a silvery luminousness when a full moon shines from the rich blue of a deep, clear sky. Whether in noontide splendor or the softer lunar radiance of nocturnal hours, the light from heaven is always a brightness. And so is it in the moral and spiritual realm: the divine holiness which streams to us from heaven not only enlightens; it irradiates whatever it penetrates. That is why Psalm 34:5 testifies, "They looked unto Him [Jehovah] and were lightened." It is always noticeable that those Christians who come into the experience of inwrought holiness have a radiance about them. The infilling Holy Spirit, by the very fact that He is the *Holy* Spirit, floods the mind with gladness. Holiness is always radiance. Think of it. These words, "God is light, and in Him is no darkness at all," means that God is incorruptibly and exquisitely holy, and that therefore (let us say it reverently) the mind of God is *radiant*.

Further, light *beautifies*. In fact there can be no visible loveliness without it. Exclude light, and every charming product of nature hangs a blighted head. Color becomes non-existent; the richest floral hue turns black; every rainbow disappears in blankness; the most brilliant tapestries of garden and orchard droop and die. Nothing has any color in itself; for what we call color is simply response to the different rays in light. The most masterly works of art have "no form or comeliness" and no optical appeal whatever unless they are bathed in light. So is it with the holiness of God: everything it touches it beautifies. Did not the psalmist have that in mind when he prayed, "Let the beauty of Jehovah our God be upon us" (Ps. 90:17)? Yes, in His holiness God is both beautiful and the imparter of beauty. That is why the psalmist adds, "Worship Jehovah in the beauty of holiness" (Ps. 96:9).

Who is the holiest ever seen on earth? Is it not our Lord Jesus? Was He beautiful? This is His description: "Thou art fairer than the children of men," the "chiefest among ten thousand," "the altogether lovely." Holiness both reveals and imparts beauty. The words, "God is light, and in Him is no darkness at all," mean that God is beautiful beyond all our present power of conception, and that wherever His outshining life quickens human minds, it sheds that moral beauty.

Light *exposes*. As nothing else, it uncovers and lays bare ugliness. As John 3:20 observes, "Every one that doeth evil hateth the light, neither cometh to the light, lest his deeds should be exposed" (R.S.V. et al). In the dark, sin or snare or foulness can lurk undetected. Light lays bare all such evil, showing what it really is, and making us wise to the avoidance of it. In the light there is safety: in the dark there is danger. In the light there is perception: in the dark there is deception. Light and darkness are mutually hostile: they simply will not cohabit. That is why godliness and ungodliness can never make a truce. That is why Christian spirituality and mundane carnality are in uncompromising antagonism. They can never unite, any more than divine light and Satanic darkness can ever blend in reciprocal toleration. That is why the New Testament distinguishes Christian saints as "the children of light" who have been translated from "the power of darkness" (Col. 1:13).

It is because "God is light," sheer purity, penetrating holiness, that many believers, when they are seeking the blessing of experiential sanctification, become shocked at the exposure of hitherto unsuspected sin in their hearts as they lay themselves open wide to God. That is why, also, to evildoers the holiness of God is unbearable. As the ultra-violet rays of a sun-lamp are torture to the eyes of rats, and are used to protect warehouse grain from them, so is the holiness of God intolerable to the minds of those who love "darkness...because their deeds are evil" (John 3:19). The same sun which calls the garden to blush with loveliness and exude fragrance is a scorching flame to the arid desert.

Yet another attribute of light is its *freeness*. Gas and electric companies may charge us for the artificial light which they produce for us, but natural light is always and everywhere free. The money of the wealthy cannot purchase it. The skill of the artificer cannot manufacture it. The labor of the hardest worker cannot earn it. The poverty of the poor need not debar it. Without any social discrimination light equally gilds the woodman's hut and the millionaire's mansion. An undesirable feature observable in many English houses of the eighteenth century is the small size and small number of windows. It is due to the "window tax," one of the most senseless taxes ever levied by a ruling power, first imposed by William the Third in 1695. Notwithstanding its injurious effect on ventilation and health, it was not repealed until 1823. Houses with seven windows and over were hard hit, and later those with six or more. One wonders at such stupidity as charging for the use of natural light. The government certainly needed a bit more of it! Thank heaven, light as it comes to us fresh from God has no price-ticket on it. Around the year and around the world it is free.

Even so is it in the spiritual realm. "God is light." God is utterly holy; and although it may sound strange to put it this way, the holiness of God is free—free to every godly heart. Did not our Lord Jesus say, "How much more shall your heavenly Father give the Holy Spirit to them that ask Him?" (Lk. 11:13)? Is it not scripturally true that God calls us to holiness (Eph. 1:4, etc.) and provides holiness for us in Christ (1 Cor. 1:30), so that we become "partakers of His holiness" (Heb. 12:10)?

Light is wonderfully *productive*. Those regions where the sun most rarely shines are usually the sparsely productive places: vegetation languishes; trees wither; foliage dies. However drenched with rain they may be, unless there is the light and warmth of the sun, they fight a losing battle with darkness and remain infertile. The light of the sun brings resurrection. Responding to its heavenward pull, life leaps up from dark death; flowers and plants, cereals and fruits luxuriate, smiling their gratitude to genial skies. Correspondingly so is it with the light of holiness. It is like productive sunshine: it is both light and warmth. Where holiness enters, a glow is kindled; the "fruit of the Spirit" begins to develop in the character and to show forth in gracious behavior.

Is it not true that light is the harbinger of *joy*? What is it the psalmist tells us?

Weeping may endure for a night, but joy cometh in the morning
(Ps. 30:5).

When the ninth plague plunged Egypt long ago into that three
days of "darkness which could be felt," sight failed and motion ceased;
so did all laughter and singing. It was as joyless as it was lightless.
What a dreary time, also, was Paul's hazardous voyage to Rome,
when "neither sun nor stars in many days appeared" (Acts 27:20)
and all aboard became gloomily dispirited! Instinctively we associate
darkness with mental gloom, and light with gladness, as in Psalm
97:11,

> *Light* is sown for the righteous,
> And *gladness* for the upright in heart.

Let every Christian heart rejoice in it: "God is light, and in Him
is no darkness at all." The light of divine holiness which shines upon
us from God the Father, through the glorious face of our Lord Jesus
(2 Cor. 4:6) and is shed within us by the communicating Holy Spirit
(Rom 5:5) is the joy and gladness of our infinite creator! That holiness
is meant to infill our minds and hearts. That is the inward light
which is incorruptible, radiant, beautiful, fruitful, glowing, and
which so transforms us that we "show forth the praises of Him" who
has called us "out of darkness into His marvelous light" (1 Peter 2:9).

[1] For instance, if a ray of light hits a piece of aluminum, an
electron of aluminum of exactly equal energy to that of the
light-ray is displaced from the aluminum. This seems to indicate
particles of light displacing equals in the aluminum.

8

The Holiness of God, Part Two

B
esides being expressed in symbols and similies, as we have seen, the holiness of God is made vivid to us through *visions*, which are recorded in Scripture for our learning. I mention just one of them here as representative. It is recorded in Isaiah 6. All Bible readers are familiar with it, yet it somehow always repays a further, thoughtful reading.

> In the year that king Uzziah died I saw also the Lord sitting upon a throne, high and lifted up, and His train filled the temple. Above it stood the seraphim: each one had six wings; with twain he covered his face, and with twain he covered his feet, and with twain he did fly. And one cried unto another, and said, Holy, holy, holy, is the Lord of hosts: the whole earth is full of His glory. And the posts of the door moved at the voice of him that cried, and the house was filled with smoke.

> Then said I, Woe is me! For I am undone; because I am a man of unclean lips, and I dwell in the midst of a people of unclean lips: for mine eyes have seen the King, the Lord of hosts. Then flew one of the seraphim unto me, having a live coal in his hand, which he had taken with the tongs from off the altar: And he laid it upon my mouth, and said, Lo, this hath touched thy lips; and thine iniquity is taken away, and thy sin purged. Also I heard the voice of the Lord, saying, "Whom shall I send, and who will go for Us?" Then said I, "Here am I; send me" (Isa. 6:1-8).

The vision has three aspects: its nature, its impact, its outcome. It is with its nature that we are here the more concerned.

Before all else, it is a vision of the deity. Isaiah says, "I saw...the Lord." That enthroned Lord was Jehovah, as verse 5 certifies: "Mine eyes have seen the King, Jehovah of hosts." Let wonder possess our minds, for that suddenly visible figure, wrapped in blinding splendor, was none other than the pre-incarnate Christ who eight centuries later was born of a human mother on this earth. We know this because we are plainly told so in John 12:41, "These things said Isaiah when he saw His [Christ's] glory, and spake of Him."

But it was notably a vision of sovereignty, for it was of "the Lord sitting upon a throne." It was equally a vision of transcendent majesty, for it was a throne "high and lifted up." It was also a vision of a wing sanctity, for "above it stood" those flaming guardians, the seraphim.

Oh, the holiness of that throne! The plural, *seraphim*, means "burners" or "burning ones," indicating their own sheer purity. Yet see how even those exquisite spirits behave. Each had six wings, with two of which he veiled his face, as if the sight of that beautific throne was too sacred to look upon; and with two other wings each seraph covered his feet, as if that scene of infinite resplendence was too awesome to trespass upon; and with the remaining two wings each seraph hovered in readiness for swift-winged prosecution of the King's commands. Note and learn: four wings for worship; only two for service! Today, most of us have four for service and only two for worship. We are so busy—and so wrong! So much quantity—and such poor quality! So well-meaning, but so undiscerning! We forget that it is prayerful worship which gives practical worth-ship to service, and that service without the prior prostration is presumption. Once for all, young Isaiah learned that truth as he gazed on that supernal super-throne.

But his vision was not only optical, it is audiovisual. He not only saw those wings of pellucid flame and those seraphic faces like stars on fire, he suddenly heard voices of such tone as he had never heard from Israel's temple choirs—voices which seemed to fill everywhere, which thrilled through his ears and rang through his deepest being. Yet it was loudness without harshness—like "the sound of many waters"; or like rolling thunder-music: "Holy...holy...holy is Jehovah of hosts: the whole earth is full of His glory!" It was the continually repeated antiphonal of the seraphim; and as it reverberated around the throne the "foundations of the thresholds" shook, as though the very building was awed into trembling at the sound; and "the house was filled with smoke," as though the whole temple sought to veil itself from that utter glory of the divine holiness. To the astonished Isaiah it was unbearable. He sank down overcome, crying, "Woe is me! For I am undone! I am a man of unclean lips...!"

Perhaps the devout Isaiah, like others both before and since, had often wished that he could be given a vision of God. Maybe he had prayed for it. Yet now, when such a vision came, how different the effect of it from what he had presupposed! One blinding yet revealing flash from that all-eclipsing, celestial holiness, and Isaiah is flat on his face in self-abasement. With electrifying clearness his Adamic vileness was thereby exposed to him. It was suddenly intolerable. He knew now what a sinner he was. There was a sudden, new *conviction*—"Woe is me! For I am undone!" There was an intense, new *confession*—"I am a man of unclean lips...." There was a prostrating new *conception*—"I have seen the King, Jehovah of hosts!"

The total impact of this new conviction, confession, conception, was utter self-abasement. Isaiah had always known that as a member of Adam's fallen race he was a sinner, but now the humiliating contrast between that flame-white throne and his own sinfulness shocked him with a sense of vileness never experienced before. He had been a devoutly godly young man, but his very sincerity now made the torture of that exposure all the more acute. There was the dismaying discovery of sin scarely even suspected before.

A vision of the divine holiness *always* has that same effect. No man who is given a glimpse of it ever talks about his own sanctity again!

> Mine eyes have seen the King!
> Jehovah throne on high!
> Adoring myriads sing,
> Veiled seraphs "Holy!" cry:
> Ah, woe is me! Undone am I!
> Before the throne I prostrate lie.

It was the same with Ezekiel (Ezek. 1); with Paul (Acts 22:11; 26:13,14); with John (Rev. 1:17); with the heavenly "elders" (Rev. 4:10; 5:8). None but the cleansed and holy can abide the sin-devouring rays of that ineffable holiness.

It takes the guilt-removing blood of a Savior and the soul-sanctfying fire of the Holy Spirit within us, and the translating power of the coming Rapture to prepare us for our presentation there.

> Now oft on earth the spirit faints
> And mourns o'er inward sin!
> But yonder the enraptured saints
> Know sinless bliss within!
> Oh, for the robes of spotless white!
> That realm of ageless day!
> Oh, for that pure, unshadowed light!
> That life beyond decay!

Holiness in Incarnation

Yet even when it has been pictured to us in symbol and simile and vision, we still cannot clearly enough grasp the meaning of the divine holiness. All spiritual concepts such as holiness remain more or less elusive until they move visibly before us in some personal form. Beauty is a mere abstraction until expressed in some lovely flower. Music is mere fantasy until some instrument gives it speech. Art is ethereal until embodied in picture or sculpture. Even the idea of love is ephemeral until we see it tangibly displayed in some personal attachment or sacrifice. Similarly the holiness of God needs some vehicle which somehow makes it realistic to us beyond what symbol and similitude and theatrical presentation can say. We need to see it lived out here on earth in a person. God's answer to that is Jesus.

In Jesus the divine holiness does indeed take human form and become visibly observable to human eyes and minds! It lives, walks, looks, speaks, acts and reacts before our careful inspection. We who live at this late date can survey it only retrospectively now, in the Jesus of the printed page. But the pen-photography of Matthew, Mark, Luke and John has reproduced the matchless manhood so superbly for us that we can still clearly see and hear Him. It is continually surprising how vividly He still comes to us in those four gospel memoirs; but what must it have been to be actually with Him in His bodily presence! In Him we certainly see the "*beauty* of holiness." There never was another life so beautiful as His. Neither the friends who knew Him best nor the enemies who hated Him most could ever detect the faintest flaw in His moral character. It was because He was so beautiful that He was loved as no other by the sincere, and hated as no other by the hypocrite. There was not only sinlessness (which is negative) but glorious goodness (which is positive). The garden was not only weedless; it abounded in loveliest flowers and fruits. There was such meekness, sympathy, tenderness, compassion, self-sacrifice for others—and Calvary! In Him holiness is moral beauty expressed so clearly that we cannot help but recognize its true nature even though it is beyond our present capacity to truly comprehend it.

Yet there was also the *fire*! It flashed out early in the first year of His public ministry when He made a scourge of small cords and drove the mercenary traffickers from the temple, overthrowing the tables and pouring out the changers' money. Why did they not resist Him? They were afraid. There was such a flash of fire in His eyes as they had never seen before, and such holy ire on His reverend face that they cowered before Him. Children loved Him, but pretenders cringed before His penetrating gaze. That fire flashed out again in His "Woe unto you scribes and Pharisees, hypocrites!" (Matt. 23:13ff.)

And there was the *light*! Was there ever such light as we see in *His* teaching and example? Ever such stainless purity? Just as light is never defiled by what it passes through, so He passed through this sinful world as a sunbeam passes through a hovel, lighting hearts wherever He shone, yet never absorbing the faintest speck of contamination. "Which of you convinceth Me of sin?" (John 8:46). He challenged the Pharisees who maliciously dogged Him to find a fault. "This is my beloved Son, in whom I am well pleased," came the attesting voice from heaven (Matt. 17:5). "I am the light of the world" (John 8:12), said Jesus, and He was, or, rather, is. There is no such light for mind and soul anywhere else. It was because He was pure light, with "no darkness at all" that He could mediate with God for us. Had there been even a wisp of sinful shade in Him, He would have needed atonement for Himself and could never have saved others; but His was perfect holiness. It was the holiness of God.

Oh, the holiness of Jesus! Not only was it seen, it was felt. Demoniacs who had never before seen Him recognized Him at once by it. The occupying demons quailed and cried out in alarm, "Jesus of Nazareth...I know Thee who Thou art: the *Holy* One of God!" (Luke 4:34). "Jesus of Nazareth, art Thou come to destroy us?" (Mk. 1:24). Their power collapsed before that holiness. To them it was like the searing of a branding iron. When our Lord crossed over to Gadara, the legion of demons sensed His presence even a great way off, and by a strange compulsion they came tearing down the road, crawling before Him, in the person of their human victim (Mk. 5:6, 7). And why did the unchaste woman in Luke 7 steal into the Pharisee's house and kneel at Jesus' feet, anointing them with precious ointment—and laving them with her tears? It was her remorseful, deep-down wonder at a purity which condemned her, yet drew her like a resistless magnet. Why did Peter suddenly fling himself at Jesus' feet one day exclaiming, "Depart from me; for I am a sinful man, O Lord" (Luke 5:8)? It was because that holiness both enamored him and convicted him. Why did the armed band of officers who came to arrest Jesus in Gethsemane suddenly fall backward to the earth (John 18:6)? They were struck down by a strange light which made their lanterns and torches absurd. That unearthly flame could have scorched them into instantaneous Gehenna had our Lord so determined; but He withheld it that the Scriptures might be fulfilled.

The holiness of Jesus was *ambivalent*. It caused both attraction and repulsion. It attracted the true and repelled the false. Yet there was nothing cold or steely about it. There was a warm glow in it, for the light which shone through it was love-light. As we have elsewhere observed, it is error to think of the divine holiness and the divine love as being opposites, with the former blazing against sin and the latter excusing it. God is not part holy and part love: He is all holy, including His love; and He is all love, including His holiness. Not only because He is love, but because He is holy, human sin *hurts* God.

Yes, sin hurts God, and therefore it hurt the holy Jesus—more than we finites can ever know. Have you ever tried to imagine the ghastly shock it must have been to the utterly pure soul of Jesus as the ugly totality of the race's sin intensified its pressure upon Him from Gethsemane to Calvary? Matthew tells us that as He went into the garden agony He "began to be sorrowful and very heavy" (Matt. 26:37). Mark says that He "began to be sore amazed" and "exceeding sorrowful unto death" (Mark 14:33-34). Luke tells us that "His sweat was as it were great drops of blood falling down to the ground" and that there appeared "an angel...from heaven, strengthening Him" (Luke 22:43,44). It would seem as though, when the final hours of that substitutionary sin-bearing actually came, the black horror of it was such a staggering shock that Jesus might have died before ever getting to the cross. The help of an angel was needed. There are known cases of men who, on being awakened to the heinousness of their former sinning, have become so strickened at the sight that they have gone insane. What must the totality of the whole race's sin and guilt and moral disease have been to the holy soul of God the Son? There were two infinitely profound factors which made that racial sin-burden the crushing shock that it was to our dear Lord. One was His infinite capacity for suffering; the other was His exquisite purity, His holiness. The worm cannot suffer as the bird, nor the bird as the dog, nor the dog as a man. The degree of capacity to suffer increases as the scale of intelligence and consciousness grows higher. What then must the immeasurable suffering have been in the infinite mind of Christ?

But even that was intensified by our Lord's sheer holiness! The capacity to suffer usually corresponds to the degree of refinement. That which occasions no discomfort at all to a vulgar, savage mind can cause razor-sharp pain to a sensitively refined person. What then must the horror of that racial sin-bearing have been to the superbly sensitive mind of the sinless Jesus? We may get some faint idea, perhaps, from certain Scripture references. The Book of Numbers, in chapter 12, recounts a sad episode during the wilderness wanderings of the Israelites. Although Moses was "meek above all men which were upon the face of the earth" (verse 3), his own sister and brother, Miriam and Aaron, fell to envying him. They complained, "Hath Jehovah indeed spoken only by Moses? Hath He not spoken also by us?" (verse 2). God commanded them, along with Moses, to present themselves at the door of the tabernacle, where He came down in a cloud and rebuked them for their jealousy. Miriam seems to have been the more jealous of the two; and as the cloud departed, Moses and Aaron saw, to their grief, that Miriam had been stricken with leprosy! That leprosy was not only a punishment, it was a revelation. It was meant to show us what jealousy looks like to the holy eyes of God! That jealousy became ugly, loathsome leprosy!

Many years later, in 2 Kings 5, when the prophet Elisha had been used of God to cure Naaman of his leprosy but had refused to accept any part of the reward which the Syrian military man urged upon him, Elisha's servant, Gehazi, followed after Naaman and secretly solicited part of the reward. Thereupon he, too, was stricken with leprosy. We are meant to see thereby what covetousness looks like to God—the repulsive leprosy! Years later again, (in 2 Chronicles 26), when King Uzziah ill-advisedly trespassed into the holy place of the temple and presumed to offer incense on the altar, even he was suddenly smitten with the dread disease, and was a leper to the day of his death; wherein we see what such irreverence looks like to God—ugly leprosy.

All such instances add up to this, that sin is moral leprosy. That is why leprosy has such distinct significance in Scripture. Have you noticed that although leprosy is a disease, nowhere in Scripture was it ever said only to be healed; it was "*cleansed*." Leprosy was not only disease; it was uncleanness. Leviticus 13:44 makes the direct statement, a leprous man "is unclean," to which it adds, "his clothes shall be rent, and his head bare, and he shall put a covering upon his upper lip, and shall cry, Unclean! unclean!" Of all diseases, leprosy was meant to be a walking parable of sin as moral filthiness, and of divine judgment upon it.

Refer all this now to what happened in Gethsemane and on Calvary. The whole vast sin of the human race, like a millionfold dose of the filth of leprosy, pressed down upon the lovely, holy, heavenly mind and soul of the meek and lowly Jesus. Somehow, as our sinbearer, He became so expiatingly identified with our fearful sin and shame that as the Father saw Him on the cross, that pain-racked figure hanging there assumed the appearance of some monstrous, repulsive, leprous being, from which the Father turned away His face in abhorrence. And out of the depthless darkness the Eternal Son cried, "My God, My God, why hast Thou forsaken Me?" (Matt. 27:46). The very holiness which made Jesus our acceptable substitute was that which made His bearing the race's mass of vile guilt a shock of piercing anguish beyond all human imagining. How unspeakably awful, ugly, painful, intolerable must that loathsome load have been to that immaculately holy heart! Our Lord had known beforehand that His atoning death would be hurtful and costly, but it would seem as though even He did not fully realize until Gethsemane what a staggering horror it was for that concentrated aggregate of darkness and uncleanness to swamp that exquisitely pure and sensitively holy soul. What happened in Gethsemane and on Calvary is a mystery of human sin and divine holiness beyond finite comprehension; yet somehow we cannot help praying,

> Oh, make me understand it,
> Help me to take it in,
> What it meant to Thee, the HOLY ONE,
> To bear away my sin!

Holiness Imparted

Let us now sound a final chord. In the biblical teaching there is not only the divine holiness in symbol, in simile, in vision and in incarnation; there is the divine holiness in *impartation*. I mean that according to Scripture there may be a transfusion of the divine holiness to ourselves, bringing a transforming experience of it, if we are born-again Christian believers and are truly yielded to our Lord. Although this may seem at first to be beyond credence, it is nevertheless true. It is the most precious mystery of the Christian life; something which spiritually unintelligent worldlings cannot understand, but which is a heaven on earth to Christian hearts.

Hebrews 12:10 speaks of us as becoming "*partakers* of His holiness." In a book like the New Testament, where the very words are part of a selective, sovereign inspiration, that word *partakers* is arresting. The Holy Spirit put it there. In the Greek it is a verb, and it really means "to partake." It is part of a teaching which connects right through the New Testament Epistles (can we ever cease to marvel at it!) that the Holy Spirit of God indwells us, and seeks to infill us! It would be remarkable enough even if the Holy Spirit were only an impersonal emanation from God; but He is the personal Holy Spirit of our divine Savior and our heavenly Father, distinct from them yet one with them, so that in having Him we thereby have Them. Mystery? Yes, indeed, but none the less a millionfold proven reality.

> Sent from the Father, by the Son,
> Come forth our guide to them to be;
> For Thou we know with them art One,
> And we have them in having Thee.

"They were all filled with the Holy Spirit" (Acts 2:4). "Be filled with the Holy Spirit" (Eph. 5:18). Because He is the *Holy* Spirit, what He fills is thereby made to partake of His holiness. "God hath elected us in Him [Christ] before the foundation of the world, that we should be holy" (Eph.1:4). God knew that we could never effect our own holiness, so He elected us "in Him" in whom holiness is provided for us. As 1 Corinthians 1:30 says, "Of him [God] are ye in Christ Jesus, who of God is made unto us...sanctification." 1 Thessalonians 3:13 calls us to be "unblameable in holiness before God," to which chapter 5:24 adds, "Faithful is He who calleth you [to this holiness] who also will do it." This is so truly the holiness of God imparted that 1 Corinthians 3:16 calls us temples of God because "the Spirit of God dwelleth in you."

Oh, this experience of imparted holiness is real! And it has just the results one would expect. It brings *light* which illumines and purifies the mind; for "God is light, and in Him is no darkness at all." It brings the heavenly *fire* which purges and refines our motives and desires through and through. It brings *radiance* to the heart and life, for the holiness of God is that of a beaming sun at everlasting zenith. Holiness never shouts: it *shines*. It never advertises itself, yet it can no more be hidden than a sunlit hilltop. Holiness also brings *beauty*—beauty of character. It wreathes the temple pillar with lilywork. It turns severity to kindness, and egocentricity into gracious otherism. It brings fragrance, fruitfulness, joy. This imparted holiness atmospheres one's personality with a spiritual influence which is much more than any self-generated forcefulness. By that, of course, I do not mean anything ghostly or eerie, some peculiar aura or imaginary halo. True holiness makes us intensely spiritual but perfectly natural, and thoroughly practical. It is the most up-in-heaven yet down-to-earth of all spiritual conditioning. It never makes reclusive, self-occupied mystics or pious solitaires like diamonds set apart to be admired in isolation. Its shining is never merely selfward, but always otherward. It not only is light; it spreads light. Without trying to do so, it gleams like a sunbeam, and diffuses itself like the fragrance of a rose. In a modified way it invisibly enwraps and then emanates from a Spirit-filled Christian just as it suffused and made its presence felt through our Lord Jesus. Unclean spirits knew it at once, and winced. Hypocritical Pharisees keenly sensed it and were jealously irritated by it. The God-hungry, the sincere, the spiritually yearning, and even the badly fallen who longed for a purer life were instinctively drawn by it and turned heavenward.

I have known unforgettable instances of that radiant influence in persons who have crossed my own pathway. If ever there was a none-too-handsome preacher who was handed over to Christ and living in the experience of inwrought holiness, it was the late Reverend Samuel Chadwick, a former principal of Cliff College, Derbyshire, England. I remember a public meeting in our home town, Ashton-under-Lyne, Lancashire, where he was the main speaker, when I was but a youth. When he commenced his address he was not too impressive in appearance or in voice or in his preliminary remarks; but as he proceeded there somehow spread through the whole of that large building an atmosphere, a realized presence of God which gripped and bowed every one of us in the large crowd. So far as I myself am concerned, the influence of that meeting has lasted ever since. I remember, too, that Samuel Chadwick had to leave just after his message, to be in time for a railway train to another town; and when he left us it seemed as though that wonderful influence went out of the building with him. We all sensed it to be so; and we were rather sorry for the minister who had to bring the closing address after Samuel Chadwick had gone. We felt gloomily sympathetic with him as he apologetically began: "My dear friends, it is a comfort to some of us that when the sun has gone, the stars come out to twinkle!"

I recall a strange incident in those same youthful days, when I was pianist to the National Young Life Campaign in Britain. We were holding a campaign in a new civic hall which seated five thousand, in an English city. The "feel" of the meetings was good until the second Saturday night, when the atmosphere suddenly changed—for a strange reason which we did not understand at first. It was just as though, all around us, there were invisible forces of evil struggling to defeat what we were trying to do in our evangelistic gathering. Lest you should think me over-imaginative, let me say that every Christian in the building felt likewise. It was oppressive. The hymns dragged, and the choral pieces fell flat. After struggling through his evangelistic address and seemingly futile appeal, Frederick P. Wood, the preacher, sank down exhausted like a defeated wrestler.

But why? Well, the reason was downstairs! Underneath the main hall where we held our meeting was a large but lesser hall in which a dance was in progress until after midnight. It was a godless voluptuous affair, with much drinking and unchaste "goings on." Whether the atmosphere of *our* meeting got down there I doubt, but *their* atmosphere certainly rose to where we were! Every now and then, when certain doors swung open we could hear the blare of the jazz and the thud, thud, thud of the big drum; and the odor of beer would somehow waft itself upstairs. It is not extra-sensory perception running wild when I say that it seemed as though a horde of invisible demon-personalities were sweeping up and violently objecting to our presence in the building. I have never forgotten it, nor ever will. It was an eye-opener to me, a young Christian, as to the utter hostility of holiness and evil. Both are essentially personal, and each detests the other. There can never be any truce between moral light and darkness. Holiness and love always go together; so do evil and hate. Holiness and love are the stronger, and in the end will win outright. We know this because the crucified Jesus rose from the dead, and not all the powers of darkness were able to prevent Him!

Long before our Christian era, those who wrote the Old Testament Psalms had clear-sighted spiritual perception. They knew well enough, even then, that the holy war of light against darkness was one of absolutely no compromise. I am not surprised that one of those psalmists wrote, "Ye who love Jehovah, *hate* evil" (Ps. 97:10). Since such a holy God is ours, holiness of heart and life should be the sacred passion of every Christian. Nothing less than such holiness in us can satisfy our holy Savior. That very holiness which is intrinsic in God is not meant to become secondarily reproduced in us. As 2 Corinthians 4:6 says,

> For God who commanded the light to shine out of darkness hath shined into our hearts to give [i.e., through us to others] the light of the knowledge of the glory of God in [i.e., shining from] the face of Jesus Christ.

Oh, to live looking at that dear, radiant, wonderful face; looking at it with such steady gaze of the heart that we become reflectors of it everywhere! "Be ye holy, for I am holy, saith Jehovah." That holiness truly becomes ours when we are so fully yielded to Jesus that the "Spirit of holiness" (Rom. 1:4) can unobstructedly *fill* us. Is not this the language of our hearts?

Spirit of holy light infill
My yielded intellect and will;
This waiting temple now possess
And may Thy radiant holiness
My inmost self refine:
Pervade, suffuse, renew, inspire
Burn through me, penetrating Fire;
My deep-down motives purify,
Inwardly, outwardly sanctify;
Through all my being shine.

9

The Love of God—Its Outreach to Us

I f there is one truth more than another which I deeply wish we could somehow make real to the minds and hearts of people today, it is that God loves them; that the one and only true deity, the infinite creator whose almighty arms embrace the starry spaces, and in whose hands our very breath is, loves us *all* without exception, and loves us *each* in individual distinction. That is the most profoundly elevating and comforting news which ever flashed from the throne of the Most High and broke like a super-sunrise on planet Earth.

When once that superlative wonder really grips the mind and is gratefully responded to, one's whole outlook is transformed. God, the universe, history, mankind and human life, all assume new meaning. There is a new light in the mind, a new song in the heart, a new calm in one's spirit, a new restfulness amid adversity, a new horizon stretching before one's inward eyes and a new confidence concerning the unfolding future.

The love of God to men is the high pinnacle of biblical revelation. Everything else is a climbing up to it. Our Lord Jesus is the peak expression of it. The cross is the intense focal-point of it. The redemption of man is the most extraordinary demonstration of it. The gospel, with its "whosoever" message of blood-purchased salvation, is the magnanimous outflowing of it. Those of us who have been to Calvary and have found there the love that is bigger than our biggest sinning, the grace that forgives transgressions beyond counting, the pierced hands that give release from the heaviest burden of guilt, and the precious blood that washes away the ugliest stains—how can we ever cease singing of the love that sought us, and the blood that bought us, and the compassion that brought us back to the great heavenly Father? It was there, at that green hill outside a city wall, that we first heard the heartbeat of an infinite love in the bosom of the Eternal; and with utter gratitude we have been singing of it ever since.

> My glorious God, the King of all creation,
> By whose command all worlds and wonders are;
> Thy boundless rule controls each constellation,
> Surrounds all space, enrings the farthest star.

> Yet greater far than suns and stars to me,
> The love which bled to make me Thine;
> Yes, greater far than suns and stars to me,
> The love which bled to make me Thine.

> And when in heav'n, I gaze on glories yonder,
> The sapphire throne and splendors past compare,
> Surpassing all will be the depthless wonder
> That God Himself once bled to bring me there!

Yes, God loves us. But in saying so, we are a million leagues away from meaning anything like the sickly, sentimental caricature which is often called love today—the Hollywood counterfeit of it. We mean love in the truest, highest, deepest, richest connotation of the word. Never can it be too strongly emphasized that by the love of God we do not mean merely an indulgent fond feeling, too soft or sentimental ever to be angry with the perverse. We mean a love which, besides going to the uttermost in self-sacrifice for others can be awful in its rebound against Godward treason and infidelity. True love never indulges that irrational weakness which we call "temper" (which is deranged emotion), but it can react with righteous anger (which is controlled and healthy moral indignation) against evil. The very fact that the divine love has such impelling concern to save the sinner from damnation is the reason why it can be an outflaming retribution against sacrilegious distorters of the truth.

By the love of God we mean the purest, strongest, wisest, most thoughtful and self-abnegating love which ever glowed in the heart of the noblest father or mother on earth—only a myriad times purer and sublimer—a mighty, tender, boundlessly outreaching compassion that has no parallel. In final focus, we mean the "love so amazing, so divine" that once descended from the royal palace of universal government in the heaven of heavens to a gory cross of brutal mockery and deepest anguish here on earth, in order to save us human sinners from Gehenna and make us regenerated inheritors of heavenly glory!

Oh, the wonder of that love divine! Never can I forget the overpowering effect of it on my own mind when, in one of those sudden flashes of illumination which come to most of us at one time or another, I saw it inwardly with startling vividness as the biggest fact of the universe and the all-eclipsing truth of the biblical revelation. Everything shone with reassuring new appearance in the light of that brilliant moment. I realized it in a way which thrilled through every fiber of my being. "God is LOVE." Since then, I have never again been afraid of the universe. The astronomical magnitudes which float across the eye of our latest telescope may be awesomely bewildering, but with a loving divine fatherhood back of everything (as Jesus taught) and with Calvary as the guarantee, I know that I shall never get lost in those frightening spaces. As a blood-redeemed, born-again Christian, with the promises of inspired Scripture before my eyes and the witness of the Holy Spirit in my heart, I can sing in the Pauline succession, "Neither death, nor life, nor angels, nor principalities, nor powers, nor things present, nor things to come, nor height, nor depth, nor any other creature, shall be able to separate us from the love of God, which is in Christ Jesus our Lord."

> His forever, only His;
> Who the Lord and me shall part?
> With what peace and rest and bliss
> Jesus fills the loving heart!
> Heav'n and earth may fade and flee,
> First-born light in gloom decline;
> But while God and I shall be
> I am His, and He is mine.

Perhaps after my expressing such decidedly Christian convictions, it may seem superfluous for me to remind you that our approach in these studies is not metaphysical or in any way philosophical, but purely biblical and expository. Yet such a reminder is peculiarly appropriate at this point for a noteworthy reason. The Bible is the only place in all the world and in all history where we learn this greatest of all truths: God loves us.

Start back with Aristotle, from whom the very term, "metaphysical," derives, and then travel down the winding river of metaphysical disquisition to the present day (when modern materialists would relegate the labors of the metaphysician to the lumber room of useless effort). What do you find? In all the metaphysics of a thousand poor and perspiring heads there is not the faintest fleck of apprehension that the great First Cause of all things is a God who loves. Tramp down the long, circuitous pathway of philosophy in the larger sense— including ontology, epistemology and other kindred "ologies,"—from Thales and Heraclitus amid the misty beginnings of man's endeavors to solve the riddle of the universe, and where do you eventually find yourself? You are in the bogs of modern existentialisms, disillusioned and wearied, with not even the foggiest clue as to the one true solution of the big riddle. Nay, the riddle has become a muddle. After all the trek through one philosophical system after another, there is not even a hint of that greatest, simplest, truest and most profoundest explanation of man and his star-surrounded domicile which the Bible states in three short words: "God is love."

Nor is it much use looking to modern *science* to learn that God loves us. Each branch of enquiry has its axioms from which it starts, but after all, science is solely phenomenal, not metaphysical. It deals only with the facts of the material universe as revealed to the senses. Its sphere is limited to the finite by facts based on physical experiment. It is concerned with causes rather than reasons: with "what" rather than "why". Therefore it can never fully answer the deepest quest of the human investigator, for in the human spirit there is an inextinguishable persuasion that behind the chain of facts that science links together, there are absolutes and ultimates beyond the furthest ascertained links of natural phenomena—spiritual originals which scientific probe and test can never uncover. So indeed there are. But even if some optical invention could see further than our biggest telescope or more minutely than the finest microscope, neither they nor the most brilliant mathematics could ever lead us to that purely spiritual origin of all life and being behind all energy, motion and phenomena. Where do all the originating electrical charges come from? From what? Nay, from *Whom*? The whole universe begins to sing a joyful anthem to us when we learn from the Bible—and from nowhere else—that before and behind, above and beneath, within and around, and forever beyond all creature-life and being is God, and that "God is love."

Shall we patiently peruse the sacred writings of the nonbiblical religions to find the love of God enunciated? Long before Moses dictated the Pentateuch, China's wise man, Confucius, was compiling his six canonical "Classics" and four "Books" of Confucianism. But do you find anywhere in them even the slightest suggestion that God is love? On the contrary, Confucianism discourages belief in a personal God and advises against the practice of prayer. To Confucius God is a pale shadow, farther off and less knowable than the faintest nebula on the farthest fringe of the Milky Way.

Will you find that God is love in Hinduism or Buddhism? The very question has a sad humor in it. Love implies warm personality. How can that bleak, characterless, pantheistic "Everywhere-Everything" called "Brahma" love, or that impersonal cosmic power called "Karma" feel compassion?

Perhaps, then, Mohammedanism will teach us that God is love? We might have expected so since Mohammed was born six centuries after Jesus had left this earthly scene and he (Mohammed) was to some degree, at least, acqainted with both the Hebrew and the Christian Scriptures. But does Islam's *Koran* recite the love of God to us? Those of us who have read through its repetitive and wearisome pages know the answer. Of the 114 Suras which comprise the *Koran*, every one except the ninth begins with the stereotyped formula, "In the Name of Allah, the Compassionate, the Merciful," but you will have to read long and closely to find even scraps of real compassion and mercy, and you will look in vain for any love of Allah to women or to those who dare oppose the blood-dripping sword of Islam.

Will you find the love of God in Shintoism or Zoroastrianism? One has only to call out the question, and the sad-toned echo brings back an empty negative.

But did not the gods and goddesses of the inventive Greeks have love? Those fantastic deities of Mount Olympus were certainly prodigies of love and hate, of passion and intrigue—among themselves. But their loves and hates were merely mythical magnifications of our own human emotions. The Greek Zeus is as much like Jehovah as a monster beetle is like a sinless seraph, and the Roman Jupiter is as much like the God and Father of the meek and lowly Jesus as a thunderbolt is like a soft-hued rainbow. Oh, we have good reason to thank Heaven that ever our dear old Bible said, "God is love," for we find it nowhere else.

The Threefold Outreach

With the foregoing contemplations as a preparation, we turn now to the Bible, especially to the New Testament, to see what those precious pages actually tell us about the love of God. In doing so, we are turning away from all abstract reasoning about God to learn from God Himself as He is self-declared in those inspired writings, and completively self-revealed in His incarnate Son.

Inasmuch as the New Testament is the full-flowering of Old Testament anticipation, I purposely overleap the earlier and fewer references to the divine love during the Old Testament era, and turn at once to the four Gospels and the apostolic Epistles. In those immortal documents we see the love of God reaching out in a great, threefold movement: the love of God *to* us, the love of God *in* us, the love of God *through* us. Or, in other words, the love of God projected, imparted, transmitted.

THE LOVE OF GOD TO US

Again and again, the New Testament sings of the love of God *to* us. In more than a few places, that love is expressed or implied even where the actual word love does not occur. Here, however, I am more concerned with specific statements of it. Like great shafts of golden light from a brilliant sunrise striking up into the sky through dispersing clouds, the magnanimous declaration of the divine love breaks on us at intervals through the New Testament. Romans 5:8 says, "God commendeth His love toward us, in that, while we were yet sinners, Christ died for us." Ephesians 2:4, having told us that by nature we were "children of wrath" (v. 3) goes on to add, "but God, who is rich in mercy, for His great love wherewith He loved us...quickened us [to new life] together with Christ." 2 Thessalonians 2:16, 17, utters the encouraging benediction, "God, even our Father which hath loved so, and hath given us everlasting consolation...comfort your hearts." 1 John 4;10,11, pointing to the cross, tries to describe what none can define when it says, "Herein is love, not that we loved God, but that He loved us, and sent His Son to be the propitiation for our sins. Beloved [i.e., loved ones] if God *so* loved us...."

In Titus 3:4, there is a noteworthy word used to express this outreaching love of God. "The kindness and love of our Savior God toward man appeared...." Paul uses the Greek compound, *philanthropia*, which is made up of the two words, *philos* (loving) and *anthropos* (man). Our English word "philosophy" is made up of *philos* (loving) and *sophia* (wisdom); so philosophy is the love of wisdom. Our word "philology" is made up of *philos* again (loving) and *logos* (speech, discourse); so philology is the love of words, language, literature, linguistics. In the same way our word, "philanthropy," comes from that same *philos* (loving) and *anthropos* (man, mankind). So philanthropy, strictly, is the love of man. Think of it: *philanthropia* (man-love). Now read Titus 3:4 again: "Our Savior-God's kindness and *love of man*..." What a name of God—"our Savior-God!" And what a word to indicate His tender feelings toward us, His "love-of-man"! This is no stern love. Nay, the Greek *philos* has the sense of fondness and tender feeling in it. His love *to* us is the active, outward expression of a deep, fond, tender love which He feels in His heart toward us.

Contraction and Expansion

But among the New Testament statements of the divine love there is one. which stands out above all others. It is a resplendent concentration point and epitome of them all. It is the most famous text in the Bible: John 3:16.

> For God so loved the world that He gave His only begotten Son, that whosoever believeth in Him should not perish, but have everlasting life.

Doubtless it is bad form for an author to quote from his own earlier writings, but may I transgress just once? Back in the 1940's I wrote a book, *God So Loved.* The whole of it gathered round John 3:16. As I then commented, this resplendent text is not only the most remarkable convergence-point of the gospel message; its *wording* seems to make it uniquely representative of the whole Bible. Observe again the ten meaningful terms which are the building-blocks of it. (1) "God," (2) "loved," (3) "world," (4) "gave," (5) "Son," (6) "whosoever," (7) "believeth," (8) "perish," (9) "have," (10) "life."

Those ten are surely an arresting union of terms. Would it not be true to say that they are the ten *distinctive* words of biblical revelation? The whole message of the Scripture library seems to be comprehended in them as in no others.

As many thinkers and scholars have acknowledged, one of the most impressive features of the Bible is its over-all unity amid diversity. Centuries marched by in the penning of it. Two score and more writers contributed to it—persons living in different places, at different times, having sharply different social levels, different professions and occupations, different idiosyncrasies and vocabularies, writing to different persons, about different concerns, and for different purposes—not to mention other dissimilarities. Yet the superintending divine Spirit who was the invisible compulsion behind each writer has so overruled every part that, despite all the variety and diversity, certain great words and truths run through the whole sixty-six component documents of the Bible like the links of a shining chain. And the riveting peculiarity is that all those big, distinctive words seem to have been picked out and packed into this one, peerless verse (John 3:16) as though the Spirit of God wished to gather up into focal expression the most dominant truths of the Bible and the Gospel.

Nor is that all. Closer inspection finds that those ten words go together in five significant pairs. The first pair, the two words, "God" and "Son," shows us two members of the ever-blessed divine triunity cooperating in the effecting of human redemption: God the Father and God the Son—the supreme Giver and the supreme Gift. The second pair of words shows us the twofold outreach of the Father's heart—He "loved" and He "gave." The third pair shows us the twofold direction of God's loving and giving—the "world" and "whosoever." The fourth pair shows us the two things which all human beings are privileged and invited to do—"believe" and "have." The fifth pair shows us the two ultimate alternatives of human destiny on the other side of the grave—"perish" and "life." Truly those are five profoundly challenging pairs!

But analyze a bit further, and you will find that in each of those pairs the second term grows out of the first. That is obvious in the case of the first pair, "God" and "Son." The word God is the comprehensive name for the deity. But emerging from the mystery of the divine being and coming to us through the miracle of the incarnation is one who, although being "very God of very God," is the Son who, for our redemption, becomes "bone of our bone and flesh of our flesh."

Take the second pair of words, "loved" and "gave." The giving grows out of the loving. Had God not first loved, He would never have given. How important it is for us humans to keep hold of that! The incarnate Son did not suffer on Calvary in order to induce the Creator-Father to love us, but because that boundless Father-heart already loved us. Calvary is not the cause of God's love, but the proof of it. Many people have held the erroneous idea that God the First Person is a hard, cold, vengeful Judge who looks down on this world of sinners with nothing but stern determination to sentence and punish, and that the tender-hearted Jesus in pity for us came between this wrathful Judge and ourselves, suffering on our behalf so that the offended Judge might feel merciful relentings toward us. Oh, what a caricature of the real truth that is! Let us glory in it: He loved, and He gave. Aways keep the two in that order! See, now, that third pair—the "world" and "whosoever." Again the second grows out of the first. The "world" is *all* of us. "Whosoever" is *each* of us. The one is collective, the other individualistic. It is good to know that God loves us all without exception; but that which emerges from it is even better, namely that He loves us each as the particular object of His heart's concern.

Next note the fourth pair of words, "believeth" and "have." How clearly again the second grows out of the first! It is by believing that we have. Yet how stupidly slow many of us are to grasp it! How many there are who think that if only they might first have, they could then believe! They think, for instance, that if only they could first have all their intellectual hurdles removed, then they could believe. If only they would act on what they already know of the gospel; if only they would believe with their hearts the gospel promise which has so much to recommend it, the problems in their heads would be answered by the logic of experience—an inward proof which is the greatest of all Christian apologetics. An ounce of real experience is worth a ton of hypothetical objections. Yes, that is the true order: believe, and thereby have.

Finally, the same is true of the fifth pair, "perish" and "life." That word, "perish" covers all outside Christ, for there is no eternal life outside of Him. A perishing world! Nay, there is another word to add, for emerging from the ranks of the human race there comes forth a mighty host which "no man could number" who have found salvation and eternal life in that wonderful Savior. Oh, that mighty multitude! Not only is it such as "no man could number," but perhaps it is far, far bigger than many of us suspect. As F.W. Faber says,

> For the love of God is broader
> Than the measures of man's mind;
> And the heart of the Eternal
> Is most wonderfully kind.

The Outgoing Message

And now, having looked at the text internally, so to speak, look at it again *externally*, i.e., at its tremendous, outgoing message to mankind. (1) God loves! (2) God gives! (3) God saves! Those are the three mighty wonders that here blend to make the one "Gospel of God" (Rom. 1:1; etc.). Is not that again the whole Bible in threefold miniature? Are not those the three supreme inspirations, the triune driving force of divine revelation and human redemption?

Look at that indefinite particle, "so." "God *so* loved." There is an infinite elasticity in it. It stretches as long as eternity, and is as uttermost as the capacity of God.

"God *so* loved." Our little human minds can never guess the cost, the hurt, the pain to God the Father which that immeasurable "so" betokens. It is not easy for us to think that God can suffer, *really* suffer. He has nothing to regret, nothing to fear. He cannot die. He always has His own way (which, of course, He must, for it is always perfect righteousness). There is none who can resist Him, except by momentary permission. All must submit whenever He chooses to require it. He has no need of anything. He *gave* existence to all that exists outside of Himself. His universe expresses Him, but is not in the least a completion of Him. His vast universe of energy, motion, phenomena, of space plus matter plus time does not add the tiniest mite to Him; nor could its self-destruction even infinitesimally deplete Him. He is utterly complete in Himself, with absolutely no lack and no unfulfillment. How then can He *suffer*?

Strange paradox though it may seem at first, that which causes suffering in God is that which gives Him highest joy, namely, His love. But that immediately raises a big question. If God created the universe, then the universe had a beginning. The Creator is distinct from and prior to His creation. How then could God love before there was anything else in existence to love? Is it not true that love must have an object ouside of itself which awakens it and draws it? Is it not true that love is never inlooking, but always outgoing? That love never loves itself, but always another? How, then, could God love in that pre-universe aloneness?

There would be no answer to that question if God were monadic, that is, an absolute unit, an indivisible *one*, as the Unitarians suppose. But God is not a unity in simplicity; He is a trinity in unity. God is the divine *tri*unity: one in three, and three in one. Furthermore, in His very being, God is a fellowship, a fellowship of ineffable love between the Father and the Son and the Holy Spirit. To us (especially while we are in these restrictive flesh-and-blood bodies) it is a mystery beyond all sounding, but it is a divinely revealed reality. That the fatherhood of God is eternal, the Holy Scriptures plainly teach. For instance, in John's prologue the *God* who created all things through "the Word" is the *Father* from whose bosom came the "only-begotten Son." The identification is unmistakable: the God from whom came "the Word made flesh" is identically the Father from whom came the "only-begotten Son." The implication is absolutely inescapable: That eternal God is the *Father*, that eternal Word is the *Son*. They were together *as such* before "all things" were created (John 1:1, 3, 14, 18; Col. 1:12-20; Matt. 11:25; John 5:26; 1 John 1:2; etc.). The eternal God did not *become* the Father. The eternal Word did not *become* the Son. The eternal Creator did not *develop* into triunity. The fatherhood and the sonship and the triunity are eternal absolutes in God as revealed in the Bible.

So, then, the eternal fatherhood and the eternal sonship imply each other; and God is eternally love because in the very triunity of the Godhead there is an eternal object of that love. There is a six-way reciprocity of perfect love. The Father loves the Son and the

Spirit. The Son loves the Father and the Spirit. The Spirit loves the
Father and the Son. Thus the divine love is not dependent for its
activity on the universe which the divine power created. God, who
is infinitly in threefold personality, has eternal self-fulfillment in
the interior communion of that triunity.

Think, then, what it must have cost the Father to give up the
eternal Son of His love. Again and again, the New Testament speaks
of the Father's love for the Son.

> This is my Son, the beloved, in whom I have found delight (Matt.
> 3:17, 17:5).
> My beloved, in whom my soul has found delight (Matt. 12:18).
> The Father loved the Son, and has given all things into His
> hand (John 3:35 RSV).
> The Father loves [*filei:* fondly] the Son (5:20 RSV)
> As the Father has loved Me, so have I loved you (15:9).
> Thou, [Father] lovedst Me before the foundation of the world
> (17:24).
> That the love wherewith Thou [Father] hast loved Me may be
> in them, and I in them (17:26).
> He [God the Father] hath made us accepted in *the Beloved* (Eph.
> 1:6).
> He [God the Father] hath translated us into the kingdom of the
> *Son of His love* (Col. 1:13).

It is quite impossible for us, the hereditarily and innately selfish
members of Adam's fallen posterity, to imagine the utter felicity of
complacent love which exists in the holy community of the triune
Godhead. But knowing the revealed fact of it, we can perhaps grasp,
to some small degree, that when the Father so loved this world as
to give His only begotten Son to save it—with all the suffering which
that involved—it cost God. It hurt the Father-heart; it shot pain
into the consciousness of God.

We think of statements like Romans 8:32. "He who spared not
His own Son, but delivered Him up for us all, how shall He not with
Him also freely give us all things?" Halt at that clause, "He delivered
up." It was not only the giving that cost. Far, far more was the
giving Him *up* to all that His incarnation as a human being included—the self-imposed limitations of humanhood, the poverty and
hardship, the being "despised and rejected," the pain of sensitive
sympathy with sick and suffering humanity, the hostile "contradiction of sinners against Himself," the jealous hatred of Israel's religious leaders, the incessant pressure of temptation by the subtle, dis-
guised, relentless, powerful prince of evil, the agony and bloody
sweat of Gethsemane, the excruciating transfixion and forlorn grief

of Calvary and the "outer darkness" of "My God, my God, why hast Thou forsaken Me?" Yes, think of it: God "spared not" His own Son, but "delivered Him up" to all that! Oh, how it hurt the Son! How it cost the Father! "He spared not..."! What a world in a word! What a cloudburst in a sob! What a whirlwind in a sigh! What an ocean in a tear! What an eternity of meaning in one verb! "He spared not..."! "God *so* loved the world that He *gave* [to all that] His only-begotten Son" from His very bosom (John 1:18). It shook the interior of the very Godhead when the Father plucked the Son of His eternal delight from that boundless "bosom," and allowed Him to tread those grief-bestrewn miles to Calvary. How can we ever think of it without tears of adoring wonder and gratitude!

Furthermore, what the giving of that greatest of all Gifts by the greatest of all Givers cost the heavenly Father may be all the more appreciated when we realize that the heavenly Father suffered *in* all the sufferings of the Son. The iron spikes which those Roman soldiers hammered through the hands of Jesus went right through that wooden transom into the heart of the Father. The spear which a calloused hand thrust into the side of Jesus pierced right through to the co-suffering Father. The pinioned Sinbearer on that middle cross did not represent an absentee God who sits distantly apart, unmoved as He surveys our human woes. At Calvary, God was right in the middle of it with us. Remember 2 Corinthians 5:19, "God was in Christ, reconciling the world unto Himself." How near to us Calvary brings God—a God who could suffer so! There are those who have objected to the idea that God can suffer. Calvary proves them wrong. The fact that God is love implies the capacity for sacrifice in Him; and the capacity for sacrifice indicates the capacity for suffering.

There are three aspects of God's love revealed at Calvary which should always be in our thinking about it. On that cross God suffered *as* man, and *for* man, and *with* man. Consider those three one at a time. (1) He suffered *as* man. So now God is not only a sympathetic external observer of our human suffering, but, in the person of His dear Son, an actual participant. God was not at Calvary merely by proxy; He was in it; and it was in Him! In Jesus, God knows human suffering by experience! (2) He suffered *for* man, and in that sense He was there redemptively, taking our place as the race's vicarious substitute and sinbearer. (3) He suffered *with* man; and that means a love which feels the highest and deepest and tenderest sympathy. The more one ponders those three, the more wonderful does the love of God become.

It is indeed true: "God *so* loved..." and therefore *so* suffered. But if we would enter with the keenest perception into what it cost the heavenly Father to give His only-begotten Son, we need to reflect again on the sufferings of Jesus. What Jesus suffered to save us, tongue can never tell, nor can any human mind encompass.

From His birth in Bethlehem, and through His growth to manhood, but especially from the moment of His baptism in the Jordan, our Lord was identified by His manhood and messiahship with the sinning, suffering mankind He had come to redeem. At times the sorrow and weight of it so pressed on Him that He emitted a sad sigh. It is only too plain, also, that during His long, final trek from Galilee to Jerusalem (Luke 9:51-19:44), the shadow of the cross was falling over His mind (13:33-35, 17:25, 18:31-34). He pre-described the cross as a "baptism" (baptisma, an immersion) in suffering (12:50). The gloom of it saddened Him as He wept over impenitent Jerusalem. He knew in advance the shameful, painful kind of death He must die (Matt. 26:2, etc.).

But it was as He drew near to Gethsemane that the first full-beating of the storm broke upon Him, and (I say it with prostrate reverence) He seemed for the moment to have reeled under the grim shock and force of it. Yes, I speak with thoughtful awe as I dare to make the comment, but it would seem that, although He had "set His face like a flint" in anticipation of that awful event, and had expressed advanced sensations of it, when the reality fell on Him with its concentrated blackness and satanic frenzy, His holy manhood quailed. So far as we can gather, it was at the gate of the garden that the fearfulness of it broke with deadly vividness upon His soul. He had known it would be costly. But even He who "knew all things" was by virtue of His incarnation truly human, and seemed to have been taken by mingled surprise and horror at the enormity of the suffering involved in his Racial sin-bearing as it now becomes a concentrated experience.

We infer that it was then that the pressure of the world's sin became increasingly intense and crushingly heavy upon Him. Matthew says, "He began to be sorrowful and very heavy," to which he adds, "Then saith He to them, My soul is exceeding sorrowful even unto death" (26:37,38). In the Greek, that expression, "exceeding sorrowful," is *lupos* with the preposition, *peri*, prefixed to it, giving it the force of a going beyond, of excessive suffering. That other expression, "very heavy," (*ademonein*) speaks of pressure and dismay, the sudden dismay which comes with unexpected calamity. Perhaps Weymouth's rendering best gives the sense of the original: "He began to be full of anguish and distress, and He said to them: My soul is crushed with anguish to the point of death." He meant quite literally "to the point of death," for the doubt now was whether his humanhood could bear to the required degree the immense aggregate of the race's guilt without His body succumbing; and, indeed, as we have seen before, an angel was sent to strengthen Him.

Mark's account says that "He began to be sore amazed, and to be very heavy" (Mark 14:33). One is almost afraid to look at the Greek word translated "sore amazed." Weymouth renders it "full of terror." Our Lord saw starkly now the depth, ugliness, enormity of human sin. He felt overwhelmed as by a gigantic tidal wave of retribution through which He must plunge on our behalf. In that garden of the olive press the incarnate Son of God was appalled.

The combined effect of what Matthew, Mark and Luke tell us is that even the Son of God, in that hour, was almost swept off His feet by the shuddering horror of the ordeal. Whatever His prior premonitions had been, the ghastliness of the actual experience (as it now struck Him) seemed too much even for Him, in His humanity, to endure.

But if, to some small degree, we may gauge His suffering through the descriptive words used by Matthew and Mark, and by our Lord Himself, perhaps we may tread more deeply into it as we see and hear Him in His Gethsemane prayer. Hitherto, in His earthly ministry, our Lord had maintained singular tranquility and poise, despite calumniating enemies, unrepentant cities, turncoat disciples, bitter opposition, and the crescendo of satanic temptation. His closest friends had seen only unruffled calm. It is noticeable, too, that after His Gethsemane wrestle, He exhibited a fully recovered equanimity, so that during His arraignment before the high priest, His inquisition by Pilate, and then amid the mocking and scourging and the torture of crucifixion, He showed that self-possessed, kingly dignity and uncomplaining resignation which have been a challenging wonder to His adoring followers ever since. But there, in the black darkness of Gethsemane, the sublime serenity was ousted by an agony which shook Him to the depths of His being. Earth rejected him. Man despised him. His disciples slept while He struggled, and He knew they would soon desert Him. Satan tempted Him, taunted Him, attacked Him, pressured Him more desperately and determinedly than ever before. There was one solitary resort left: He prayed. In the words of Hebrews 5:7, He prayed "with strong crying and tears unto Him that was able to save Him from death, and was heard in that which He feared."

Oh, that Gethsemane prayer! Some of us prefer different postures for different kinds of moods of prayer. For myself, I find it helpful now and then to pray slowly walking to and fro. At other times I find it better to pray just standing. Often, during longer seasons of waiting on God, I sit in a tallish, straight-backed chair. Frequently, too, I am constrained to kneel, and bow low physically as well as spiritually in the divine presence. But with that lonely figure among those shadowy vines in Gethsemane there was no slow pacing or quiet standing or relaxed sitting. Even kneeling was not enough. Matthew says, "He fell on His face...." There was sheer brokenness. He was at the extremity of bearable pain. Never had such heart-rending cries of grief risen to the ears of heaven.

So intense now was His pleading that despite the chill of the night, He began to sweat profusely, until (can it be?) His sweat became "great drops of blood" oozing through His pores and dripping to the ground. (Remember, it is Luke the doctor who tells us this: Luke 22:44). So far as records inform us, only five or six cases of such blood-sweating have ever been known; and I have read somewhere that in each case the person died almost at once through collapse of the heart due to excessive pressure of hypertensive stress. Possibly that might have happened even to our dear Lord but for the fact that "there appeared an angel unto Him from heaven, strengthening Him" (Luke 22:43). Far more surprising than the fact of the angel's appearing is that Jesus, the Crown-Prince of heaven, should need such emergency help because of such piteous prostration.

Oh, never, never can we know
What filled that cup of bitter woe;
Nor can we ever understand
How Jesus there with trembling hand
Took hold upon that deadly cup
Which He, our Sinbearer, must sup:
No finite mind can ever know
The grief He had to undergo;
Only the Father understood
As Jesus there sweat drops of blood,
And then, amid the tears of God,
To Calv'ry from Gethsemane trod.

The Calvary Culmination

It might seem an unpardonable irreverence even to attempt an analysis of our Lord's atoning sufferings. will not commit such an impertinence here, though I will not hesitate, with a worshiping heart, to suggest that we may profitably contemplate different aspects of His sufferings.

There were the sufferings of His *body*. These were the outward and visible part only. They were but the brim of the cup that He had to drink. The bitter dregs were deeper down, too deep for any human observer to see. Although His physical pains were the least hurtful ingredient of that fearful potion, how abnormally severe they were! Even physically, did anyone ever suffer more than He? I sometimes wonder whether the usual pictures of His crucifixion give adequate portrayal of His disfigured face and lacerated body. The swipes and blows which made His face black and blue with bruises were not those of children, but of rough soldiers and others who struck with such force as only satanic malice gives. By the time He hung on Calvary His face must have been scarcely recognizable. Long before that awful deed disgraced man's history, the prophet Isaiah had forseen it. In his prologue at the "great passional" (Isaiah 53) he said that His appearance was disfigured beyond human semblance! (52:14, R.S.V. et al).

Death by drowning is comparatively painless. Death by burning is intensely painful but soon over. Death by starvation is prolongation of dying, but is attended by exhaustion rather than actual pain, and the victim gradually slips into coma. Death by bludgeoning is savage hurt, but in only moments the blow falls which knocks unconscious and leaves the body a corpse. There are many hard ways of dying, but none is more torturous than crucifixion. There are reasons for thinking that our Lord's crucifixion was the most painful ever endured. That body of His, remember, had never known pain before; for His body was as diseaseless as His soul was sinless.

Such violence, brutality, and the climactic torture of impalement by iron spikes driven through hands and feet must have registered with peculiar intensification in that sensitively refined manhood and physique.

Even among ordinary men, flagellations which can be borne in a dullish, callous way by roughened, hardened bodies are tenfold sorer to bear by those with gentler frame. For with the latter it is a tenser strain of pain which is transmitted through nerves and brain to the mind. Somewhat correspondingly, on Calvary that extraordinary manhood in that extraordinary body could experience extraordinary pain—and did so beyond our most imaginative empathy. We simply cannot gauge that suffering by comparison with any other. Therefore, even if we think only of those bodily tortures, we may well hear the words of Lamentations 1:12 coming from those parched lips: "Is it nothing to you, all ye that pass by? Behold, and see if there be any sorrow like unto My sorrow, which is done to Me, wherewith Jehovah hath afflicted Me in the day of His fierce anger."

Our Lord's physical sufferings, as already noted, began even in Gethsemane when, to the shock of watching angels, His very body so shared His grief as to sweat drops of blood. How He rose up after that and bore with regal self-command all that quickly ensued, is an awe-exciting wonder. Think of it all: the predawn arrest, being dragged before that venomous schemer, Annas, (the elderly father-in-law of Caiaphas the high priest, the chief "brain" of the anti-Jesus conspirators), being sent bound from Annas to the informal confrontation before Caiaphas and members of the Sanhedrin, the more formal arraignment before that same high priest and the fuller membership of the Jewish supreme council, the charge of blasphemy, being spat on, buffeted, and smitten, mocked, blindfolded, and repeatedly struck on the face to the accompaniment of "Prophesy, who is it that smote thee?", being bound again and dragged before governor Pontius Pilate, being hustled from Pilate to Herod and "set at naught" by Herod's armed men; being shunted back in a gorgeous robe of mock majesty to Pilate, the further interrogation by Pilate, the frenzied yelling of the mob, "Crucify Him!", the scourging until all the stripes merged into one bleeding area of torn flesh (as seen implied by Isaiah 53:5, where the word stripes should be singular), the horseplay by Pilate's men-at-arms in the praetorium, being stripped, exposed, and made to wear the purple robe of farcical royalty, the pressing of the wreath of thorns upon His head, the further spittings and smitings on the head, then the weary, weary drag along the Via Dolorosa to the mount of execution outside the city wall, the stumbling and staggering under the weight of the heavy wooden beam, being flung down backward on the wooden beam and crossbar, the hammering of the spikes through hands and feet, and that moment of excruciating torture, when the cross was hoisted up and plunged into the ground, when His body became suspended entirely on those nails, making every vein a stream of intense pain and every nerve a strand of fire, and, finally, the six hours of hanging naked in the glare of the sun, pain-racked and by now facially almost unrecognizable. Oh, the anguish of that night in Gethsemane and those precrucifixion brutalities and those hours of grueling torture while hanging on those nails! How does that visage languish which once was bright as morn! How pale is that dear face which shone like the sun on the mount of transfiguration! How is that handsome manhood mutilated! Was any suffering ever like His?!

Yet far more severe were the sufferings of His *mind*. Those sufferings, being inward, were unobservable by men. They can never be grasped by any creature-mind. They were possible only to a mind of superhuman dimension. His was not only the greatest human mind which has ever existed, it was the mentality of *God*, of God the Son who, by incarnation, had taken to Himself not only a human body, but our human nature. He was not two persons in one body. Nor was He two minds somehow temporarily co-existing with each other. In Him there were indeed two natures—the divine and the human. But His person was that of God the Son. At one and the same time, in that mysterious union of natures, He suffered both humanly and divinely. There was the suffering of an utterly sinless, exquisitely holy and refined humanhood blended with that of the boundlessly divine and therefore magnified into proportions unthinkable by any of us.

As we have seen, capacity for suffering is determined by the level or degree of intelligence and consciousness. A mouse can suffer more than a worm. A bird can suffer more than a mouse. A dog can suffer more than a bird. A man can suffer more than any of the lower animals. As a worm cannot grasp the mental capacity of a bird, nor a bird the mental capacity of a dog, nor a dog the mental capacity of a human being, so are we human beings unable even faintly to imagine the capacity for suffering in "the mind...which was...in Christ Jesus" (Phil. 2:5). Only a mind with an infinite experiential capability could have endured the vast shock, borne the incalculable weight, expatiated the monstrous evil, and exhausted the full penalty incurred by the total sin of our human race.

The mind of Jesus was and is divinely boundless, and thus His love of man not only outweathered the uttermost fury of the tempest that beat upon Him, and outloved the worst that human hate could do, but He out-bounded all that His vicarious atoning demanded and exacted. Language fails. How can we even creep within a "stone's throw" (Luke 22:41) of that deep, surging, fathomless suffering as Jesus, our God-Man Redeemer, who languished in that ignominious repudiation on Calvary?

But there was also the suffering of His *soul*. Do I seem to be making an unreal differentiation if I speak of His soul in distinction from His mind? That is the last thing I want to do. Perhaps, even in us humans, the distinction drawn between mind and soul sometimes seems superfine. For heart and mind and soul are all inseparable constituents of the one indivisible ego. Nevertheless, the distinction seems justifiable. The heart is the seat of the affections, desires and ambitions. The mind is that in us which thinks, knows and wills. And the soul is the self-aware person who is expressed through the heart and the mind. Heart, mind and soul are all aspects of man's *spiritual* being, but the soul is the basic self.

Reflect then. Our Lord Jesus is the purest personal being conceivable. His mind, heart, soul, intellect, emotion and will were all alike utterly untainted by moral defect, either hereditary or contracted. Moreover, not only was there the negative perfection of sinlessness, there was the positive perfection of holiness. There was purest light filling that mind, and purest love filling that heart, and purest personal outreach of soul toward God, toward all angel intelligences, and toward all human beings. In Scripture phrase, He was (and is) the "altogether lovely."

In hideous contrast to that, think now, if you can, of all the selfishness, envy, hatred, violence, murder—from Cain, who slew his brother not far from man's lost paradise in Eden, to the present day—all the ugly, repulsive continuity of it from then until now. Then think, if you can, of all the lust, sensuality, lechery, sodomy, erotic animalism, incest, and other moral filth that has taken place down the centuries. Think also, if you can, of all the antigodism, demonism, tyranny, rapine, cruelty, perversion, deceit, corruption, wickedness, rebellion against the moral law, and man's inhumanity to man. Yes, think of it all, if you can, and then add to it all the other aspects of the race's sin-disease, moral leprosy, and millionfold depravity. The fact is, we cannot think of it all as it is in its aggregate monstrosity. But God sees it all, as He alone can, and what a sight of vast ugliness it must be!

When our Lord, the "altogether lovely" one, hung on Calvary, He *saw* all that, and *bore* all that, and *felt* all that in His substitutionary sinbearing. He saw it, bore it, felt it, as only God could. He shuddered and recoiled from it as only exquisite purity, holy love and sensitively noble manhood could. On that cross there occurred the direst collision ever known in the universe between moral ugliness and moral loveliness, between utter foulness and utter purity, between vicious hate and virtuous love, between vile darkness and sheer light. What the heart-crushing shock of that collision must have been within the soul of our dear, holy, unresisting Savior, who shall ever say?

Again, may it not seem as though I am over-analyzing when I mention that interwoven with all those profound sufferings of mind and soul there were the sufferings of His pure and tender *heart*. Jesus, being truly human, had a human heart, i.e., human feelings, desires, hopes, concerns, and responses. He very humanly "sighed" over our human afflictions, such as deafness (Mark 7:35), and "sighed deeply" over the hypocrisy of the Pharisees (Mark 8:12). He "thrilled with joy" (how human that sounds!) when spiritual truths were revealed to the simplehearted (Luke 10:21, Moffatt). He "wept" such tears of human sympathy with Martha and Mary at their brother's tomb that the onlookers said, "How He loved him!" (John 11:35,36). His bosom heaved with human fellow-feeling as He was "moved with compassion" for the entreating leper. And, as John 13:1 says, "having loved His own who were in the world, He loved them unto the end"— or, more truly representing the Greek word, "He loved them to the *uttermost*," as He was now going to show them at Gethsemane and Golgotha.

As Jesus and the Twelve sat together at that long-ago Passover supper, how humanly upset Jesus was at the thought of Judas' imminent treachery! John 13:21 tells us, Jesus...was *troubled in spirit*, and testified "...Verily, verily, I say unto you, that one of you shall betray Me." Jesus loved Judas, which made the betrayal a sorer pain. It was a poignant hurt to Him that one of His closest confidants should become the avaricious traitor.

Why did Jesus take His disciples to Gethsemane with Him, even to within a stone's throw of His prayer-wrestle, and then take Peter, James and John even further in among those shadowy trees to be near Him? Was it not that His truly human heart longed for sympathetic human friendship, understanding, and closeness amid His lonely distress?

Even humanly, then, how He suffered! As the thick gloom of death, "even the death of the cross" (Phil. 2:8) now gathered stiflingly around Him, His human heart must have fretted keenly over being betrayed by a trusted friend, and His being loudly disowned by a cowardly Peter, over being deserted by the other ten panic-stricken disciples, over being left in the lurch by the fickle enthusiasts who only a few days before had regaled Him with their hosannas and adulations. How much must that guileless, loving, outgoing human heart of His have suffered through the virulent spite and spleen which now found full expression in atrocious misrepresentation and maltreatment! Consider the venomous jealousy of Israel's leaders who plotted His execution, the conniving duplicity and pusillanimity of Pilate, the malicious lust for His blood and obliteration by those who ostensibly represented Jehovah and the bigoted prejudice of those whom He had come to redeem, and who were bringing on their nation such an avalanche of divine judgment as had never been seen before.

And how that human heart must have recoiled from that agonized dying in public shame! What shrinking there must have been from that strange dissolution of soul and body that we call death! A human heart such as His could suffer as no other ever has, either before or since.

But whatever may be said about the sufferings of our Lord's

body, mind, heart and soul, the most unknowably grievous of all were those of His *spirit*. Once again, we are in the awing presence of that inscrutable mystery, the union of the human with the divine in our Lord's being. He had a human spirit, i.e., that attribute of the human soul which makes man *capax Dei*, capable of God, and distinctively God-conscious. But in Him the human spirit was by absorption entirely one with His eternal divinity. There was duality of experience, both the human and the divine, yet so blended as to be personally one in His deepest grief of all.

With that in mind, try to think what our Lord's communion with the heavenly Father must have been during those years on earth. His consciousness of God was far beyond that of any other, even if we try to think only of His humanhood. When He was only twelve years old, He said to His parents, "Wist ye not that I must be about My Father's business?" (Luke 2:49). During His boyhood and youth in Nazareth did He not have the deep awareness that He was wrapped around with that love which had delighted in Him before the worlds were created? Was not the heavenly Father's smile more to Him through all those years than Caesar's favor or the imperial purple could ever have given Him? He had a richer joy, a deeper peace, a sweeter satisfaction than all the pompous elevation and possessions that earthly royalty could confer. The Holy Spirit, the "well of living water," was springing up in His own pure soul before ever He talked about it to the woman at Sychar's well.

No one ever communed by prayer with the Father as did Jesus. No one ever carried such a continuous inward pledge of the Father's approval. "I do always those things that please Him" (John 8:29). Looking up to heaven He could say, "Father, I know that Thou hearest Me always" (11:42). "I and the Father are one," He declared (10:30). To Nicodemus He explained that although He had "come down from heaven" He was still *"in* heaven" (John 3:13), meaning that His communion with the Father was such that even incarnation did not interrupt His being in heaven in that deepest sense of fellowship with the Father. Uncloudedly He knew the Father, loved the Father, pleased the Father, rested in the Father, breathed the Father's love like fresh morning fragrance from heather-carpeted hills, and was encompassed by a perpetual realization of the Father's protective presence. No less than three times it is recorded that as He envisioned how He would be betrayed, denied, deserted, "despised and rejected of men" (Isaiah 53:3), He took comfort in saying, "I am not alone...*The Father...sent Me*" (John 8:16, 29; 16:32). He was saying that He could endure all things as long as the Father was with Him.

Try to imagine, then, how heavenly, how dear to Jesus was that moment-by-moment, heart-to-heart intertwine between Himself and the heavenly Father, and how confident was His repose in the luminous realization of that loving Father's presence. Then stand aghast at Calvary as you hear that pinioned, pain-racked sufferer utter that wail of piteous desolation, "My God, My God, why hast *Thou* forsaken Me?" Up to that point, even on the cross, He had been sustained by the unquenchable joy of being submissively pleasing to the Father. But suddenly, in that awful moment, there is a heart-rending rupture of communication between them. The one, last refuge is ripped away. The man-forsaken has become the God-forsaken! In that instant the warm sunshine of the Father's face gives place to a nameless horror of black darkness. More than once or twice during the three preceding years, Jesus had warned His hearers of "the outer darkness." Now, He Himself was in it and utterly alone. That was the distant point at which further endurance became impossible. It was the extreme at which, not physically but inwardly and spiritually, the heart of Jesus was broken (Psalm 22:14, 69:20, 21).

The first three hours of our Lord's six hours on the cross were in the light of the morning (9 A.M. to noon). The remaining three hours were in the abnormal midday darkness (Mark 15:25, Matt. 27:45, 46). It was amid that enshrouding gloom, and just before He expired, that He cried out in His God-forsakenness. The daytime darkness that engulfed Golgotha was symbolic of that fearful other darkness into which Jesus passed before He vacated His body. Hebrews 2:9 selects a word significantly relating to this when it says, "That He by the grace of God, should taste death for every man." That expression, "taste death," means far more than ordinary dying, more than all our Lord's sufferings of heart, mind, soul and body together. It means the bitter, bitter experiencing of *spiritual* death, the essential meaning of which is separation from God. For to be cut off completely from the face of Him who is "the light of life" is a horror of unrelieved darkness and destitution. As our sinbearer, and for our sakes, our dear Savior underwent even *that* which was the uttermost which the holy law of God could demand, and the uttermost to which even the divine love could go.

We can but gaze in speechless wonder, or else vent our hearts by exclaiming again, "Oh, the sufferings of our meek and lowly Lord Jesus!" For those sufferings are "a deep where all our thoughts are drowned." The holy angels and principalities and powers in the heavenly places must have looked on in dumb amazement and with a sympathy beyond tears. But outside of Jesus there was only one place where there could ever be suffering equal to that which He endured, and that was in the heart of the heavenly Father. What it all cost Jesus is the measure of what it cost the Father, for the Father suffered with Him through it all. Every pang and pain, every throb and throe, every groan and grief, every shock and shudder, the Father jointly experienced, even to the bitter outcry, "My God, My God, why hast Thou forsaken Me?" At that point the Father's heart-response was, "My Son, My Son, how can I turn away from You, and plunge You into such darkness, even though I now see You as covered with all the moral leprosy and ugliness of human sin?"

Yes, that cross and that suffering Savior are the measure of God's love to us. That is the ocean without bound which evermore rolls in upon us through John 3:16.

> For God so loved the world that He gave His only begotten Son, that whosoever believeth on Him should not perish but have everlasting life.

10

The Love of God—In and Through Us

A s already mentioned, in the New Testament we see the love of God reaching out in a progressive threefold movement: first *to* us, then *in* us, and then *through* us. Inadequate as all our words are, and even must be about the love of God toward man, having reflected gratefully upon that in the study preceding this one, we now press forward to think about the love of God within us. By this we mean God's love imparted to us Christian believers by the Holy Spirit; imparted so as actually to indwell us in living experience. This is a reality clearly unfolded in the New Testament, and what a soul-thrilling truth it is! As mountain-climbers reach a summit and then find, to their surprise, other summits rising up beyond them which they could not see from the lower slopes, so is it we survey the scriptural disclosures concerning the love of God.

> Oh, vast surprise—that wondrous Incarnation!
> Creation's God now born in Adam's race!
> To bleed for sin, and bring us free salvation!
> A wonder dwarfing matter, time and space!

Again and again the references to God's love as indwelling the Christian appear in the Scripture pages. We think of John 17:26, where our Lord prays, "that the love wherewith Thou hast loved Me may be *in them*, and I in them." That, be it noted, was the last sentence and crowning request in the yearning prayer which He prayed just before crossing the dark waters of the then full-flowing Kedron, on His way to Gethsemane. There can be no mistaking the meaning of His words. They were not a petition merely that a love *for* God might somehow be stirred up in the hearts of His disciples, nor even that God the Father should show the same kind of love *toward* them that He shows to the beloved Son. It is a prayer that in the same way as our Lord's own peace and joy were going to be *within* the disciples (John 14:27, 15:11), so the heavenly Father's own love should be by supernatural impartation *in* them! Moreover, that high-soaring prayer has been answered. Pentecost has translated it into experienced reality among our Lord's own. It is the gladdest mystery and miracle of the Christian life. As later Scripture tells us, it brings the full bloom of Christian sanctification, wrought in us by the heavenly Paraclete, the Holy Spirit.

We think of Paul's glowing asseveration in Romans 5:5: "The love of God is shed abroad in our hearts by the Holy Spirit who is given to us." Again there can be no dubiety as to the meaning. By "the love of God" Paul is not meaning *our* love toward God. We sometimes say that a man has "the love of art," or "the love of money," or "the love of nature," and in each case we mean the man's own love toward something. Similarly, this expression, "the love of God," could mean a man's love toward God. That, however, is not the way Paul uses it in Romans 5:5. It is the love which is in the very heart of God now "shed" within us by none other than the Spirit of God Himself. Well may we wonder at it.

We think, too, of other passages such as Galatians 5:22; Ephesians 1:4; Philippians 2:2,5; 2 Thessalonians 2:5; 2 Timothy 1:7, 1 John 2:5; 4:12,18; all to the same effect. There are also various other passages where this impartation of the divine love is clearly implied even though not actually stated. It is like a golden embroidery on the New Testament teaching as to Christian holiness.

In our study preceding this one, we saw how John 3:16 gathers up and expresses all the biblical utterances about the love of God *toward* us. Similarly, there is one paragraph which expresses in representative splendor all the varied references to the love of God *within* us. It is Paul's prayer in Ephesians 3:16-19.

> That He [God] would grant you, according to the riches of His glory, to be strengthened with might by His Spirit in the inner man; that Christ may dwell in your hearts by faith; that ye, being rooted [like a tree] and grounded [like a building] in love, may be able to comprehend with all the saints what is the breadth, and length, and depth, and height; and to know the love of Christ which passeth knowledge, that ye might be filled with all the fullness of God.

The paradox here of knowing that which "passeth knowledge" is only seeming. It emphasizes that what cannot be known by the head may be known in the heart. Truths which cannot be figured out by reason may be shining reality in experience. Love is bigger than logic, and faith can intelligently grasp what intellect alone can never capture.

In this Pauline prayer see all three persons of the divine triunity blending in the deeper experience of the redeemed and sanctified. The Holy Spirit "strengthens" us in "the *inner man.*" It is that "Christ may dwell in our *hearts.*" And it is with a view to our being "*filled* with all the fullness of God!" Who can read such words thoughtfully without being overcome by mingling surprise and adoring praise that such an experience of God is open to us?

Look carefully again at what Paul prays we may know. We are to "comprehend with all the saints what is the *breadth*, and *length*, and *depth*, and *height*" of the surpassing "love of Christ," so that we may become "filled with all the fullness of God!" Perhaps if we had not become so familiar with the phraseology here it would affect us more excitingly than it does. Is it not strange that Paul should speak of our Savior's love as having those four dimensions? We do not normally speak of abstract concepts such as love, joy, peace, hope, fear, as having breadth and length and depth and height. Strictly, those four dimensions can be predicted only of material objects. They do not belong to the mental, moral, spiritual. Is there some special allusion in Paul's peculiar use of physical measurements here? I think the Bible can best interpret that for us.

Think back to those earlier Old Testament times when God gave to Moses the specifications for the Israelite tabernacle in the wilderness. Although comparatively small and outwardly unimposing, was there ever a more extraordinary structure? Right down to its smaller appurtenances it was divinely invested with symbolical and typical meanings, some of which reach right on through the centuries to our own so-called Christian dispensation. When the heavenly Architect gave the plans and particulars to Moses, He instructed him to make, first of all, the "Holy of Holies," that hallowed inmost shrine where Jehovah was to reveal His presence through the shekinah flame. Its dimensions were carefully dictated in advance. It must be ten cubits long, and ten cubits wide, by ten cubits high. In other words, its breadth and length and depth and height were all to be equal with each other.

Some five hundred years later, when king Solomon built in Jerusalem the magnificent temple which superseded the tabernacle, he enlarged the Holy of Holies, but he retained the original symmetry. He made it *twenty* cubits long, but also twenty cubits wide, and twenty cubits high. So it was still a perfect cube, with its six equal square sides. Then again, right at the end of the Bible, in the twenty-first chapter of the Apocalypse where the celestial city is described—"that great city lieth foursquare, and the length is as large as the breadth...twelve thousand furlongs. The length and the breadth and the height of it are equal." So, once again, in magnific enlargement, we have the cube.

Is there some symbolic meaning latent in all this? The answer is not far to seek. This figure, the cube, because of its absolute symmetry, was to the old-time Hebrews (as probably to others) the symbol of perfection.

Now, in a flash, we catch the meaning in the cubic dimensions of the Holy of Holies in the tabernacle, then in the temple, then in the contour of the New Jerusalem which shall yet be set up on this planet. In the tabernacle and the temple the four equal dimensions bespeak the perfection of Israel's God. In the Apocalypse they fore-picture the perfection of that queen city which will be the center of God's new order of things on this earth. That surely is what Hebrew Paul has in mind when he speaks of "the breadth, and length, and depth, and height" of the love of Christ! It is that symbol of the cube again! Paul is thinking of the glorious perfection of that love which came in vast descent from the highest height of heaven to that deepest depth of woe on Calvary. Oh, this indescribably glorious, all-perfect love of God's dear Son! It matters not from whichever standpoint we view it, sheer perfection flashes forth—whether we think of its expression toward the Father, or toward us poor human sinners; whether we think of its immensity or its intensity, its eter-nity or its sublimity, its deathless strength or its exquisite tender-ness, its majesty or its humility, its profundity or its simplicity, its outward expression or its inmost motive—in its breadth and length and depth and height it is perfect with a perfection that belongs to God alone.

Dimensions of Calvary

Stand yet again before that cross on Calvary. See those cube dimensions shining out northward, southward, eastward, westward, upward, downward. Above the uncomplaining "Man of sorrows" there is a trilingual superscription: *THIS IS JESUS THE KING OF THE JEWS* (Matt. 27:37). It is written "in Greek and Latin and Hebrew" (Luke 23:38). Those three languages representatively em-braced the entire race: the language of religion (Hebrew), of culture (Greek), of law (Latin or Roman). They represented also the charac-teristic types of men in continuing generations. They thus reach out to all points of the compass. See in them the wide-flung arms of redeeming love. In them we behold the *breadth* of that love.

Linger, as Jesus hangs there, until He cries, "My God, My God, why hast Thou forsaken Me?" (Matt. 27:46). As you hear that strangest requiem which earth or heaven ever heard, let it tell to you the unmeasurable measure of the *length* to which the divine love would go for our sakes.

Keep looking. That cross stands between two others, for the Holy One of Israel is "numbered with the transgressors." He hangs there between two robbers—two insurrectionists whose hands were stained with other men's blood before being now fastened by the nails. They both have heard of Jesus many a time before. Likely enough they actually have lurked among the crowds who thronged Him to hear His teachings about the long-awaited "kingdom of heaven," and to see the amazing miracles of healing which He everywhere performed in proof that He was the promised one of God. They knew of His strong but meek and guileless character, and of His claim to be the expected Messiah. The last thing they could ever have dreamed was that they would one day hang crucified, one on each side of Him. They now observe His resignation and hear His gracious words, "Father, forgive them; for they know not what they do" (Luke 23:34). Suddenly one of them has a spiritual eye-opening. It breaks upon his mind who Jesus really is, and he begs, "Lord, remember me when Thou comest into Thy kingdom" (Luke 23:42). Can the Savior's love reach down low enough to pluck this polluted son of evil from Gehenna? Hear the reply from that middle cross: "Verily, I say unto thee, Today shalt thou be with Me in *paradise*" (v. 43). And as you listen, learn the *depth* to which heaven's love can reach—and the *height* to which it can lift even the lowest. How true it is, that the cross itself is the sublimest illustration, as it is also the most profound expression of that love divine which, in its breadth and length and depth and height, "passeth knowledge"!

"Breadth, and length, and depth, and height." Is not the pen of inspiration clearly guided in so putting the order of these dimensions? Change the order, and you spoil the sequence. When we learn of this redeeming love, what is the first thing we want to know? Is it not the breadth? "Is it broad enough to take me in?" What is the next thing we ask? Is it not the length? "How far will it go? How long will it last?" What is our next question? Is it not as to what depth it can reach? Some of us exclaim, "I have sinned against special light and peculiar privilege, so that I am really more culpable than many a murderer or blasphemer or drunkard. Can the love of God reach down even to me?" And when we get the "Yes" to that, what is the grateful further question? Is it not as to what height this soul-saving love can lift us? It is; and it completes the true sequence: "breadth, and length, and depth, and height."

Incidently, what a parallel this makes with John 3:16! "God so loved the *world*"—there is the breadth. "That He gave His only-begotten *Son*"—there is the length to which that love would go. "That whosoever believeth on Him should not *perish*"—there is the depth to which it reaches. "But have *everlasting life*"—there is the height to which it lifts us.

The High-water Mark

Looking again, now, at Paul's prayer in Ephesians 3, we note that the high-water mark of Christian experience is indicated when he covets for us that we may not only have this heavenly love abiding in us, but *filling* us. His wording seems at first almost too excessive for credence: "filled with all the *fullness of God*"! How can the Pacific Ocean be contained in a teacup? How can the Milky Way be packed into a suitcase? How can the big blue sky be housed in an Indian tepee? By comparing one Pauline passage with another, however, we soon see that what the apostle prays for is as possible as it is challenging.

We need to understand what that nineteenth verse means by "the fullness of God." Colossians 1:19 says, "It pleased the Father that in Him [Christ] should all the fullness dwell"; or as in more recent translations, "In Him all the fullness was pleased to dwell." Chapter 2:9 complements that: "For in Him [Christ] dwelleth all the fullness of the Godhead bodily." So our Lord Jesus Christ is "the fullness of God." To the same effect is Ephesians 1:22, though as it appears in our English translation it would seem to make the church the fullness. Taken with the immediate context, and with the two Colossian verses just quoted, the force of the words in Ephesians 1:22,23 is, "[God] put all things under *His* [Christ's] feet, and gave *Him* to be head over all things to the Church which is His body, the fullness of Him that filleth all in all." Yes, let it be repeated, *Christ* is the fullness, and to be "filled with all the fullness of God" is to be filled with Christ. The conclusive commentary on this is Paul's own word in Colossians 2:9,10, "*In Him dwelleth all the fullness* of the Godhead bodily. And *ye are* complete in Him."

"Filled *with all* the fullness of God." Note that preposition, "with." We are to be "filled *with*" the fullness to a certain point denoted by that little-big word, "all," which signifies entirely. So, of course, it is not a question as to whether these poor little selves of ours can hold all the fullness of God; the reference is simply to our *capacity to hold.* We are to be filled "to" our utmost capacity—completely possessed, pervaded, permeated by Him who is "the fullness of God" and "Head over all things to the Church." What a prayer! What an ideal! It is entire sanctification in its highest, purest, richest, deepest aspect—our unobstructed absorption of the life and love of our risen Redeemer-King. Oh, that we may more fully prove it in our own experience! Does it seem a height too high even to be scaled? Then listen to the doxology which Paul subjoins to it:

> Now unto Him who is able to do exceeding abundantly above ʔll that we ask or think, according to the power that worketh in us, unto Him be glory in the church by Christ Jesus throughout all ages, age without end. Amen.

Romans 5:5 Again

Our theme is running away with more pages than we allocated; so we will not attempt here to inspect all those other texts which refer to the love of God *in* us. Albeit, there is one, at least, which should be allowed to recapture our attention, even though briefly. It is Romans 5:5. "The love of God is shed abroad in our hearts by the Holy Spirit which is given unto us." What a word that is! I know of no religion outside Christianity which comes anywhere near making such a claim or expressing such an experience. Either it is credulous self-delusion or it is the most extraordinary invasion of human personality ever known.

It cannot be self-delusion. The sanity as well as the sincerity of Paul and his fellow-apostles rules that out. Besides, had it been any mere autosuggestion of enthusiasts it would soon enough have been exposed by relentless investigation, and early Christianity would never have won its expanding conquests over the plentiful skepticism which everywhere opposed it. When Paul writes, "The love of God is shed abroad in our hearts by the Holy Spirit," he is describing a genuine and verifiable experience which was common rather than exceptional among early Christian believers. Such was the true Apostolic Christianity, the intended level of spiritual experience. Should not all of us covet maximum sanctification, a flood-tide immersion?

"The love of God is shed abroad in our hearts by the Holy Spirit which is given unto us." How this emphasizes the *inwardness* of the true Christian life! Christianity is no mere list of rules, or school of ideas, or code of ethics, or set of ideals, or even a body of beliefs. It is inwardly re-creative divine presence and power. Christian holiness is nothing less than the love of God Himself inflooding and renewing a human heart.

"The love of God is shed abroad in our hearts by the Holy Spirit." This denotes, also, the *directness* of our Christian fellowship with God. It is not mediated through priests, sacraments, ordinances. Back at Pentecost, where did the heavenly pleroma, the fullness of divine excellencies and powers, descend? In the temple? No. The temple, the priests, the altar, all were bypassed. Christianity is no longer God in temples of man's building, but known and possessed in human hearts directly through the indwelling Spirit. Away with human mediaries! They are an ineffective superfluity since Pentecost.

See the *copiousness* indicated here. "The love of God is shed abroad in our hearts." As Weymouth and others translate it, "The love of God floods our hearts." Oh, rich and blessed flood-tide, swamping, submerging, flooding away our inveterate selfishness, vain pride, unholy hankerings; ridding us of doubt and fear and anxiety; purifying our whole inner life!

Obviously, a saturation such as that must be a matter of *consciousness*. I do not see how anyone could live in such an insurge of the divine love without its registering itself in the deepest awareness of the mind. Heartily do I agree that the Christian life must be lived, not in one's inconstant emotions, but in the will. It is the life of faith, not of feeling only. Yet we must not turn faith and feeling into incompatible opposites, any more than we would say that the roots and the fruits of a tree are in opposition to each other. States of mind such as joy, peace, fear, sorrow, are experiences of which we are conscious. Undoubtedly, therefore, this sanctifying suffusion of heart by the Holy Spirit is inwardly vivid. I do not say that it registers itself either most powerfully or even most usually in the *emotions*, for the emotions are neither the deepest nor the steadiest part of us. Nay, they are the most mercurial and unpredictable part. An experience does not have to be *emotional* before it can be *conscious*. When the divine Paraclete "sheds" the love from heaven within us, doubtless the emotions participate, but the far deeper impact is in that thinking part of us which we call the *mind*. Some of those who have glowed the most in mind have thrilled the least in mere emotion.

It came as a rather startling surprise to my own mind when I discovered that in every instance where the divine love is spoken of in the Bible, it is never a passive, in-looking emotion, but an active, outreaching benevolence. It is not a self-contained complacence, but a self-emptying *otherism*; not a self-contemplating ecstasy of feeling, but a redeeming compassion toward the unworthy, the unlovely, the defiled and the deformed. It is a love which gives and gives and gives again. When we read in Romans 5:5, "The love of God is shed abroad in our hearts..." we should not overlook what is said about that love in verses 6 and 8 and 10. Verse 8 says, "God commendeth His love toward us, in that, while we were yet *sinners*, Christ died for us." Verses 6 and 10 describe us as "without strength" and "ungodly" and "enemies." How those words photograph our helpless sickness, moral disfigurement and innate antigodism! Yet such are the objects of God's love!

When, according to that fifth verse, "the love of God is shed" within us, other than giving us merely some happy tempest of emotion, its heavenly magnanimity lifts right out of our self-centered littleness into large-minded concern for others. It breaks the chains of our hereditary egoism and emancipates us from the prison of self-preoccupation. It unbinds long-bound sympathies within us, and awakens long-dormant capacities to help and heal which we scarcely suspect were in our nature. In short, it releases the heart from all jealous self-interest, and immerses us in the generous, kindly otherism of Jesus.

THE LOVE OF GOD THROUGH US

That brings us to the third outreaching movement of the divine love, i.e., the love of God *through* us. Like golden sunshafts breaking through the cloud-rifts on a rainy day, the love of God expressing itself through Christian believers appears up and down the New Testament Epistles. Nor is that all; for besides being recurrently stated or implied in the teachings of the Epistles, we see it strikingly exemplified in the conduct of the apostles.

We see that love channeling its way like a fresh mountain stream through the heart and ministry of Paul, in such verses as 2 Corinthians 2:4; 5:14; 6:6; 12:15. We learn of its welling up and spilling over through the unselfish behavior of the young Christian churches and their members, in references such as 1 Thessalonians 1:3; Hebrews 6:10; 1 John 3:14; 4:19. Perhaps that last-mentioned verse is the key to all the others. Our revered old King James Version renders it, "We love Him [God] because He first loved us." It would seem, however, as though the evidence of the manuscripts requires that we omit the "Him," and read it: "We love because He first loved us." The two clauses, "*We* love" and "*He* loved," answer antiphonally to each other. Our love is His love moving through us—as verses 16, 17, and 18 have made plain.

But, as might almost be expected, if we are to see this love of God expressing itself through consecrated Christian hearts, we need to have living examples of it; and such we find in the New Testament. I pick here on Paul. Simply because he is the most prominent figure in other respects, he becomes the most prominent exemplification of the divine love communicating itself through transformed human personality. Yet although he is peculiarly conspicuous in this connection he is not exceptional, but grandly representative of all his apostolic compeers and of many another contemporary Christian witness.

Let me remind you that the Jews of Paul's time were the most egotistically nationalist, religiously bigoted, and narrow-mindedly separatist ever known. They were thoroughly right in worshiping Jehovah as the only true God, and in holding that they were His covenant people, and in believing that there was an exalted destiny for their nation in the coming reign of the promised Messiah. But they were reprehensibly wrong in the grabbing way they flaunted it all. Instead of humbly accepting that Israel had been chosen to be a nation of priests or mediators through whom all the Gentile peoples should be brought to the true God, they proudly preened themselves on being Heaven's favorites—a superior race holding the title deeds to a splendid future which they were determined the Gentiles should never share.

With conceited Judaistic arrogance they called other races "Gentile dogs." According to Rabbinist doctrine the very dust of a heathen country was unclean, and any Jew who came into contact with it was defiled by its putrescence. If a speck of Gentile dust touched an offering, that offering must at once be burned. Although Judaism itself was torn by rival factions, there was one feeling common to practically all those Jews, whether high or low, rich or poor, Pharisee or Sadducee, Zealot or Herodian; and it was an intense hatred of the Gentiles. This found expression in all kinds of ways. Three days before any non-Jewish festival all transactions of Jews with Gentiles were forbidden. To enter the house of a Gentile was a defilement. Milk drawn from a cow by Gentile hands, or bread and oil prepared by Gentile hands, might be sold to aliens, but never used by Israelites. And, of course, no Jew would sit down at the table with a Gentile.

If we would know the continual fever-heat of this Jewish antipathy toward the Gentiles we need only turn to Acts 22, where Paul, from the castle stairs, utters his defense to the Jewish crowd who had just almost lynched him. When they heard that he addressed them in the Hebrew tongue they quietened down and listened. They even seemed to be getting interested, until Paul told them how God had said to him, "I will send thee far hence unto the Gentiles" (verse

21). That was enough! At the very mention of that they yelled for Paul's blood. They "cast off their clothes, and threw dust into the air" (23). If we want a summary description of them, we have it in 1 Thessalonians 2:15,16, "Who both killed the Lord Jesus, and their own prophets, and have persecuted us; and they please not God, and are contrary to all men: forbidding us to speak to the Gentiles that they might be saved."

Now here is a superlative wonder. It was from men of that race and sort that we Gentiles received the glad tidings which brought us salvation and planted Christianity among us. All the writers of our New Testament were Jews, except Luke. They were Jews every bit as Jewish, every bit as anti-Gentile as their Israelite compatriots. They had grown up with the same narrowness and prejudices. Yet it is they, of all people, who have given to the whole world the one great, open-hearted "whosoever" gospel of salvation!

Moreover, wonder of wonders, so magnanimously concerned were those one-time Gentile-hating Jews to *share* their Gospel with us, so eager were they to welcome us as equals and partners in their God-given convenant promises, that they willingly suffered whippings, scourgings, stonings, clubbings, starvings, privations, drownings, burnings, imprisonments, tortures and excruciating martyrdoms—all for the sake of sharing the glad tidings with us!

But *why* such an astonishing change? What was it that had worked such a miracle in them? The whole explanation is found in words like those of 1 John 4:19, "*We* loved because *He* first loved us," or 2 Corinthians 5:14, "The love of Christ constraineth us." When Paul wrote, "The love of Christ constraineth us," he meant it to the last inch of meaning. With him, this love had become the dominating compulsion of his life. It had become so by a threefold process. First, he had stood amazed before that incomparable love which came from heaven's height to Calvary's depth. He had marveled with trembling to see it hanging there in agony and blood on a felon's cross, surrounded by sinister derision and vulgar mockery. He never could recover from his astonishment that incarnate Love had staggered to that ignominious public execution for such a conceited Pharisee as Saul of Tarsus.

But besides that, the more he had contemplated that thorn-crowned Love, the more had he entered into it with intense sympathy and deepening understanding, until it revolutionized his whole view of God, of men, of life and of human destiny. Then he found that by a reciprocal process the more he entered into *it*, so the more this love had entered into *him*, until he was thinking the thoughts of Christ, and feeling the same feelings; and the very compassions of

Christ were coursing through him. The love which had sent Jesus to Calvary was now sending Paul out in self-sacrificing service to make this glorious Savior the possession of others, Jews and Gentiles alike.

The degree to which this love constrained Paul may be seen in the contrast between what he formerly *was* and what he afterward *became*. Formerly he was Saul the Pharisee, a thoroughbred, well-educated Jew of the very strictest sect. The anti-Gentile bigotry which that implied was so intense that it is difficult for you and me today to believe it possible. He was a proud participant in the fanatical Pharisaical determination that the Gentiles should never share in the covenant superiorities of Israel. Think, then, of Saul, that fiercely intolerant Hebrew monotheist, that strait-jacket Pharisee, that mass of anti-Gentile prejudice, that hot-blooded champion of Judaism madly determined "in the name of God" to stamp out the blasphemous Nazarene heretics, and equally fierce against all compromise with Gentile "dogs." Then read these tender, touching words in 2 Corinthians 3:2 and 12:15, "Ye [Gentiles] are...written in our hearts...I will very gladly spend, and be *spent* for you; though the *more abundantly I love you* [Gentiles], the less I be loved!" Or see those surprising words of his in Romans 11:13, "I am the apostle of the Gentiles; I magnify mine office!" Or see his affectionate words to them in Philippians 1:7, 8. "I have you *in my heart*...I long after you all in the very affections of Jesus Christ!" Or, once again, glance at Ephesians 3:8. "Unto me, who am *less than the least* of all the saints, is this grace given, that I should preach among the *Gentiles* with unsearchable riches of Christ!"

Oh, wonderful change! Instead of bigotry, charity; instead of narrowness, magnanimity; instead of pride, humility; instead of conceit, concern; instead of jealous selfishness, open-hearted generosity; instead of hatred, love. Yea, "The love of Christ constraineth us!"

Lovely miracle indeed! The love of Christ has first conquered him, then refashioned him, and now it dominates him. With all selfish egoism buried in the grave of the old Saul, and with the self-forgetting love of Christ streaming through his heart toward others, he has now found, without seeking it, that joy of joys which comes through transition from selfism to otherism. He finds himself living next door to the heart of God, and singing:

> Oh, this is life, oh, this is joy,
> My God to find Thee so;
> Thy face to see, Thy voice to hear,
> And all Thy love to know!

A *Final Reflection*

Well, there it is: the love of God *to* us; the love of God *in* us; the love of God *through* us. That is how the never-ebbing ocean of the divine love rolls in upon the shores of human experience. Is it not full of challenge to you and me? Are you, am I, living in the cleansing fullness of it, and reaching out to others under the gracious "constraint" of it? The love of God never infloods us just that we ourselves may possess and enjoy it. God means us to be, not reservoirs, but dispersal channels. Many Christians fail to know in deep experience "the love of God shed abroad in their hearts" because (perhaps unsuspectingly) they want it for their own enrichment only. They need to grasp clearly that the Holy Spirit's surging in with the love of God is never an introversive experience. It turns us inside out. Its first big effect is to save us from ourselves. We never know a continous *in*flow unless there is a continuous *out*flow of sympathy, compassion, and service even to the point of sacrifice for the blessing of others. And it is then (as it was with Paul) that we suddenly find the purest joy this side of heaven—when we are not looking for it!

Do we sometimes wonder why the chariot wheels of Christian witness seem to drag heavily in many places today? Why among all too many churches which are soundly evangelical is there a strange poverty of fellowship and a dearth of conversions? Why do prayer meetings languish and testimony meetings become extinct? Well, one of the big reasons, if not the biggest of all, is that Christian ministers, elders, deacons, leaders, workers, and church members are not living in the spiritual glow of the Savior's love filling the heart. For when that pure love really floods into the Christian heart it bursts upon the sluice-gates of pent-up capacities for fellowship and service, releasing them in warm, sympathetic outflow to others.

Can you, can I, truthfully say, "The love of God is *shed abroad* in my heart by the Holy Spirit; the love of Christ *constraineth* me"? Perhaps someone replies, "But we cannot all be world-girding apostles like Paul, or traveling evangelists, or overseas missionaries, or full-time Christian workers. What about those of us who have to spend hours of each day, and days of each week, in what is often the tiring drag of a secular job?" Well, I know this, that when we get low before that cross, and linger there long enough with that dear Savior, and open wide our hearts to that flood-tide love of His, something happens which causes us to see everything and everybody in a new way—including our so-called "secular" job. I know this, too, that when once we begin to see things through *His* eyes, and to feel about things with *His* feelings, there comes a new motive-force into our life, a new rest of heart, a new spiritual glow, a new concern for the saving of others, a new sense of His dear presence and a new touch of immortality in our words for Him, however stammering.

Looking back over my own life, I am bound to acknowledge that those through whom the love of Christ has been communicated to me with most determining effect have not been outstanding full-time ministers of our Lord, but persons in so-called secular employ. Three stand out: my godly mother, an earnest Sunday School teacher and a commercial bank manager. It was in my precious mother that I first saw, when I was but a little boy, what Jesus can be to a human heart. It was in a diminutive, bowlegged young cotton-mill worker, my Sunday School teacher, that I first saw, as a youth, and to my strange surprise, the love of Christ weeping for me through the tears of another human being. It was through a bank manager, the most Christlike man I have ever known, that I learned in my early manhood how the love of Christ can sanctify a human personality. Oh, if only we will let that love conquer us, control us, constrain us.

11

The Fatherhood of God—
The New Testament Evidence

I n 1868 Dr. Thomas J. Crawford, Professor of Divinity in the University of Edinburgh, Scotland, published a monumental work, *The Fatherhood of God*. At the beginning of it he wrote:

> The fatherhood of God, whether in relation to all men as His intelligent and moral creatures, or more particularly in relation to those who are "the children of God by faith in Christ Jesus," has hitherto been in a remarkable degree exempted from the speculations and controversies of theology. No heresies of any note have ever risen with respect to it. No schisms or bitter contentions have been occasioned by it.

If Dr. Crawford were penning his treatise today, he certainly could not begin with such a comforting reflection, for recently the fatherhood of God has become a subject of fervid argument and wide disagreement. On the one hand, theological liberals now ascribe an undiscriminating universality to it, while on the other hand certain keen evangelicals and fundamentalists deny its universality. They rigidly limit it to those who are the regenerating "sons of God" through conversion to our Lord Jesus Christ.

That great gulf between those two characteristic attitudes, on a subject which is as immense and majestic as it is basic and vital, lies athwart our path right at the outset as we here commence this brief reconsideration of the divine fatherhood.

It is a good number of years now since I became disturbed into thinking more concentratedly about our evangelical doctrine of the divine fatherhood. Until then I had tenaciously held and preached that God is the Creator, Preserver, King, Judge of all men, but the Father of those *only* who are born-again Christians. One day I fell into a pleasant skirmish with an Edinburgh lawyer who, in biblical phrase, smote me "under the fifth rib" with the following objection: "I am not an irreligious man, sir, but your petty little fundamentalist religion I simply cannot shrivel myself small enough to believe. For one thing, do you expect me seriously to accept that out of all the thousands of millions of human beings, both B.C. and A.D., including the more than two billion souls of this present generation, God is Father *only* to the comparatively microscopic little clique whom you call 'the saved'? Why, sir, the people whom *you* call 'the saved' are only a small fraction even among the religious people who go to church! Do you mean to tell me that God is *not* a Father to all those countless millions of others, not one of whom ever asked to be born?"

I remember replying that I would sooner stay with the teachings of the Bible than go by human reasoning in the matter. Nevertheless, from then onward the question kept bothering me, i.e., "But does the Bible really teach the restricted fatherhood of God which I preach?"

Inasmuch as one of my evangelical beliefs has always been that the Bible is the inerrantly inspired Word of God, whenever my own opinions have run counter to its teachings I have resolutely subordinated my own intellect and ideas to its authority. Yet I must also testify to this, that when certain supposedly biblical doctrines have not merely contradicted my own theories but have offended the most innate intuitions and sensibilities of my very humanhood, I have always found that the Bible did not teach those things—or not, at least, in the way they were being propagated. So has it been with this doctrine of a restricted divine fatherhood. I had unquestioningly believed and preached it; yet I had no real answer to that lawyer's objection. On the contrary, a voice from the deepest within me championed him against myself. All my being seemed to cry out against such a vast, awful, cruel denial of the outreaching father-heart of the God who "so loved the *world* that He gave His only begotten Son, that whosoever believeth on Him should not perish, but have everlasting life."

At that time the problem of racial human sonship and other related aspects had not projected themselves prominently into my thinking. What I did know was that the truest and deepest within me seemed revolted by this teaching that God is the Father of Christian believers only, and that His relation to all the multi-millions of other human beings is no more than that of Creator to creature, Preserver to dependent, King to subject, Judge to criminal. The gospel message that "God so *loved* the *world*" became a problem; for if that so-called love was no more than the feeling of a king to a rebel subject, or of a judge to a law-breaker, was it really love at all?

Subsequently, the more I consulted Scripture and reflected on what I found there, the more I seemed to see that the commonly held idea of a divine fatherhood exclusively limited to Christian believers is unscriptural, fallacious and harmful. It is into this that we shall presently enquire. But, lest I should be hastily prejudged as having in any way slipped over to "modernist" or "liberalist" concepts, let me make this emphatically clear once for all: By the universal fatherhood of God I do *not* mean the sentimentally indulgent presentation of it which liberalist schools have popularized. *Their* looser idea of it stems from their more or less naturalistic view of the Bible; and their view of the Bible is not mine.

That brings us right to grips with our subject. The historical and exhaustive way of approach would be to travel first right through the Old Testament and then go through the New. But in this case, as in certain others, the fact that biblical revelation is *progressive* indicates that the Old Testament must be read in the light of the New. We are Christians! We must begin with Christ Himself. The Son has risen! "In *His* light we shall *see* light."

Even now, however, as we turn to those Scriptures, we should make sure that certain cautionary reflections temper and condition our thinking. When we Christians call God "Father," we are not just "making God after our own image," as the Greeks made Zeus "the father of gods and men," or as the Romans addressed "Father Mars" and "Father Janus" and "Father Jupiter." No; we call God "Father" because an inspired revelation of God definitely teaches His fatherhood.

Nor, when we Christians use the scriptural title, "Father," of God, are we using it in a merely anthropomorphic and anthropopathic sense? Are we ascribing to God human attributes or qualities which He does not *actually* have, but which serve as likenesses to make Him intelligible to human apprehension?

What is more, when we find our Lord and the Scriptures naming God as the "Father" we must not put upon that even the milder limitation of saying that it is merely analogous, i.e., no more than an illustration of something in God which has likeness to human fatherhood. Nay, the fatherhood which Scripture predicates of God is not something which God is *like*, but something which He essentially *is*. The really startling fact is this, that instead of the divine fatherhood being a reflection of human fatherhood, it is human fatherhood which is an intended reflection of the divine! The fatherhood of God existed before any human fatherhood, and it exists independently of human fatherhood. Even if never a human being or any other kind of intelligent being had been created, God would nevertheless have continued unchangingly as the eternal Father. What says John 3:16? "God so loved the world that He gave His only begotten *Son*..." Mystery inscrutable, but reality unmistakable: The eternal sonship involves an eternal fatherhood. Now that the human race has been created, the divine fatherhood is the sublime archetype and original of which ideal human fatherhood is the counterpart and correspondent. Is not that what Paul has in mind when he says in Ephesians 3:14,15, "For this cause I bow my knees unto the Father of our Lord Jesus Christ, of whom every family [or fatherhood: *patria*] in heaven and on earth is named"? The divine fatherhood *originates* all others.

Obviously the fatherhood of God assumes the *personality* of God; but it equally assumes, also, a certain spiritual *community* between God and ourselves as His human creatures who are made "in His own image" (Gen. 1:27). It is a reciprocal community which makes the fatherhood of God both possible *toward* us and responsively realizable *within* us. For since God is pure spirit, our being after His "likeness" must mean that there are in Him mental and moral qualities corresponding with our own. When God is revealed to us in His holy Word as a God of justice, holiness, love, compassion, what can it mean but that the same qualities exist in God as those which are called justice, holiness, love, compassion, in men—only that in God they are infinitely sublimer?

So, when God is revealed to us as the heavenly Father, can His fatherhood toward us creatures who are made in His own image and likeness mean *less* than all the highest and loveliest aspects of ideal human fatherhood? There are those who say glibly enough, "Oh, yes, God is the Father of all men, but only in the sense that He is their Creator." That, however, is as superficial as it is glib; for if the fatherhood of God is thus equated with bare origination, it becomes no more than a "euphonious synonym for causation," and the real content of fatherhood is evacuated.

Yet on the other hand we must guard against over-liberalizing fatherhood as applied to God. It is important to distinguish between fatherhood as the inherent nature of God Himself, and fatherhood as a divine *relationship* toward man. Let it ever be borne in mind that all *earthly* relationships (including fatherhood) which are used to represent *divine* relationships are necessarily imperfect. Therefore all of us should understand that when we speak of the divine fatherhood, we mean a real quality and relation of which human fatherhood, *but only at its best*, is an approximate parallel and emblem. Indeed, human fatherhood, even at its best, is *only* a poor approximation to that ineffable divine fatherhood which has now become supremely expressed in our Lord Jesus Christ.

With such reflections in mind, we turn now first to the four Gospels, to find and ponder our Lord's teaching on this subject. All will agree that this wonderful fatherhood is the outstanding feature in His teaching as to the divine being. In fact, the word, "Father," is the characteristic name for the Most High on the lips of Jesus. No less than 167 times, according to the Gospel records, He thus designates God. It breaks on us like a shining avalanche of new revelation. And as a glorious accompaniment there comes with it a new revelation of the divine love; a love not just for the covenant people, Israel, but for man, for the race, for "whosoever"; a love from the heart of God which ignores ethnic divisions, and compassionately engulfs us all!

The Sermon on the Mount

That inevitably sets us asking: Did Jesus, then, teach that the *fatherhood* of God is likewise *racial*? Let us probe into that somewhat here. Our Lord's greatest single utterance concerning the fatherhood of God is the Sermon on the Mount. Those who would limit that fatherhood to Christian believers assert our Lord's famous discourse was addressed to none but "disciples"—meaning by "disciples" an inner circle of our Lord's hearers who were definitely believers on Him—and they base this assertion on the fact that Matthew, in introducing the sermon, says: "...and when He was set His disciples came unto Him" (Matt. 5:1).

Yet obviously those "disciples" were not born-again Christian believers in the evangelical sense which belongs to the present dispensation. Nor were they, as is wrongly supposed, some inner circle of our Master's followers. They were simply all who desired to hear and learn of Him—for He was as yet right at the beginning of His public ministry, and had not yet even appointed the Twelve to accompany Him. However, we scarcely need to point that out, for there is proof positive that the Sermon on the Mount was in the widest sense a public utterance, and was addressed without discrimination to the assembled crowds. This is how Matthew introduces the sermon: "And seeing the multitudes He went up into a mountain: and when He was set, His disciples came unto Him; and He opened His mouth, and taught them, saying...." Mark that expression, "the multitudes." In the Greek it is *hoi ochloi*; and besides coming just before the sermon to explain its occasion, it comes just after it to show its effect—"And it came to pass, when Jesus had ended these sayings, the people [*hoi ochloi*, the multitudes] were astonished at His doctrine: for He taught *THEM* as one having authority, and not as the scribes" (Matt. 7:28-29).

Surely there is no getting over that. Moreover, as has been discerningly observed, other than being only a spiritual legislation for avowed disciples the sermon is a criticism of the worship and conduct of the scribes and Pharisees. That criticism has its ground in the fact of God's universal fatherhood. Those pretentious religionists were making a wrong response to that magnanimous fatherhood. But if that divine fatherhood did not really exist, how *could* they be expected to make a response which only fatherhood could evoke? As for our Lord's disciples, the very basis on which He exhorts them to a right response is that because God is indeed the Father of all, He is the Father of each one of them individually, and they should respond to Him accordingly.

So far as I can find, the objections of those who would limit the Sermon on the Mount to "disciples" are strangely poor. One such is that, according to Mark 4:11,34, and Luke 8:9,10, our Lord did not speak to the multitude except by parables. He used non-parabolic utterance such as in the Sermon on the Mount only to His "disciples."

The answer to that is clear. If our Lord addressed the people at large only in parables, what about the following *non*-parabolic preaching (not to mention others) all of which are plainly said to have been to the crowds: Matthew 11:7-30; and 12:38-50 (see verse 46 with 15:10, etc.) and 23:1-39; Mark 12:35-40 ("great crowd heard him gladly":37); Luke 7:24-35; John 5:18-47; 6:22 and onward (note "crowd" ing verses 22 and 24); 7:14-53 (note "crowd" in verses 40); 8:1-58; 10:1-39.

Any attempt to limit the Sermon on the Mount by reference to our Lord's use of parables is bound to fail. Not only did our Lord speak mainly in non-parabolic utterance to the crowds, as is abundantly evidenced, but His special employment of parables did not begin until a certain point of time considerably later than the Sermon on the Mount. It was not until His moral teaching on the kingdom of heaven had been rejected in Galilee that parables became a more dominant feature in His teaching (rejection-point being time-marked at Matthew 11:20-30). That He did not resort to the larger use of parables until then is clearly indicated by the surprise of the twelve apostles as they then asked Him, "Why speakest Thou unto them in parables?"—in answer to which our Lord told them *why* the change-over to a more parabolic method (13:11-13). Surely, therefore, to suggest that the Sermon on the Mount was not addressed to the crowds because it was not all in parables is puerile.

There is a further objection, however, to those who would limit the Sermon on the Mount to "disciples." They argue that Luke's version of the Sermon (6:20-7:1) was not to the people in general because it is prefaced by the comment, "He lifted up His eyes to His *disciples*, and said...." Therefore (it is urged) neither is the Sermon in Matthew to any but "disciples."

Yet surely such an idea is almost too feeble to need rebuttal. What we have in Luke 6:20 to 7:1 is not Luke's version of the Sermon on the Mount, for it was preached in a different place (6:17) and at a different time (verses 6 to 19). So even if the discourse reported by Luke could be proved to have been only to "disciples" it would not prove the same to be true of the Sermon in Matthew. What is more, we are informed in unmistakable wording that this somewhat similar discourse in Luke 6 was to the whole *crowd*. Verse 17 says, "And He came down [from a mountain] with them [the Twelve] and stood in the plain, and the company of His disciples, and a *great multitude* out of all Judea and Jerusalem, and from the sea coast of Tyre and Sidon, which came to hear Him, and to be healed of their diseases...." *That* was the huge assemblage He addressed; for right at the end of the peroration Luke adds, "Now when He had ended all His sayings in the audience of the people...."

Still more, from verse 24, which begins, "But woe unto you that are rich!" it is as clear as daylight that the bulk of what our Lord says is to those who were not disciples. And to crown the matter, it is to those that our Lord says, in verse 36, "Be ye therefore merciful, as *Your Father* also is merciful."

In truth, the whole basis of that discourse, as with the Sermon on the Mount, is that God is the Father of *all*. In that characteristic it *is* like the Sermon on the Mount, where we find verse after verse which simply cannot have been intended only for "disciples" (e.g., 5:20,29,30; 7:2-5,13,14) unless, as already remarked, we take the word "disciples" in the widest sense of all who desired to hear and learn of Jesus.

Finally, even if we were to concede that the Sermon on the Mount was to "disciples" only, who would claim that those disciples were "born–again" believers in the way that Christian believers of the present dispensation are? It is of those very same that we read in John 6:66, "From that time many of His disciples went back, and walked no more with Him." Remember, they lived before ever Calvary and Pentecost had brought in the present age of grace. They did not know or even suspect at that time the deity of our Lord Jesus—that He was none other than God the Son incarnate. They were not believers in the sense that we now are. Yet all the way through His preaching, our Lord teaches them that God is their *Father*.

My own careful conviction is that the Sermon is in the widest sense racial in its outreach, and that its doctrine of the divine fatherhood is correspondingly wide-embracing, as implied in the following excerpts.

> Love your enemies, bless them that curse you, do good to them that hate you, and pray for them which despitefully use you, and persecute you, that ye may be the children of your Father which is in heaven (Matt. 5:44, 45).

Translated most precisely, the last clause is, "that ye may *become* sons of your Father...." Our Lord is telling those hearers not that they *are* sons, but how they may *become* sons of the heavenly Father who "sendeth rain on both the just and the unjust" (45). The point is that the divine fatherhood is assumed by our Lord as already *prior* to their "becoming" sons by emulating God's indiscriminate fatherly goodness. In other words, our Lord is saying in effect: God is your Father, but you (unless you live as I am saying you should) are *not* truly His sons.

Let me repeat for emphasis: Not one of those who then listened believed on Jesus as we now do. Not one of them believed on Him as the crucified, resurrected, ascended, interceding Savior. Not one of them could be classified as a regenerated child of God in the sense of Paul's words in Galatians 3:26, "For ye [born-again Christians] are all the children of God by faith in Christ Jesus." Yet Jesus repeatedly speaks to them of "your Father who is in heaven." But see now verses 47 and 48, where we find further confirmation of this.

> And if ye salute your brethren only, what do ye more than others? Do not even the publicans so? Be ye therefore perfect [i.e., in impartiality] even as your Father which is in heaven is perfect.

There again the point is that, whether they practice this impartiality or not, God is the Father whose impartial fatherhood is meant to be the inspiration of their emulating Him. And this prior divine fatherhood is obviously assumed all the way through our Lord's use of that phrase, "your Father who is in heaven."

Does not the same truth shine through again in chapter 6:14, 15?

> For if ye forgive men their trespasses, your heavenly Father will also forgive you: but if ye forgive not men their trespasses, neither will your Father forgive your trespasses.

Yet even though He cannot forgive the unforgiving, it is nevertheless as "your Father" that He cannot do so. And so we might further quote, but is there need? All through the great discourse it is the all-inclusive divine fatherhood which is the underlying reality, comfort, appeal, challenge.

The Parable of the Prodigal

As the Sermon on the Mount is the most famous of our Lord's discourses, so is the story of the prodigal son the most famous of His parables. And as the former is the most outstanding statement of the divine fatherhood, so the latter is the most remarkable picture of it. Both the sermon and the parable teach us that the fatherhood is not restricted to the regenerate. If we turn now, with open mind, to that parable of the prodigal son, we cannot help seeing how clearly it exhibits a wide-sweeping fatherhood of God which takes in *all* of us human sinners.

We always need to guard against pressing to extremes any dogmatic interpretation of the parable. But in this story of the prodigal son the central truth is so clear that to dispute it would surely make language meaningless. The parable is addressed to "the publicans and sinners" (Luke 15:1) and to the murmuring "Pharisees and scribes" (verse 2). Those tax-gatherers and sinners, as plainly as can be, are shown to stand in the same relation to God as did the prodigal to his father. If God be not the Father of those tax-gatherers and sinners as pictured in the prodigal, and of the Pharisees and scribes as figured in the unsympathetic elder brother, then surely this parable has no meaning at all.

Very well, when did the prodigal's father *become* his father? Was it only after the return from the far country? A thousand times, No! He was the father before ever his wayward son left home; and he *remained* the father even when that ungrateful wanderer was degrading himself those many leagues away. His father-heart all the while was yearning over him, reaching out after him, longing for him, waiting to forgive and forget and welcome him back.

Nothing is more regrettable than the casuistical treatment of Scripture in order to defend an orthodox theory. Yet that is how this parable of the prodigal son is being treated today in a well-meaning but perverted determination not to yield any concessions to the liberalist idea of the divine fatherhood. It is realized that if indeed the prodigal represents the unconverted sinner, then the parable undoubtedly does teach the universal fatherhood of God. So, in order to dodge that implication, there are those who now call the story the parable of the *returning backslider*!

Alas, as is always the case when we try to save a doctrine by such expedients, those who thus wrench this parable only land themselves in further difficulties. For if it is a parable of returning backsliders, then it teaches that a saved and regenerated Christian believer may become completely lost and unregenerated again. It actually uses the words "dead" and "lost" of the prodigal—"This my son was *dead* and...was *lost*...." Can we honestly believe that this supposed demoralization of born-again Christians is what the parable meant to teach?

Is not the parabolic picture transparently clear: that the prodigal, having become "lost" and "dead," had *forfeited* sonship, while the fatherhood of the grieving father remained unchanged? The son was no longer a son in the true meaning of sonship; but in the truest meaning the father was still the father. However, there are those who demur, as the following shows,

> Did the son remain a son while in the far country? I would say, a thousand times, yes. When he was in the far country he still thought of himself as a son, as we see in verses 17, 18, 19. Therefore I see in the story, not the fatherhood of God to unconverted sinners, but a wonderful message for *backsliders*, that is, "*born-again*" wanderers. For that reason this parable does not close, like the two preceding it, with the words, "one *sinner* that repenteth."

Not a few, latterly, have united in that objection. Yet the contradictoriness of it is so patent, I marvel that it could be put forward seriously. Can any open-minded reader seriously doubt that the prodigal represents those tax-gatherers and sinners whose presence occasioned the parable? Can anyone seriously contend that those longing tax-gatherers and sinners were "born-again" backsliders? Can anyone seriously take this parable as purposing to teach that born-again Christian believers of the present dispensation, washed in "the blood of the Lamb" and regenerated by the Holy Spirit, and spiritually incorporated into the true Church, can become "lost" and "dead" to God again as pictured in that prodigal? How can any of us accept such strange reasoning? For what a miserable contradiction it is of our Savior's promise to safe-keep those who are His own!

As for the idea that the prodigal "still thought of himself as a son" while in the far country, the three verses which are supposed to say so (17,18,19) do nothing of the kind; in fact two of them point the other way. In verse 17 he compares himself with his father's hired servants; and in verse 19 he asks to be given employ simply as one of those hired servants because he is "no more worthy" to be called a son. Why, according to those verses, the uppermost thought in his mind is that of *lost* sonship. As Edgar Y. Mullins says, "The poignancy of his grief arose from his recognition of this loss of sonship."

As for that final point in the foregoing quotation, namely, that this parable does not end with the words, "one sinner that repenteth" (as do the preceding two parables), it is imagining a significance where none exists, as can easily be shown. In conformity with common custom, I have here called the story of the prodigal a parable; but strictly speaking it is one of three stories which together comprise one threefold parable: (1) the lost sheep, (2) the lost coin, (3) the lost son. All three are covered at the outset by the one introductory word, "And He spake this parable unto them." It is when we take the three together that we catch their full significance. To begin with, in those three stories we see, in turn, the three persons of the Godhead engaged in man's salvation. In the first story the seeking shepherd is God the Son. In the second the lighted candle is the revealing Holy Spirit. In the third the compassionate parent is God the Father. Or again, in those three stories we see a triple picture of man in his lost condition. In the first, like the sheep, he is lost foolishly. In the second, like the coin, he is lost unconsciously. In the third, like the prodigal, he is lost knowingly and deliberately. We might mention other striking points, but all we are concerned to show here is that as the lost sheep and the lost coin undoubtedly represent the lost *sinner*, so by unmistakable parallel does the prodigal in the third story. To make him a regenerated Christian of the present dispensation who has backslidden, even to the point of having become "lost" and spiritually "dead" again, is simply playing about with Scripture. There is no need at the end of the third story for the repeated statement that there is "joy over one sinner that repenteth," for the obvious reason that the "joy," instead of being merely stated, is vividly described in the kiss, the robe, the ring, and the feast.

But perhaps the most decisive factor of all in repulsing the extraneous idea that the prodigal represents Christian backsliders is that if such was our Lord's meaning, then the story had *no* relevance to those "tax-gatherers and sinners" to whom it was spoken. For what did they then know about the post-Calvary and post-Pentecost gospel of salvation through the slain and risen Lamb of God? It is as clear as can be, that the parable was intended to be intelligible and directly applicable to *them*, then and there. Therefore the prodigal must represent *them*; and the love of that forgiving father, also, must represent the divine fatherhood and attitude toward *them*.

So, then, to round off the matter thus far: who can read the Sermon on the Mount with its benign preaching of the divine fatherhood to the multitude, or the parable of the prodigal son with its clear picture of God as the Father who yearns over prodigals, without seeing that the fatherhood of God embraces all men?

Some Further Confirmations

I readily appreciate that there is often good motive behind the attempted curtailment of the divine fatherhood to Christian believers. It is feared that to teach a divine fatherhood of *all* men would nullify the vital New Testament truth that the sinful members of Adam's fallen race can only become sons of God by the "new birth." Such fear would be justified if by the racial fatherhood of God we meant the wishy-washy caricature of it which is fawned on congregations by certain liberalist intellectuals. But we need have no such fear if we adhere closely to that fatherhood of God which Jesus and the New Testament writers teach us.

Let me re-emphasize at this point that I myself repudiate the modernist fond idea of a divine fatherhood which winks at human sinfulness and carries the supposed corollary that all men are already sons of God. However, I do not think we are driven to a choice between that and the ultra-evangelical view, as I shall try to show. Certainly, only such as have become "new creatures" in Christ have come into the *enjoyment* of the divine fatherhood; yet nowhere are we taught that thereby they have the exclusive *title* to it. I leave that there for the moment, in order to mention here some further confirmations of the universal fatherhood.

Let me pick out several texts where the racial fatherhood of God seems so clearly taught as to put it beyond doubt. They are not the only such, but I select them because they are representative. Take first our Lord's words to the woman at the well of Sychar, in John 4:21,23. Reflect: That woman was an outsider so far as Israel and the covenants were concerned; one of a mongrel race detested by the Jews. She was also a loudly immoral woman, as the context discloses. She was not only unregenerated, but even according to merely human standards was badly *de*generate and living in adultery. Her mind was spiritually dark. She had never seen Jesus before, and had no idea who He really was. Surely our Lord will not speak of God as Father to *her*. But He does!

> Jesus saith unto her, "Woman, believe Me, the hour cometh, when ye shall neither in this mountain, nor yet at Jerusalem, worship *the Father*....The hour cometh, and now is, when the true worshippers shall worship *the Father* in spirit and in truth: for *the Father* seeketh such to worship Him" (John 4:21,23).

Who can fail to see that our Lord is there speaking of our loving Creator as the Father of *all* His human creatures, even of those who are most astray?

Next I turn to John 5:22,23,45, where Jesus is addressing unbelieving and hostile Jews. Four times here we encounter our divine Master's use of that appellation, *"the* Father," in a way which may well set us pondering.

> For *the Father* judgeth no man, but hath committed all judgment unto the Son: that all men should honour the Son, even as they honour *the Father*. He that honoureth not the Son honoureth not *the Father* which hath sent Him....Do not think that *I* will accuse you to *the Father*: there is one that accuseth you, even Moses, whom ye trust.

In those verses our Lord refers to the divine fatherhood without the slightest suggestion of any boundary line. Such words as "the Father judgeth no man" lose all point unless God is indeed the Father of every man—even of those unrepentant and hostile Jews. That expression, *"the* Father," on the lips of Jesus is a kind of standard title for the First Person of the Godhead, indicating a relationship which is at once constitutional and all-inclusive.

Another such instance immediately comes to mind: John 14:6, where Jesus says, "I am the way, the truth, and the life: no man cometh unto *the Father*, but by Me." Can we evade the obvious? By that negative, "no man," our Lord means positively any man who would fain come to the one and only true God; also that God is "the Father" to every such man prior to that man's coming. The truth here is not that God becomes a Father after the man has repentantly come. He already is the Father to whom men come through Jesus. The plain sense is that whether a man comes to God or not, God the Father is the Father of all men.

Passing on from those specimen pronouncements by our Lord, I refer briefly to a few other such, made by the New Testament writers. In Acts 2:33 Peter says,

> Therefore being by the right hand of God exalted, and having received of *the Father* the promise of the Holy Spirit, He [the ascended Jesus] hath shed forth this which ye now see and hear.

There, again, that descriptive designation, "the Father," speaks of a substantive fatherhood which was a basic divine relationship to all those thousands of Jews who were as yet unregenerated, but to whom the message of salvation was now being proclaimed. In fact, all those as-yet-unconverted Israelite throngs did already look upon Jehovah as the Father of them all (as seen, e.g., in John 8:41, "We have one Father, even God").

That same extensive fatherhood gleams out again in 1 Corinthians 8:6, where Paul writes, "To us there is but one God, *the Father*, of whom are all things, and we in Him; and one Lord Jesus Christ, by whom are all things, and we by Him." Are we not obliged to see that in this incidental manifesto the fatherhood of the Father and the lordship of Christ are co-extensive?

> One God, the Father, of whom are all things.
> One Lord Jesus Christ, by whom are all things.

Clearly the fatherhood of the heavenly Father is meant to be understood as being equally racial as the supreme lordship of that cosmic Christ.

Even more strikingly the same flashes out from 1 Corinthians 15:24. "Then cometh the end, when He shall have delivered up the kingdom to God, even *the Father*; when He shall have put down all rule and all authority and power." The Greek, reproduced with verbatim fidelity, is,

> Then the end, when He shall have given up the kingdom to *Him* who is *God and Father*.

It is just as tremendous as it is brilliantly clear, that the Godhead and the fatherhood are eternally inseparable. God the Father is constitutionally the Father, not a merely so-called "fatherhood" watered down into meaning nothing more than Preserver, but in the full, warm, rich, tender meaning of the word. He is "God and Father" to all His myriads of intelligent creatures.

We have the identical Greek construction in Ephesians 5:20: "Giving thanks always for all things unto God and the Father in the name of our Lord Jesus Christ"—and with just the same implication.

I pass over more or less similarly significant texts (Matt. 18:14; 28:19; Luke 10:22; 11:13; John 5:44,45; 8:27; 14:9-11; Phil. 2:11; Col. 1:12; Jas. 1:17) and halt at Hebrews 12:9. "Furthermore, we have had fathers of our flesh which corrected us, and we gave them reverence: shall we not much rather be in subjection unto *the Father of spirits*, and live?" We at once notice that the phrase used here is not "the Father of *our* spirits," as though the inspired writer were referring only to Christian believers. The fatherhood is a belonging relationship which embraces *all* free-willed and responsible intelligences. What less can it mean? Nay (if we think penetratively) what less could we expect of such a God as is revealed in Holy Scripture and crowningly in the incarnated Son?

But further: What about James 1:27 and 3:9? There, strictly rendering the Greek, we have the phrase, "the *God and Father*," with the clear meaning: "the God who *is* the Father." In neither context is there any specific limitation to Christian believers.

What about 1 John 2:15? "If any man love the world, the love of *the Father* is not in him." So the man who is an earthy-minded worldling does not have in him the love of the Father, yet the Father still remains the Father even to that forgetful ingrate. And is not chapter 2:23 to the same effect, "Whosoever denieth the Son, the same hath not *the Father*"? The denier of the Son certainly cannot be a Christian; yet the Father still remains "the Father." Perhaps even more strongly we have the same in chapter 4:14, "*The Father* sent the Son to be the Savior of the world."

Do I need to requisition further such data? If so, let me submit this additional comment: I believe that if anyone will look up and impartially weigh many of those New Testament instances where we have that epithet, "the Father" (in the Greek some 98 times), the impression will be irresistible that the fatherhood of God is intrinsic in His very being, and basic to every other relationship which He sustains to all of us, His human creatures.

We shall be returning to this subject in our next study, submitting further supports for what we have here postulated, and answering objections raised by those who deny the racial fatherhood of God. We shall encounter certain false alternatives which are suggested, and finally reflect on some of practical issues involved. For the moment, being persuaded (I hope) as to the truth of what we have found thus far, let us with adoring gratitude reverently worship, love and serve that wonderful heavenly Father who "so loved the *world* that He gave His only begotten Son, that whosoever believeth on Him should not perish, but have everlasting life."

> Heav'n above and earth around
> Now with meanings new abound,
> Since, O God, all-wise and good,
> I have learned Thy fatherhood:
> Flaming sun at zenith high,
> Silver lamps in midnight sky,
> All with richer meanings glow
> Since Thy fatherhood I know.

Singing bird and soaring wing,
Cooling brook and crystal spring,
Plaintive sigh of evening breeze
Wandering 'mid the leafy trees,
Stormy wind and thunder's roar,
Pounding waves on ocean shore;
Are not all, in calm or flood,
Voices of Thy fatherhood?

Absent loved-one, vacant chair,
Empty purse and larder bare;
Stony path and lonely road,
Smarting sorrow, painful load;
These I scarcely understood
Till I learned Thy fatherhood;
Now through all I learn to see,
Father-God, Thy care for me.

J. S. B.

12

The Fatherhood of God— Further Considerations

T he love of God to the whole world, and the fatherhood of God to each human being, are the crowning revelation of God in the Bible. There are fairly clear, even though sparse, references to that fatherhood in the Old Testament (e.g., Ps. 68:5; Isa. 63:16; 64:8; Jer. 31:9; Mal. 1:6; 2:10), but its full-flowered expression comes with the supreme manifestation of God in our Lord Jesus Christ. This has a correspondingly deep significance.

We should digest this thoroughly, that the biblical revelation considered as a whole presents first the *power* of God—as seen in the Creation, the Flood, the Babel dispersion, the Exodus; next the *holiness* of God—as seen especially in the Mosaic law the subsequent divine dealings with Israel, notably through the ethics of the prophets; and then the *love* of God—as exhibited through the Gospel of Christ. The truth is at once suggested thereby that the revelation of the *love* of God must be safeguarded by a due recognition of His power and holiness.

As already noted, the characteristic word of God, on the lips of Jesus, is "Father"; but let it be remembered that not until Jesus came as the culminating self-revelation of God was the divine fatherhood given prominence. The wonderful truth of that divine fatherhood is not safe for fallen man to possess without the earlier expression of God's awesome power and holiness. In nothing is the wisdom of heaven more clearly observable than in this progressive tuition of man, and the postponed disclosure of the heavenly fatherhood. In ancient religions where there has been no such safeguard as that which we see in the biblical pattern, no conception is less ethical than that of divine fatherhood, with the result that the whole character of the deity is correspondingly degraded.

Such are the moral necessities of the case that it is only safe for man to say "Our Father which art in heaven" when he has learned immediately to add "hallowed be Thy name." One of the faults of certain modern theology is the mental divorcing of the divine love and the fatherhood from that sin-abhorring holiness which atmospheres it.

The Ultimate Relationship

Let me here reiterate that this fatherhood of God is His *basic* relationship to all of us, His human offspring; and that brings me to a new angle on the subject. I stand by it as an irrefutable proposition, that the fatherhood of God is the relationship which underlies and gives meaning to all others. Based on the biblical revelation (so I contend) our only true philosophy of God must make His fatherhood the *ultimate* relationship.

Reflect on that thoughtfully here for a moment or two. By general concurrence, God sustains four main relationships to mankind: (1) Creator, (2) King, (3) Judge, (4) Father. Which of these four is the one that is fundamentally determinative of the others?

Take the first: God is *Creator*. But did He create us merely to sustain our existence? No: motive inadequate. Take the second: God is *King*. But did He create us only to rule us? Surely no: motive inadequate. Take the third: God is *Judge*. Did He create only to adjudicate rewards or penalties? No: motive inadequate. Take the fourth: God is *Father*. Did He create us to love us and to be loved *by* us? Surely, yes: motive thoroughly adequate.

Is it not true to say that the fatherhood *includes and sublimates* the meaning of the other three relationships? Is it not true that the fatherhood gathers up the other three into a larger and higher explanation of the universe? Take away that fatherhood and the universe becomes a vast prison. The divine creatorship without it loses its highest motives and loftiest ends. Similarly, the divine kingship without that fatherhood loses its worthiest authority and weightiest influence. Equally so, the divine judgeship without that fatherhood loses its purest compulsion and truest safeguard.

Yes, let me underline it: The fatherhood is the basic, ultimate, inclusive relationship in which God stands to ourselves. Never must we think of Him as only Creator, King, Judge; for He did not create merely to sustain, to govern, to judge. There is a motive and an end, and a method toward the realizing of that end which proceeds from His fatherhood. The fatherhood of God is not subordinate to, or comprehended by, His other relationships as Creator, King, Judge; but, on the other hand, those other relationships *are* subordinate to, and comprehended by, the fatherhood. They are the expression of, and are conditioned by, the fatherhood.

The fatherhood includes kingship: for fatherhood minus kingship is imperfectly exercised. The fatherhood also includes the legislative and the judicial; for its vigilance of love involves its inviolable maintenance of those laws which condition the well-being of the family. From His own infinite life and being God has given existence to us human beings who by the very way He has made us are at once kindred with Himself, made in His own image, yet having free-willed individuality. In that outgoing movement of God the motive is love, the purpose is fellowship, and the method toward the realizing of that end is the education of the family; and all those have their ground in and are the expression of the divine fatherhood.

Have we not already seen how conclusively presented that is in the teaching of Christ? It has been said with truth that this revelation of God as Father is "the *characteristic* revelation through Christ." As such, it culminates all former revelation, and in so doing makes known with finalizing clearness that which is sublimest and infinitely deepest in the being of God.

Fatherhood Implicit in the Triunity

Surely, too, the universality of the divine fatherhood is implicit in the very triunity of the Godhead. The deity exists in the eternal triunity of the Father, the Son and the Holy Spirit, the primacy, as it were, being with the Father. We think of the Father as the self-existent *source* of the divine life; of the Son as the eternal *expression* of it; and of the Holy Spirit as the ever-continuing *completion* of it in the inner fellowship of the divine love.

Now the outward acts of God in creation and redemption have their ground in and reflect those inward relations of the Godhead. The *creation*, so to speak, is originated in the Father; it is constituted in the Son; it is vitalized by the Spirit. And because the creation reflects the triunity of the Creator, the *primacy* of the Father in the inward life of the Godhead implies the primacy of fatherly purpose in the outreaching creativity of the Godhead. We should see a fatherly purpose in the universe, and a father-relationship toward all that which is constituted in the *Son*.

Similarly, *redemption* has its source in the Father; it is accomplished through the Son; and it is communicated to human experience by the Spirit as regenerator. Redemption is ours because the Father *thought* it, the Son *bought* it, and the Spirit *wrought* it.

Glancing back at that wonderful concentrate of the gospel, John 3:16, can we ever read its "God so loved the *world* that He gave His only begotten *Son*" without sensing this fundamental priority and racial sweep of divine fatherhood expressing itself through the eternal Son? Such utterly sublime and self-giving love as that simply cannot be the expression merely of creatorship or kingship or judgeship, but only of fatherhood!

Fatherhood and Atonement

It has often been asked: If God is our Father, why did He need to give His only-begotten Son to suffer for us on Calvary? Why could He not forgive us, as our Father, without that fearful sacrifice? The reply is, that the fatherhood of God, rather than rendering Calvary needless, is that which more than anything else *necessitates* it, as careful consideration soon convinces us.

It has often been argued (and rightly so) that the necessity for the Atonement, from God's standpoint, arises from the different relationships which He sustains to our human race: Creator, King, Judge, Father. Which, then, of those relationships is it in virtue of which He demands atonement? Strange as it may seem at first, it is His fatherhood. Yes, more than His power as Creator, and more than His sovereignty as King, and more than His severity as Judge, it is His fatherhood which requires that cross outside the city wall.

But *how*, then, does this fatherhood of God necessitate atonement? The question has often been put: Does fatherhood, either human or divine, require "satisfaction" before it will forgive? Many have replied no. The old Socinian argument was that if any earthly father worthy of the name will forgive his child for wrongs without first demanding a "satisfaction," surely the compassion of the heavenly Father cannot be less.

It is surprising and disappointing to find the Puritan theologians, and even later evangelical princes like R. W. Dale, accepting this paltry idea of fatherhood—a fatherhood shorn of all its nobler and more virile qualities, as representing the fatherhood of God. It is pathetic to find them, instead of repudiating such an inadequate conception of fatherhood, resorting to the reply that the Atonement is made necessary by one of those sterner relationships which God sustains to men, i.e., His being moral Governor and Judge as well as Father. This, as though the different acts of God spring from His different relationships, so that at one time He is acting as Judge, at another time as King, and at another time as Father.

It is many years since I read the late Dr. J. Scott Lidgett's book,

The Spiritual Principle of the Atonement, but I retain a quotation from it which is much to the point here.

> The relationship of God to man is a unique and living whole. Each purpose and act of God towards men is founded upon the whole of His nature and the whole of His relationships, and not upon a part of them. It is less possible for the heavenly Father to divest Himself of fatherhood in any of His dealings with men than for an earthly father to do so in his dealings with his child. Different aspects and functions of His fatherhood may, no doubt, be abstracted from the whole, for purposes of thought. We may set, for example, in the forefront for the moment His legislative or His governmental or His judicial activity. But we must not suppose that the entire action of God proceeds from, or is explained by, any one of those aspects or functions in severance from the fatherhood which is over, in, and through them all.

The true reply to those who say that the fatherhood of God does away with the necessity for an atonement is that they are *arguing from a conception of fatherhood which is strangely inadequate*; a conception of fatherhood which is far removed from that divine fatherhood which is taught by our Lord Jesus and the writings of the New Testament.

In dealing with a disobedient and rebellious child, a conscientious father must observe four sacred principles. First, he must do justice to his own character. Second, he must maintain the authority of his own will for the good of the family. Third, he must assert the sanctity of the law which has been broken. Fourth, he must bring home to the child a penitent consciousness of wrong. Apply those four considerations to the heavenly fatherhood and it will be seen at once that it is the very fatherhood of God, even more than His regal governorship or judicial rectitude, which necessitates the Atonement. And further, the more deeply we ponder the cross of Christ, the more do we become convinced that there could be no other way whereby those four inviolable principles of true fatherhood could be observed and vindicated in the divine dealing with mankind. That cross upholds those four principles.

First, it upholds the *character* of the divine Father, for it magnifies both His holiness and His love. Second, it exalts the *authority* of the divine will, for our vicarious representative who hung there thus "became obedient unto death, even death on the cross." Third, it asserts the *sanctity* of the law which has been broken, for it is the means whereby full satisfaction is rendered. Fourth, it also brings home to our hearts, as nothing else ever could, a truly penitent *realization* of our sin.

Yes, that cross is a necessiy of the divine fatherhood; but the ineffable coronation of that is this: The very fatherhood which necessitated it is the fatherhood which also, at inconceivable cost, *provided* it. As the late Bishop Handley Moule put it, the Atonement "liberated His mercy by satisfying His law." That is why it ever came to be written, "God so loved the world that He *gave* His only-begotten Son...." What a giving that was! For the Father Himself suffered in all the sufferings of the incarnate Son!

But further: In our thinking upon this profound and utterly sublime fatherhood of God we need to guard against making a false alternative, as though we had to make a hard and fast choice between the liberalist view of it and the ultra-evangelical view which confines it to Christian believers.

Again and again in the history of the Christian Church much harm has been done because theologians have made antitheses of concepts which are not really antithetic. Good men, in their zeal to disprove error, have gone to exaggerated opposites and thus made it appear that the choice was between two polarities, neither of which are the real truth. We think of Nestorius in the early fifth century who, in his ardor to refute Apollinaris' denial of our Lord's dual nature, went to the opposite extreme believing that there are really two persons in Christ, and thus occasioned one of the most troublesome heresies of the earlier centuries. Or again, we think of Augustine who, in his vehemence against the Pelagian doctrine of human free-will and moral ability, rebounded to such an excessive opposite in his predestinarianism that he has been charged with religious fatalism.

We see the same war of inflamed opposites in the post-Reformation controversy between Arminianism and Calvinism, with the hyper-Calvinists so violently repudiating the Arminian emphasis on human free-will as to run to the erroneous opposite of reducing the human will to unresponsible passivity amid the sovereign scheme of the divine purposes. With good reason we may marvel now that theological thinkers could so censoriously have made sheer antitheses of things which are not necessarily antithetic at all. Are human free-will and divine sovereignty mutually exclusive beyond all thought of their being parallel realities? May they not be complimentary aspects of one great truth?

Something similar has happened with this doctrine of the divine fatherhood. In order to counter the liberalistic version of it which rubs out any need for individual regeneration, fundamentalists have reacted to the opposite extreme of denying the real fatherhood of God to all except a tiny fraction. Yet the surest way of destroying the liberalist error is not by thus swinging to a contrary extreme which fails to do justice to the full data of Scripture, but by adhering solely and wholly to the plain meanings of the inspired Scriptures.

A Crucial Discrimination

If I see the matter discerningly, the choice is not between the liberalist caricature of the divine fatherhood and the ultra-conservative restriction of it exclusively to believers. There is a positive between the two, which, to my own judgment at least, is the truly scriptural position.

Let me call attention to what I believe is a most necessary point of discrimination. I consider it a discrimination so important that it can hardly be over-emphasized. It is the center-point of the whole issue, yet on it there is sadly obscure thinking. Many of us evangelicals seem to misunderstand it; but the crucial fact is this:

> The universal fatherhood of God does not imply the universal sonship of man.

However vague our thinking may have been as to that, it should henceforth become axiomatic in our interpretation and preaching of the divine fatherhood. If we keep close to the Scriptures we shall not err. Does not that parable of the prodigal son suddenly flash back to mind at this point? While that wayward young ingrate was in the far country the father still remained the father, but the son did not remain a son—not in the true sense of sonship, for he is described as "lost" and "dead." He needed to repent, to return, to be reconciled and to be reinstated by the father if there was to be a restoration of true sonship.

Going with this there are many New Testament texts such as the following. "As many as received Him [our Lord Jesus] to them gave He power to *become* the sons of God, even to them that believe on His name: which were born [i.e., born again by regeneration] not of blood, nor of the will of the flesh, nor of the will of man, but of God" (John 1:12,13). "Of His own will begat He [God] us" (Jas. 1:18). "For ye are all the children of God through faith in Christ Jesus" (Gal. 3:26). "And because ye are sons, God hath sent forth the Spirit of His Son into your hearts, crying, Abba Father" (Gal. 4:6). "For as many as are led by the Spirit of God, they are the sons of God" (Rom. 8:14).

So true sonship is restored only by a regenerating union with the Savior. The same Lord Jesus who uttered the parable of the prodigal son also said to the religious Nicodemus, "Marvel not that I said unto thee, Ye must be born again" (John 3:7).

Let it be underscored, therefore: The members of Adam's fallen race, whether the religious or the dissolute, are far from sonship in the vital, moral and spiritual meaning of the term. Indeed, the Lord Jesus said to a group of Pharisees, "Ye are of your father, the devil," by which, of course, He did not mean that the devil was their father in the sense of being their creator. He meant that in their moral condition and behavior they were like the devil and therefore "of" the devil (further reference to this later). The present state of all Adam's posterity, apart from saving grace and spiritual rebirth, is (1) physically mortal, (2) morally perverted, (3) spiritually dead. Yet, as shown in the parable of the prodigal, this does not negate the fact that the fundamental relationship of God to all men is that of fatherhood. We simply cannot account adequately for God's dealing with sinful men on any other basis than that of fatherhood.

Supposed Incongruity

I know only too well how many there are who keep insisting that if we preach the racial fatherhood of God, we thereby necessarily *imply* the racial sonship of man. They brand it as an incongruity when we say that man has lost his sonship yet God retains His fatherhood. Yet it is not one whit more incongruous than saying (as they all earnestly do) that our Lord Jesus is "the Savior of the world" when in reality only those in the world who accept Him are saved. Get the parallel:

(1) Is Jesus the Savior of the world? Yes.
   But are all men saved by Him? No.
(2) Is God the Father of all mankind? Yes.
   But are all men sons of God? No.

With my New Testament open before me I cannot believe in a broken-down, limited divine fatherhood, but I do believe in a broken-down, limited human sonship. The very fact that man has fallen from an original sonship (Luke 3:38) aggravates the tragedy of the Fall, and heightens the sinfulness of sin. Man's fall is not from mere creaturehood or servanthood or judicial accountability, but from a *filial* fellowship with a Creator-Father. Man is the prodigal who, like Esau, has despised his birthright. And now, instead of being children of God, it is written of the many that they are "children of disobedience" and "children of wrath" (Eph. 2:2,3).

Spiritual Paradoxes

If to some it should seem paradoxical that there can be a divine fatherhood on the one hand, without a corresponding human sonship on the other hand, we would give a reminder that there are many such paradoxes in spiritual concerns, as the two words, "predestination" and "free-will," or the two words, "justification" and "forgiveness" will recall.

Take those two words, "justification" and "forgiveness." It has been argued that they express two concepts which so sharply contradict each other as to make them mutually exclusive. If I am justified, and therefore acquitted, how can I need forgiveness as well? For to be justified means that I am declared righteous; and if so, how is there any call for forgiveness? As the Socinians of the sixteenth century used to argue: If the cross of Christ was indeed a "satisfaction" for sin to the law of God, then the divine law has exacted all that is due—which leaves neither room nor requirement for forgiveness.

Well, maybe it is not so easy to reconcile these seemingly contrary aspects of truth intellectually; yet we know that they are reconciled without the least difficulty in spiritual experience. Yes, for while I rejoice to know that I am justified, and that the divine law has been forever satisfied on my behalf, yet I am just as vividly conscious that through Christ I have a loving heavenly Father's forgiveness. Justification has to do with a *legal* responsibility. Forgiveness has to do with a *filial* relationship. However separate they may seem objectively, they are a soul-thrilling blend subjectively in the experience of the saved.

Our touchstone must ever be what the Scriptures clearly teach. In this matter of the divine fatherhood I, for one, cannot tear away the very heart from the parable of the prodigal son, or from other pronouncements of our Lord Jesus, and constrict that fatherhood to one small class. The great, wide, compassionate fatherhood of God for all human souls is plainly recorded there in Holy Writ, unless I am strangely mistaken. I glory in it, and in the wonderful gospel which emanates from it.

Some Objections

But there are objections. One of them is that to preach the universal fatherhood of God dangerously softens down the warnings of Scripture and robs evangelism of those sterner appeals which have always been powerful persuasives. If God is indeed the Father of all, how can we preach the divine anger against the ungodly, the "wrath to come," the terror of a judgment day, and a Gehenna beyond?

That complaint, however, is in my judgment a sample of the superficiality which clings around the subject. It arises from a failure to grasp what Scripture actually teaches about God as the Father. Instead of *lessening* the severity of the biblical warnings, the truly preached fatherhood of God *intensifies* them.

Which is the more awful: the stern sentence of a judge, or the righteous anger of a *father*? Which is more frightening: the penalty exacted by violated law, or the eventual vengeance of outraged *love*? What is it that makes the "wrath to come" most of all fearful? Is it the strokes of retributive justice—or the prostrating reappearance of a despised *Savior*? At the end of the present age why do the Christ-rejectors of Christendom hide in dens and call on the mountains to fall on them? Is it the coming from heaven of a regal lion? No; their cry is, "Hide us from...the wrath of the *LAMB*!" What is the sin above all others which sends souls to the damnation of Gehenna? Is it the breaking of Moses' law? No; it is the rejection of what the Father and the incarnate Son did on *Calvary*. *That* fatherhood, other than reducing the terror of the judgment day, makes it all the more to be dreaded by the unbeliever and wrongdoer. Oh, that fatherhood! Oh, that saviorhood!

"If God Were Your Father"

Perhaps the strongest-seeming textual argument against the universality of the divine fatherhood is an utterance of our Lord Jesus which is recorded in John 8:42. Those who avail themselves of it apparently regard it as enough in itself to refute the racial fatherhood of God, without need for further words.

Speaking to some of the scribes and Pharisees and other hostile Jews, our Lord said, *"If God were your Father*, ye would love Me; for I proceeded forth and came from God." It is claimed that here our Lord Himself settles the question as to the extent of God's fatherhood. He cannot be the Father of all men, because according to clear statement He was not the Father of those Pharisees. How can we argue against that?

"If God were your Father..." The words may well have startled those arrogant Pharisees, yet there is nothing in them, when rightly understood, to disturb our belief that Scripture teaches the racial fatherhood. All will accept it as a sound principle of exegisis that a

text must be interpreted in the light of its context. If, then, we take John 8:42 with its context, we see that when Jesus said, "If God were your Father," He was merely repudiating that God was their Father in the way those Pharisees were hypocritically claiming it.

In the immediate context (verse 39) our Lord uses the practically parallel words, *"If ye were Abraham's children,* ye would do the works of Abraham." Yet who would argue that our Lord was denying that they really *were* Abraham's posterity? That our Lord was not denying it is settled by the fact that almost in the same breath (verse 37) He says, "I know that ye are Abraham's seed." Obviously, then, when He says they are not Abraham's children, He means it in one particular way, namely, that they were not Abraham's children in the sense of moral and spiritual *likeness* to their venerable ancestor. Yet mark this well: While they could not honestly claim Abraham as their father in that sense, the fundamental fact remained that Abraham was their father, for in verse 56 our Lord says, *"Your father Abraham* rejoiced to see My day."

Even so is it with verse 42, "If God were your Father." Our Lord no more denies the fatherhood of God to them than He denies to them the fatherhood of Abraham. But He does deny to them the fatherhood, both of God and of Abraham, in the way they were boasting it, namely in the reciprocal sense of moral and spiritual likeness.

Our Lord's words to those Pharisees no more question the fundamental fatherhood of God than His words, "ye are of your father, the devil," (verse 44) imply that Satan was their father in the fundamental sense of being their creator. In that reference to the devil as their "father" Jesus meant that the devil was their father and they were his children in the sense of moral correspondence, as the remainder of the verse shows— "and the lusts of your father ye will do." Again, in verse 47, our Lord says, "ye are not of God"; but would anyone argue therefrom that God was not their Creator?

The whole context shows that our Lord was concerned solely with that relationship which is determined by the response of the *heart* and the correspondence of *character.* Would any of us dare to say that God did not love those Pharisees as human beings? No; but if God loved them, how can we explain that love? The divine creatorship, kingship, judgeship will not account for it, for those relationships could only call forth wrath. There is only one real explanaton, and that is the divine fatherhood.

We must add one further word to complete our demolition of the foregoing objection. If we would be finally convinced that in John 8:42 our Lord never meant to deny the racial fatherhood of God, we

only need to look up other places in the same Gospel according to
John where the same wonderful teacher tells us about that fatherhood. We have already lingered over His words to the woman at the
well of Sychar, and to those hostile Jews in chapter 5 verses 22,23,45;
but there are others similarly impressive, as any of us can easily
ascertain.

Slanting off, for a moment, to another aspect, let me mention
an objection which I came across only a few weeks ago. The writer
of it asks: "How can we believe in the racial fatherhood of God when
God Himself says,'Come out from among them' and only *then* 'I will
be a *Father* unto you, and ye shall be My sons and daughters'?" (2
Cor. 6:17,18).

Frankly, I marvel that such a feeble argument could be seriously
submitted. It is lame on both legs. First, those words of Paul were
written to Christian believers. Are we to understand, then, that God
is not the Father even of born-again Christians who may not be
living the wholly separated life? But again, the words are a composite
quotation from the Old Testament, where they are addressed to the
people of Israel in general. In these words God pledged His fatherhood
to all who would live godly lives—quite apart from regeneration as
taught in the New Testament. So the words favor, rather than contradict, the racial fatherhood of God. As for 2 Corinthians 6:17,18,
the meaning, purely and simply, is that even to Christian believers
God can only give full expression of His fatherhood when they are
living the separated life.

Some Practical Issues

As we said at the beginning of these reflections, our yes or no
to the racial fatherhood of God is no mere matter of abstract theological theory with no practical bearings. The very opposite is the truth.
The crucial discrimination which we have made, namely, that the
universal fatherhood of God does not imply the universal sonship of
man, rescues this profound and precious doctrine of the divine fatherhood from the liberalist degradation of it on the one hand, and from
the unwarranted impoverishment of it on the other hand. The practical importance of that cannot be overstated; for a right or wrong
concept of the divine fatherhood will color and flavor a Christian's
believing and a minister's preaching more than anything else, and
affect the whole atmosphere of a church.

I am not alone in having noticed that there is a certain repellant
hardness in the preaching of many who refuse the fatherhood of God
to any but believers. Some of us have been conscious of it as we have

listened to them, and have felt that the fatherhood of God was too big and tender and sublime to be cramped within their narrow dogmatism. For my own part, I know that since I came to realize more clearly the God-like inclusiveness of the heavenly fatherhood, I have entered, as I never did before, into the compassionate yearning of the great Father over all the sinning, suffering prodigals of this sin-sick world. My own heart has become borne along in the big, wide flow of Heaven's parent-hearted concern over all the souls of men and women. With this soul-expanding larger view of the divine fatherhood there found its way into my preaching a new note of tenderness, and I will not hesitate to say that I seem to find a readier inclination in my hearers to come back to the gracious Father by way of the Savior's cross.

Sometimes, when I approached thoughtful, upright, but unconverted men with a view to winning them for my Savior, I was respectfully but firmly repulsed with such words as, "I really cannot accept the narrow view of God, of providence, of history, which you preachers say the Bible teaches. I just cannot believe that God is a Father to just a privileged few, and not to *all* His creatures."

Quite recently I found that this was the main stumbling-block to one of the most respected men in my own neighborhood. He had been brought up under such teaching, and had become repelled by it. His business friends included many who, although they seemingly had no religious convictions, were upright men, honest in purpose, and a good deal better than many professors of Christianity. He simply could not think that all those were outside God's fatherhood just because they were not so-called "believers." The narrow dogmas drummed into him in earlier years he had now rejected as absurd. He had rebelled and practically given up any belief in the Bible. And that man is by no means the only spiritual casualty of such a sort.

If men of the kind I have mentioned were merely pretending, or dodging realities by voicing such objections, their words would not cut us so keenly; but the fact is, they are speaking what they really feel. One well-educated man put it to me that "this circumscribed idea" of a fatherhood which is "limited to a select little circle" contradicts "the very instincts and intuitions of human nature." Such genuine protest may well make us think pretty hard.

What, then, of the more usual evangelical teaching that the fatherhood of God is restricted exclusively to Christian believers? It is supposed to be what the Bible teaches. Does it really represent what the Bible teaches? I think not. Does it offend the deepest intuitions and sensibilities of our moral nature? I think it does; and I cannot but sympathize with those men I have mentioned who just cannot accept it. What do we do? Must we make the Bible fit to what *we* think or even feel in our deepest being? No; but we have cogent reason to re-examine the Bible in that connection. And when we do, what do we find? I submit again that it does not teach a specialistic fatherhood to an exclusive few.

I am well aware, of course, that many evangelicals easily dismiss the matter by such rejoinders as "Oh, well, you know, God is Father to all men in a general sense as Creator, but not in the special way that He is to Christian believers." That is just a camouflage for blurred thinking. The word "Father" is retained, but it is emptied of its real meaning. Where does the New Testament teach any such *thinned out* fatherhood of God? If He is Father, then He is Father in the full meaning of that wonderful word. As we have said, it is impossible to think of the creatorship at all apart from the fatherhood. It is the fatherhood of God, not His creatorship, which is the reality of fundamental value; for His creatorship springs from what He has *done*, whereas His fatherhood is that which He *is* in His very being. We can think of God apart from creatorship, but we simply cannot think of God apart from those qualities of being which constitute His fatherhood. Therefore, those who confine the fatherhood of God to Christian believers only, yet admit that in a kind of "general" way the fatherhood of God is racial (but only with debilitated meaning) are in reality both admitting and denying fatherhood in the same breath.

Of course, God does have special relationship toward regenerated Christian believers. It is they who, through spiritual rebirth, have been restored to true sonship. It is they who enter into the enjoyment of the divine fatherhood; for in them there is a divinely renewed consciousness of it and a response to it. Yet (let me finally stress) that does not impair the other truth, i.e., that the moral and emotional qualities of fatherhood remain in God toward all men. The father of the prodigal remained the father all the way through.

I believe that to preach this true, universal fatherhood of God is of large importance to the effective propagation of the gospel and the drawing of human hearts to the Savior. The unscriptural though common idea that God is Father only to a comparatively tiny community within the race savors of Phariseeism, and easily leads to it. No privileged class has the monopoly of God's fatherly love. As the Cretan poet, Epimenides (sixth century B.C.) said, and as the later Greek poet, Aratus (third century B.C.) echoed, and as Paul said (approvingly quoting them both in Acts 17:28), "In Him we live, and move, and have our being: as certain also of your own poets have said, *'For we are also His offsping.'* " So it is indeed. There is the one God and Father of us all. In these days when there is a recrudescence of barbarous nationalisms, such spacious Christian truths as the universal fatherhood of God, the universal saviorhood of Christ, the universal efficacy of the cross, and the universality of the gospel invitation need to be proclaimed more supra-ethnically and undiscriminatingly than ever before, and we must keep insisting that the only true brotherhood of man is that which is grounded in a recognition of this true fatherhood of God.

A Personal Experience

I cannot close this study without reflecting, even though briefly, on the preciousness of the divine fatherhood to us Christian believers. Trusting that it will not be considered an impropriety on my part, let me speak of it by relating an unforgettable experience of my own.

I go back to October 1973. The memory of that day will never pale. My dear wife and I were just home after a lecture-tour in Greece, Turkey, Patmos, Crete, Cyprus, Lebanon, Israel. Sadly she looked at me as she said, "Sid, I have disturbing news for you. It's about myself: I have cancer." Not even a thunderbolt could have shaken me more—not, at least, in mind and heart. My Ethel and I had grown up together since we were little neighbors five and six years old. All the years of our lives had been intertwined; and now we had been married forty-five years. To think that she had cancer, and that I might now be losing her was as though the heavens were falling in.

We hastened to our doctor, who gravely confirmed that it was indeed cancer and then called in the surgeon. It was mastocarcinoma. The cancer had eaten right across until it was under the right arm and into the lymph system. Surgery was performed on December 13, 1973, by way of single mastectomy on the left side. I had enough reason to think her days were numbered, for already three other members of her family had been casualties of fatal cancer.

She came through the surgery well; but when I enquired if the malignancy had been entirely removed I gradually gleaned otherwise. In fact, there was a whole mass of cancer in her chest and it was quite inoperable. Thereupon my beloved was put on chemotherapy; but no hope of cure could be given.

I will not describe the effects on my beautiful and hitherto well-favored wife; but it was heart-rending to me as I saw her suffering, gripped by that fear which often accompanies cancer, and wasting away until she was little more than a shadow of her former self. With intense sympathy I cosuffered with her through it all, until my own sense of heart-desolation was such that I could scarcely maintain the disguise of comforting hopefulness which I was endeavoring to wear.

Suddenly, as never before, I needed the fatherhood of God. It is not easy to put it into words, but I needed God, not so much as God, but as a *Father* who was really near me, with a father-heart which suffered with me, and a loving, sympathetic bosom on which I could lay my weary head. Alas, just when I needed that fatherhood I discovered that I had lost it! Yes, I had *lost* it; and I will tell you how.

I am no astronomer (I wish I were), but I have always been fascinated by astronomy. I am no scientist (I wish I were), but I have always been entranced by the wonders of scientific experiment and discovery. Especially, for years, I had been gripped, intrigued, spellbound by the magnificent *immensities* of the universe as revealed through the modern telescope; those staggeringly stupendous stellar marvels, and those seemingly boundless expanses beyond all measurement even in "light years."

By an unsuspected process, my thinking had eventually so linked God with the vastnesses of His material creation that now, when I suddenly needed Him closely, as my heavenly "Father," and needed Him as such all to my own poor, little, suffering self, I found that I had lost Him in the immensities of His own universe! I simply cannot express my sense of pitiful bereftness in that hour.

But it was precisely then that God brought home to my weeping heart the wonder of His fatherhood in a way I had never known before. As I knelt before Him, crying after Him, as it seemed, into unanswering space and remoteness, He suddenly became near to me in my deepest awareness, as a "very present help in trouble" (Ps. 46:1). If I may reverently say so, He sympathetically conversed with me in a mind-to-mind language which I inwardly heard and easily understood.

"Sid," He asked, "did you ever hear of anyone called Abraham?"

"Yes," I replied, "I have sometimes preached about him."

"Sid, did he have a son?"

"Yes, O God, his son was Isaac."

"Sid, did Abraham love his son, Isaac?"

"Yes, indeed. No human father ever loved a son more than Abraham loved his 'beloved Isaac,' the miraculously born son of his old age."

"Sid, when I needed to make a final proof of Abraham's love and trust toward Me, did I tell him to take his beloved son and offer him as a sacrifice on Mount Moriah?"

"Yes, Lord God; and although it was with a broken heart, he

proceeded to obey without any word of rebellion."

"Sid, do you believe that Isaac was an advance-type of the Lord Jesus Christ?"

"Yes."

"Then do you believe also that father Abraham in that incident was a type of Myself as the *heavenly* Father?"

"Yes."

"All right, Sid, answer me this: When Abraham lifted the knife to slay his unresisting son on that rough altar, who (do you think) suffered *more*—Isaac in his mute helplessness, or Abraham, his agonized father, who would fain have died in Isaac's place?"

I had never thought of it before in such stark delineation; but as I then reflected on it, kneeling there in the enveloping awareness of God, I could only say that I now began to think that Abraham so suffered in the suffering of his son that his own grief must have been as great as, if not greater than, that of Isaac.

"Sid, did you ever hear of a place called Calvary?"

"Dear God, yes."

"Sid, who (do you think) suffered *more* on Calvary? My only begotten *Son* who hung there for you? Or I Myself, His *Father*, and yours?"

There and then, in that rapt moment, the vapory mists in which I had lost my sense of the heavenly fatherhood melted away. A lovely sun-break of rediscovery flooded my mind and heart with joy and gratitude. I saw the saviorhood of the eternal Son, and the fatherhood of the heavenly Father, and the soul-subduing splendor of Calvary as I never had before. Oh, that wonderful, wonderful cross! The very saviorhood of the Son is the supreme demonstration of the Father's *fatherhood*! Did Jesus weep at the tomb of Lazarus? Then does He not weep among the mourners at a million other graves on earth? And does not the heavenly fatherhood weep through Him? As 2 Corinthians 5:19 says, "God was in Christ, reconciling the world unto Himself." On that awful yet glorious cross God suffered, not only *as* man, and *for* man, but also *with* man; and if He suffered with us then, does He not suffer with us still, in our sufferings on earth? Oh, those three wondrously expressive names of our triune God: "Father," "Savior," "Comforter!"

As I lingered there with God, in prayer, there poured down over my mind like a delightful cascade, some of those many sayings of Jesus about the heavenly Father which bring Him so near. "Thy Father which seeth in secret shall reward thee openly" (Matt. 6:6). "Your Father knoweth what things ye have need of, before ye ask Him" (Matt. 6:8). "Your heavenly Father feedeth them [the birds].

Are ye not much better than they?" (Matt. 6:26). "How much more shall your Father which is in heaven give good things to them that ask Him?" (Matt. 7:11). "Are not two sparrows sold for a farthing? And not one of them shall fall on the ground without your Father" (Matt. 10:29). "The very hairs of your head are all numbered" (Matt. 10:30). "It is not the will of your Father which is in heaven, that one of these little ones should perish" (Matt. 18:14). "He that hath seen Me hath seen the Father" (John 14:9). "The Father...shall give you another Comforter" (John 14:16). "The Father Himself loveth you" (John 16:27).

Oh, yes, the fatherhood of God was mine again! And since then it has been an atmosphering reality in a way it never was before. If I want to know how infinitesimal I am, all I need to do is look at those illimitable spaces through the telescope. If I want to know how precious I am to God, and how close He is to me, all I have to do is listen to that heavenly fatherhood which talks to me through the lips of Jesus, the incarnate Son, and through that cross on Calvary's brow. There is not a square inch of the universe where my Creator-Father is not present. There is not a throb of experience which my heavenly Father does not share with me.

Did you happen to remember that in Titus 3:4 the phrase, "God our Savior," is, in the Greek "our *Savior-God*"? What that verse actually says is, "The to-man-love of our Savior-God appeared." What a name for God! What a love for man! Deep in the being of the Eternal is a *philanthropia*, a profound love-to-man which wells up from that infinite Father-heart to *all* men, and which once poured itself out for man in that measureless self-sacrifice on Calvary. Thus it came to be written in human mid-history,

The *Father* sent the *Son* to be the Savior of the *world*.

13

The Faithfulness of God

Like sunlit peaks His mercies rise
Before my grateful, wondering eyes,
Then let me trust Him and confess
His glorious, endless *faithfulness*.

For mercies past, and mercies new,
For kindness fresh as morning dew,
For faithfulness far more than gold,
How can I fervent praise withhold?

My Maker, Father, Savior, King,
Thy grace and goodness will I sing,
Until my song with heaven's blends
For faithfulness which never ends.

J.S.B.

I n 1 Peter 4:19, we find the following sympathetic advice:
"Wherefore let them that suffer according to the will of God
commit the keeping of their souls to Him in well doing, as
unto *a faithful Creator*." What a consoling designation of God that
is! "*A FAITHFUL CREATOR!*" Let the gaze of your heart linger on
it as though you had suddenly found a priceless gem; for such it
assuredly is.

In this present study it will be our privilege to open up slightly
a much-to-be-prized theme of which there is none nobler or grander
in the Bible. That subject is *the faithfulness of God*. In Psalm 37:3
we read,

Trust in Jehovah, and do good; so shalt thou dwell in the land,
and verily thou shalt be fed.

At least, that is how it reads in our King James Version, but I doubt whether it brings out the original Hebrew to best advantage in that last clause. Instead of "verily thou shalt be fed," the American Standard Version renders it, *"feed on His faithfulness."* Yes, "feed on His [God's] faithfulness"! That is the best diet for the soul at all times, especially so in times of trouble. In this present study I want us to "feed on His faithfulness" as it is set forth in the pages of Holy Writ.

What mental relief and repose it engenders, to know that back of our human suffering and back of the staggeringly vast universe in which our own planet is an almost unperceivable speck, there is a "faithful Creator"! This prodigious universe can be frightening if we view it apart from some such guarantee as that; but when we are assured that its infinite Architect is the "faithful Creator," then the frightening becomes friendly. Every dark cloud has a silver lining, and every thunderstorm has a rainbow arching it. Every mystery holds a hidden benediction, and every permitted teardrop glistens with a gracious new meaning. A streak of powerful light strikes even across the monster problem of sin, suffering and death, so that we sense a divine fidelity even beneath *that.*

THE SEVEN PILLARS

In the Book of Proverbs, chapters 8 and 9, there is an impressive passage in which wisdom is personified. In chapter 9:1 we read, "Wisdom hath builded her house, she hath hewn out her *seven pillars.*" Those seven pillars of wisdom always remind me of seven other wonderful pillars, the seven pillars of the divine faithfulness. To my own mind, the faithfulness of God is like a gigantic archway spanning human history from its beginning to its ending; and that resplendent archway is supported on seven glorious, immovable pillars. Those are:

1. The divine righteousness
2. The divine omnipotence
3. The divine truth
4. The divine immutability
5. The divine holiness
6. The divine wisdom
7. The divine love

We can see at once how the faithfulness of God rests on that first pillar, i.e., the divine *righteousness*, for the righteousness of God guarantees His absolute fidelity to every obligation which He assumes. If God were not inexorably righteous, He might go back on His own word; but His absolute integrity utterly excludes that such could ever happen, and it assures us that our faith in His word will never be dishonored.

Equally obviously, the faithfulness of God rests upon that second pillar, the divine *omnipotence*. If God were not omnipotent, He might essay to do a certain thing and then discover that He did not have the required resources by which to expedite it; but because He is omnipotent He has the inexhaustible ability to accomplish all that He engages Himself to do.

Just as clearly, we can see how the faithfulness of God is securely upheld on that third pillar—the divine *truth*. God is not only adjectivally true; He is substantively *the* truth, the shadowless totality of truth, whose every word is truth, who therefore could never possibly be false or faithless.

Further, the faithfulness of God rides securely on that fourth pillar: the divine *immutability*. That eternal unchangingness gives us the assurance that there is never any deviation of His perfect goodness, and never any countermanding of any promise He ever makes.

Again, can we not readily realize how the faithfulness of God is inviolably supported by that shining fifth pillar: the divine *holiness*? The holiness of God is His moral and ethical perfection. Because God is ethically perfect, all that He ever thinks or says or plans or purposes or promises at any given instant in His eternal continuousness is always faultless. Therefore He never has to correct or revise or improve it, which means that He can always be fully faithful to it.

As for that sixth pillar, the divine *wisdom*, the faithfulness of God can never be thought of apart from that. The omniscient wisdom of God engages that He not only fulfills His pledged word, but that He always does so in the wisest conceivable way.

And, of course, the faithfulness of God simply must rest upon that resplendent seventh pillar, the divine *love*. As soon as I know that "God is love" and that He loves *me*, I know that all His thoughts toward me, all His prior foreplanning and present permitting and long-term predetermining emanate from pure beneficence and for my everlasting wellbeing. Supremely, the infinite love of God vouchsafes His never-failing faithfulness to His written Word, to His sworn covenant, to His redemptive purpose, to His gracious promises, and to all my highest interests forever.

These, then, are the seven magnificent pillars upon which rests the age-to-age faithfulness of our glorious Creator: (1) the divine righteousness, (2) the divine omnipotence, (3) the divine truth, (4) the divine immutability, (5) the divine holiness, (6) the divine wisdom, (7) the divine love.

THE SEVEN CORRESPONDING TEXTS

Now it is a striking peculiarity that in the New Testament the expression, "God is faithful" occurs just seven times, and those seven remarkably correspond with those seven pillars on which, as we have said, the divine faithfulness rests. When we reflect on it, are not those seven pillars the seven principal aspects in the biblical revelation of our Creator-Redeemer? If someone were to ask unexpectedly, "Can you, as a Christian believer, tell me in one sentence what your Bible teaches about God?" what would you reply? I think you could not answer more truly than to say (with those seven pillars in mind) "The God of the Bible, in His boundless being and moral nature, is a God who is (1) utterly righteous, (2) inexhaustibly omnipotent, (3) absolutely truth, (4) eternally immutable, (5) ineffably holy, (6) infallibly wise, (7) infinitely loving.

Such, indeed, is the God of the Bible. Where could you find, anywhere outside the Bible, any such true, clear, full, lofty, sublime revelation of God? Nowhere. Does not such a revelation of God argue the supernatural inspiration of the Bible? Such truth about God could never have been humanly discovered; it could only have been divinely disclosed. And when once it is thus communicated to us, does it not answer to the deepest and most native cry of our human hearts? There cannot be a God higher or sublimer than that—to which the corollary is that any supposedly divine being who is less than that cannot really be God at all. The God of the Bible is the one and only true God. The idols of heathenism and the mythical gods of ancient Greece and Rome cause one part of us to groan at such human gullibility, and another part of us to react with derision at such grotesque, squabbling, voluptuous, semi-human gods and goddesses. The pantheistic, soulless, impersonal Brahma of Hinduism, and the mindless, grinding karma of Buddhism leave me starved, shivering, frightened, hopeless. When the deep need of my being cries out to such feelingless abstractions nothing comes in reply but the hollow echo of my own voice in a universe which is a vast, dark dungeon. But when I turn to the Bible and to the God of the Bible, to the personal, all-sovereign, all-seeing, all-caring, all-loving Creator, a satisfying threefold answer comes to me from the fatherhood of the Father, and the saviorhood of the eternal Son, and the mother-like comfort of the Holy Spirit! To that sublime, triune

Creator-Father-Savior the deepest within me instinctively cries out, "Yes, yes, that is the God I need, both for my searching intellect and for my needy heart. No other will do—but if I have *that* God, I need no other."

> Hear, everyone, my grateful song,
> And publish it around;
> The God I blindly sought so long
> I now at last have found!
>
> Strangely I sensed Him everywhere,
> The God I ached to find,
> Yet could not find Him anywhere,
> Above, before, behind.
>
> Myst'ry amazing! Love unknown!
> In human form He stands!
> He calls with tender human tone,
> Uplifting nail-torn hands!
>
> Yes, for in Jesus, God Most High
> Has come from heaven above,
> To answer all my aching cry
> With His redeeming love!

So, let me now invite your eager interest as we go through those seven New Testament occurrences of the expression, "God is faithful," after which we shall see how they parallel with those seven pillars on which the divine faithfulness rests.

1 John 1:9

We begin with the First Epistle of John, chapter 1, verse 9:

> If we confess our sins, He [God] is *faithful* and just [or righteous] to forgive us our sins, and to cleanse us from all unrighteousness.

Observe: it does not say in thus pardoning our sins God is faithful and *merciful* or even faithful and *compassionate*. Thank God, He *is* merciful and compassionate, but the notable feature in this verse is that God is "faithful and *righteous* to forgive us our sins..." That word "righteous" in the text is music to those of us who know in experience the forgiveness of which it speaks. It continually reminds us that because our dear Savior, the Lord Jesus, made a full and final atonement for our race's sin and guilt by His substitutionary death on Calvary, He thereby constituted a basis on which our righteous Creator can *righteously* pardon and save even the worst of human sinners who repent and accept what that sin-bearing Savior did on our behalf.

There are some people who say they cannot understand why God, if He is a God of mercy, cannot forgive sin without demanding such an atonement; but such persons surely have a superficial view both of sin and of God. In essence, sin is monstrous rebellion against that holy law of God which alone makes the universe safe. God cannot contradict His own holy nature or undermine His own holy law by condoning sin. If God were to treat sins as mere peccadilloes—whether those of Satan and the demons or those of Adam's fallen race—the whole universe would be an inferno. Such a possibility, however, is unthinkable simply because God is just what He is, a God of inflexible righteousness. The supreme marvel is that the God whose justice *demands* atonement is the God whose love *provides* it. The Judge Himself becomes the Savior! For in the person of our Lord Jesus it was God Himself who was nailed to the cross as our suffering Sin-bearer! Oh, the wonder of that cross! Oh, the mighty marvel of that substitutionary sacrifice! Because of it God can be "faithful and *righteous*" in pardoning us. God be praised for His mercy and His compassion. But, oh, it is so good to know that in forgiving me and receiving this sorry prodigal back to His bosom as a reinstated child He is *righteous* in so doing! The law can no longer point its condemning finger at me. Satan can no longer accuse me to God. As Romans 8:31-34 words it, "Who shall lay anything to the charge of God's elect? It is God that justifieth [i.e., counts us *righteous*]. Who is he that condemneth? It is Christ that died, yea rather, that is risen again, who is even at the right hand of God, who also maketh intercession for us."

Yes, God is faithful and righteous in pardoning us; faithful to His own holy nature; faithful to the moral law which human sin has outraged; faithful to the Calvary atonement of His incarnate Son; faithful to His precious promise in the gospel; faithful to the human race which Satan treacherously tricked into disobedience; and faithful to all my own eternal interests.

Nor is that all: the text says that He is "faithful and righteous to forgive us our sins, and to *cleanse* us from all unrighteousness," which means that along with the righteous pardon, the blood of God's Calvary Lamb washes away all the ugly stain of my sinning, and so wipes out all my legal guilt that in the sight of the divine law my record is now as white as an angel's wing! How wonderful indeed, then, is the faithfulness of God in this first aspect of it! "He is faithful and just [righteous] to forgive us our sins, and to cleanse us from all unrighteousness"! Let it be well underscored in our grateful thinking: God is faithful in *pardoning*.

2 Thessalonians 3:3

In our King James Version this verse reads, "But the Lord is *faithful*, who shall establish you, and keep you from evil." But although that is a true translation of the Greek, I am not sure it brings out the meaning with enough color. It is preferable to read the wording of it in the American Standard Version:

> But the Lord is faithful, who shall establish you, and *guard* you from the *evil one*.

Yes, the Lord does something more than keep us. He guards us; and well He needs, for it is a being guarded not just from evil, but from Satan himself, the evil *one*.

So, if in 1 John 1:9 God is faithful in *pardoning*, here in 2 Thessalonians 3:3 He is faithful in *protecting*. The Greek word translated as "keep" or "guard" is a military term. God garrisons us around; and not even the powerful Lucifer can breach the bulwarks of omnipotence which surround us and protect us as the elect of God. Again and again Satan is allowed to attack; and, alas, all too often our outward human defenses are pierced; but inside those there is an invisible wall of fire around God's elect before which Satan is scorched and thwarted. He may penetrate right to that innermost citadel, ripping away everything else to get there, as he did in the case of the patriarch Job; but there he always reaches the impenetrable, and slinks back in discomfiture, while the Lord's beloved comes through wiser and stronger, even as gold tested and purified.

Some years ago I heard a rather amusing tid-bit about a redcap working for one of the American railroad companies. He was a good-looking young lad, and it was in the days when passenger travel by rail was much more common than it is today. This young redcap was a new convert to the Christian faith. He knew that through the cross of our Lord Jesus his sins were forgiven, that he was reconciled to God; and that he was now his heavenly Master's property. But after several months as a young Christian he was at wits' end because of temptations which simply would not leave him alone. He was finding that although he had given up the old way of living, Satan never lets young converts slip out of his hold without a struggle. One morning the young redcap's besetment by inward temptation was evidently so acute that while he was pulling a truck-full of passengers' baggage he suddenly stopped, looked pleadingly up to heaven, and, regardless of bystanders, exclaimed, "Oh, my blessed Lord, help! *Your property is in danger!*"

That brother had got hold of a great truth. "Lord, Your property is in danger." He knew that he was now the Lord's property, and that Jesus had promised to protect him. If I had been present at the time, I would love to have whispered in his ear the words of 2 Thessalonians 3:3, "The Lord is *faithful*; He shall establish you, and guard you from the evil one." The Savior who saved you is the risen Conqueror who guards you.

I have sometimes thought that the brilliant Lucifer, who later became the archfiend Satan, is perhaps the most powerful intelligence God ever created, and that his very super-splendor was that which provoked his blasphemous rivalry of God. There seem to be indications pointing that way. But whether that be so or not, Satan has been beaten flat by man's new champion, "the man Christ Jesus." Even the powerful devil is no match for that almighty God-Man Savior. Therefore God is faithful not only in pardoning, but also in protecting.

Hebrews 10:23

Our next reference is Hebrews 10:23, where again the faithfulness of God is significantly spotlighted. I quote once more from the King James Version.

> Let us hold fast the profession of our faith without wavering;
> (for He is *faithful* that promised).

Note particularly that word "promised." In the two texts already consulted we have seen that God is faithful in pardoning, and then in protecting. We are now told that He is faithful in *promising*.

Look carefully at the wording here in Hebrews 10:23. It exhorts us to "hold fast the *pro*fession of our faith without wavering." The truer rendering of the Greek, as later translations show, is "Let us hold fast the *con*fession of our faith." There is a sharp difference between *pro*fession and *con*fession. Profession is something one believes without necessarily witnessing to it in word; whereas confession is believing it and saying so. I can be a professor of the Christian faith without opening my lips in vocal testimony. In fact that is true of all too many professing Christians. They are like the arctic rivers in winter—frozen at the mouth! What we are needing is not just silent professors of the faith, but eager confessors of it.

What is it that we are to confess? Observe the wording again. "Let us hold fast the confession of our faith." Once again we must respectfully prefer the ASV, "Let us hold fast the confession of our *hope*," which at once fits the subject of the paragraph. Read the text with what follows it.

> Let us hold fast the confession of our hope without wavering;
> for He is faithful that promised....

So we are to hope without faltering for something yet future which God has promised.

> And let us consider one another, to provoke....

What successful provokers many of us are—in the wrong way! We are so provoking by unsanctified and inconsiderate speech and behavior as to make fellowship with us a prickly problem at times! But here is a lovely kind of provocativeness:

> Let us consider one another to provoke unto love and to good works... (verse 24).

Lord, increase the guild of such provokers! It is a choice ministry indeed when by our own exemplary likeness to our meek and lowly Master we continually provoke others to love and good works. But read on:

> Not forsaking the assembling of ourselves together, as the manner of some is [in these days of television and other diversions which have invaded our Christian Sabbath]; but *exhorting* one another...

Perhaps some of us may not care too much for those words, "exhorting one another." We resent being continually corrected or admonished (though I have often noticed that those of us who are least ready to receive such admonition are most adept at giving liberal doses of it to others!). However, the truer reading is "*encouraging* one another" (see later versions). That sounds much more attractive. Although we may not like perpetual exhorters, most of us are deeply grateful for sympathetic *encouragers*. Lord, help us to be encouragers of the brethren amid these difficult days!

...encouraging one another; and so much the more as ye see *the day* approaching (verse 25).

Which day? Do I need to say that in New Testament eschatology "the day" always means one and the same climactic day? It is the day of our Lord's return in the whelming shock and splendor of His second advent to resurrect His own believing people and to bring in His millennial earth-rule.

Oh, day of days which brings back our King! Oh, bliss of Christian hearts, to see those hands which bear the nail-prints wielding that global scepter from David's throne! All around us today, so I believe, there are converging signs that at last the long-overdue enthronement is at hand. Quite so: But what if the day is to be still longer postponed? Why, this: "Let us hold fast the confession of our hope, for He is faithful that promised." However long and puzzling the seeming delay, "hath He not said? and shall He not do?"

> The voice that rolls the stars along
> Speaks all the promises.

We need have no doubt: God always keeps His appointments. As He is faithful in pardoning, and faithful in protecting, so is He faithful in promising.

2 Corinthians 1:18

Next we turn to Paul's Second Epistle to the Corinthians, chapter 1, verses 18-20. In the Authorized Version it reads,

> But as God is true, our word toward you was not yea and nay...for all the promises of God in Him [Christ] are yea, and in Him Amen, unto the glory of God by us.

Look at that first clause: "But as God is true..." Although most translations include that qualifying word "as," it does not occur there in the Greek. Also, the word "true" is the same Greek adjective which in other places is translated as "faithful." Read that first clause, then, as a simple, positive statement: "God is faithful." The *reason* behind that assertion is given in Paul's further words,

> For all the promises of God in Him [Christ] are yea, and in Him Amen, unto the glory of God through us.

These words bring to light a wonderful principle which operates through the Scriptures. All the promises which God ever made, whether to Abraham, Moses, Joshua, David, Jeremiah, or anyone else, are all *ours* now, in Christ, if in any way they fit our need and can be to our spiritual benefit. We find repeated evidence of this in the New Testament. For instance, in Hebrews 13:5,6, we read, "He hath said, I will never leave thee, nor forsake thee. So that we may boldly say, The Lord is my helper; I will not fear..." Notice the juxtaposition of the two little clauses, "He hath said...we may say." Faith is never presumption. It never asserts "We may say" until it has made sure there is a "He hath said." But once it has made sure of the "He hath said" it responds, "So we may *boldly* say."

But why dare we take that promise, "I will never leave thee, nor forsake thee," and appropriate it to ourselves? Was it not spoken to Joshua, hundreds of years before Christ? On what authority do we claim it as belonging to ourselves? It is ours on the newly disclosed principle that "*all* the promises of God," including that one, are now "yea and Amen" unto *us*, in Christ. Interestingly enough, in Hebrews 13:5,6, just quoted, there are two, possibly three, Old Testament assurances (Josh.1:5; Ps. 118:6; 54:4) and each is appropriated with a sense of perfect propriety as belonging now to the Christian believer. To inherit such a fortune of divine promises is more than wonderful. There it is; and it makes the Old Testament all the more significant and valuable to us. The modernist or liberalist type of preacher or believer may find the Old Testament of little present relevance, but to us evangelicals it is rich with "exceeding great and precious promises" all of which are now our blood-sealed legacy in Christ!

But take just another look at our text in 2 Corinthians 1:18-20: "God is *faithful*," for all those promises are now "yes and in Him Amen, unto the glory of God by *us*." In other words, this is magnificent *fulfillment*. God not only promises, He *performs*. He is not only faithful in pardoning, and faithful in protecting, and faithful in promising, but equally faithful in *performing*.

> But as God is true, our word toward you [therefore] was not yea and nay....

That is, our word was not sometimes yes, sometimes no; sometimes positive, sometimes negative; sometimes certain, sometimes doubtful. It was an unwavering, thoroughly reliable yes.

> For all the promises of God in Him [Christ] are *yea*, and in Him *Amen*.

The "yea" and the "amen" together mean positive and certain.

That is what all the promises now are "unto the glory of God, through us" Christian believers. Let it be always in our minds: The proof that God is faithful in promising is that the promising is always crowned by a sure and full performing.

I know of a saintly old grandma who lived in an English town years ago. Gradually she became too decrepit to take much part in the household goings on, but her presence was a benediction, for she was always genial and her conversation was spiced with kindly sagacity. She loved to sit in her rocking-chair reading her favorite passages of Scripture. Often she would doze off for a few minutes with her spectacles still on and her Bible open on her lap; and often she would talk with glowing face about the promises of the Bible which she had trusted through the years. One day she slipped into a deeper doze than usual, and forgot to come back. She wakened in heaven, having peacefully "passed over Jordan" into the land that is "fairer than day." She left her Bible still there, on the lap of her now untenanted body, in that rocking-chair. From then onward that Bible became a treasured family heirloom. Her married son and his wife often read it together and were much interested in the observations she had jotted down in the margins. For some time they were puzzled by the two letters "T & P" which they found dotted here and there in the well-thumbed pages. By and by they noticed that the "T & P" always came at the side of some Scripture promise. A bit later they found one place which was the key to all the others: She had written the two words represented by "T & P." There it was, in the dear, familiar handwriting: "Tried and proved!"

1 Thessalonians 5:23,24

That brings us to the fifth of these texts in which the faithfulness of God is avouched. See Paul's First Epistle to the Thessalonians, chapter 5, verses 23 and 24.

> And the very God of peace sanctify you wholly; and I pray God your whole spirit and soul and body be preserved blameless unto the coming of our Lord Jesus Christ. *Faithful is He* that calleth you [i.e., to this sanctification] who also will do it [by implication: "if you will let Him"].

This is a clear call to an experience of entire sanctification divinely wrought within the heart and then evidenced externally through one's daily life. It is not something which cannot be known until we have departed into the life beyond. It is meant to be Christian experience here and now—even "unto the coming of our Lord

Jesus Christ." When God calls us to this entire sanctification He is not mocking our human weakness by alluring us to some exalted spiritual level which, although beautiful to contemplate, is unrealizable. No; for in thus calling us, "He is faithful." Inward sanctification, or holiness, is not something we attain by strenuous self-effort: It is something we *obtain* in Christ. Our heavenly Father knows that we ourselves could never achieve holiness, however intense and persevering our struggles; for it is psychologically axiomatic that in the basic sense self cannot change self. If any deep-down change is to be wrought in the basic self, it must be by the Holy Spirit. You and I cannot change what we hereditarily are, no matter how we discipline or repress or culture or flog ourselves. But the Spirit of God *can* change us, and *does* change us when we become entirely yielded to our dear Lord. Sanctification means set-apartness. On *our* part entire sanctification is our entire set-apartness of spirit and soul and body in consecration to God, and in faith that He will fulfill His promise within us. On *God's* part entire sanctification is His taking and setting apart what we yield to Him, and His then effecting within us by the Holy Spirit a deep-going renewal into holiness.

"Blessed are the pure in heart: for they shall see God," said our Lord Jesus (Matt. 5:8). Oh, how many of us have longed for such purity of heart! The only true way to it is that which is indicated in 1 Thessalonians 5:23, 24—an utter set-apartness to Christ by our own free choice, and then the inward renewing, refining, *purifying* of our moral nature by the infilling Holy Spirit. That indeed is "the way of holiness." It is real! It works! Millions have found so—because God is "faithful" in calling us to it.

Do I now address some who have sought holiness for years without ever seeming to find it? Let me sympathetically counsel you. Instead of trying to attain it by yourself, learn that you may obtain it in Christ. Instead of thinking you can achieve it, be persuaded to receive it. Instead of struggle, struggle, struggle, let there be surrender to the complete monopoly of yourself by our dear Lord. Sanctification is not a goal at which you aim, but rather a gift which you accept. So, instead of weary working, praying, pleading, wrestling, let there be a once-for-all yielding. And then, instead of grimly resolving again to be better, let there be a humble, grateful, simple receiving of sanctification through the infilling Holy Spirit. Where there is really a full yielding and a simple enough trust to receive, the blessing always comes, for the God who calls us to it is faithful in so doing.

Mark well the progress: God is faithful in pardoning, in protecting, in promising, in performing, and now, in 1 Thessalonians 5:23,

24, faithful in purifying.

1 Corinthians 10:13

There are still two other places where we find that hope-inspiring clause, "God is faithful." They both occur in Paul's First Epistle to the Corinthians. In chapter 10, verse 13, the apostle writes,

> There hath no temptation taken you but such as is common to man: but *God is faithful*, who will not suffer you to be tempted above that ye are able [to bear], but will with the temptation also make a way to escape, that ye may be able to bear it.

We may well be thankful that there is a pledge of God's faithfulness in connection with this thorny problem of temptation. As we all know, temptation of one sort or another simply will not quit on us. Temptations big and little, bold and subtle, outward and inward, morning, noon and night, surround us, allure us, attack us, from January first to December thirty-first, non-stop. Temptation has never been known to take a vacation; and whenever we ourselves take a vacation, temptation insists on being a travel companion.

Secretly wrapped up in every temptation is an inner, secondary temptation to doubt that God is faithful in permitting us to be so tempted. Therefore it is helpful to get certain cautionary and comforting considerations clear in our thinking. The first is that temptation never comes from God. As James 1:13 says, "Let no man say when he is tempted, I am tempted of God: for God cannot be tempted with evil, neither tempteth He any man." Inasmuch as the Holy One can never be the author of moral evil, God could never tempt any of His creatures to sin.[1]

A second relieving consideration is this: God super-controls all the temptations which Satan or demon-intelligences or circumstances may bring upon us; and He restricts temptation to what He knows is our maximum capacity to endure. That is what our text here plainly denotes: "God is faithful: He will not suffer you to be tempted above that ye are able [to bear]." That is heartening. God not only strengtens us for battle, He says to the enemy, "Hitherto shalt thou come, but no further: and here shall thy proud waves be stayed" (Job 38:11). Wave after wave may roll in, but God draws a line beyond which the foaming surge dare not pass.

When I was just a laddie I was fascinated with railway trains. I used to climb a wall and sit on it to watch them. One thing which used to interest me was the notice in white paint on most of the goods wagons. It read, "Maximum capacity" and then gave how much load in hundredweights the truck could bear. May we never forget: God has His "Maximum capacity" sign on you and me in this matter of temptation—even when we think He has forgotten to notice it!

But there is another factor for our benefit. The text says that along with any temptation God "will with the temptation make a way to escape...." Thank heaven, that is consistently true. One of Satan's deadliest tricks is to convince us that in this or that or the other situation we are cornered; that we simply *have* to do what he is tempting us to do, because (so he says) there is just no other way out. He says to that young man or young woman who has become involved in some shameful wrong, "You are in a mess, and no mistake. There's only one thing you can do now, whether you like it or not. There's no alternative, no escape. If what you have done comes to light it will shame your father and break your mother's heart and disgrace the family name. You cannot, you dare not allow that. You simply must do this further thing as a cover-up. There's no way of escape." But Satan is the master liar. There is never any situation in which there is no escape from further yielding to sin. Always, when there is further yielding to what is morally wrong, the eventual results are measurelessly more shameful and damning, while Satan gloats over a bigger downfall and useless remorse. I say to any young man or woman in any situation: You do *not* have to commit the further wrong which is supposedly necessary. There *is* a way of escape. You cannot undo the evil already done, but you *can* let the next step be right and honest. And however keenly it may hurt, or however impossible it may seem, you can do it, from which point God will somehow overrule it in your favor, bringing results beyond your hopes.

Nor must we forget to add that there is a richly profitable ministry in temptation. When bravely endured, perseveringly resisted, and increasingly overcome, it has an educative and ennobling effect upon human character. As resistance to rough winds and stormy blasts strengthens the young sapling, causing its roots to grip more firmly, its trunk to become sturdier and its branches stronger, so does the enduring and overcoming of temptation develop Christlike strength and beauty of character. Cheer up, tempted, buffeted pilgrim! God has His eyes on you amid your battlings. The blasts which you think will be the breaking of you are meant to be the making of you.

During the battle of Crecy, the Black Prince, who was then only eighteen years old, led the van of the battle. His father, with a strong force, drew up near by, watching but as yet taking no part. The young prince was hard pressed by the enemy, and in considerable danger. Again and again he sent hurried appeal to his father for assistance. The king sent word, "Tell my son I am not so inexperienced a commander as not to know when help is needed, and not so careless a father as not to send it." Even so does our heavenly King and Father watch us in our battling against temptation. He knows our danger far better than we ourselves do. Often He is on the field of battle with us most attentively when His presence is least suspected; and, as 2 Peter 2:8 says, "The Lord knoweth to deliver the godly out of temptations." The hardest pressure is meant to bring us the biggest profit.

But there is another aspect. How often we bring temptation upon ourselves, or cause God to permit some trial, because we will not give up some selfishly prized, unworthy thing! One day, when a young father and mother were entertaining a few friends for an evening meal and a time of social conviviality, their young son got his hand fast in the neck of a valuable vase with which he had been playing, unnoticed by the busily chatting group of adults. Then the little fellow began to cry. Daddy tried to get the laddie's hand out. Mommy tried. Two or three of the visitors tried. None succeeded. They were thinking they would have to break the vase, valuable though it was, when daddy made a last try. "Son," he said, "open your hand and put your fingers straight out like this...and then draw your hand out slowly." With a tear sparkling in his eye the little rascal replied, "Daddy, I can't do that, I'd drop my penny." Oh, how many a precious vase has had to be broken because we would not let go of some mere penny!

Christian, learn it well: never a temptation or trial is permitted but there is in it some overruling, gracious purpose of God toward us, even though little detected by ourselves. Never was any mortal tempted, tested, tried more than Job, but what an outcome! Yet not even Job's temptations could compare with those of our Lord Jesus— even to that sweat of blood in Gethsemane: and see the outcome of *that*! See that dear King of love and lowliness, with the Calvary scars still in His hands and feet, but with eternal diadems flashing on His brow! Even He, the "Captain of our salvation," was made complete as such by the "temptations" and the "sufferings" which He victoriously "endured." Never doubt it, harassed disciple of that Master, "God is faithful" even in permitting temptation and trial. Such permitting is a part of the sevenfold faithfulness of God toward us: faithful in pardoning, in protecting, in promising, in performing, in purifying, and even in *permitting*.

1 Corinthians 1:8,9

Finally, look up 1 Corinthians 1:8,9, but allow me to read those two verses in inverse order. If we read verse 8 and then verse 9 we have the grammatical order, of course, as framed by the pen of Paul, but we get the logical sequence if we transpose the two verses, thus:

> God is faithful, by whom ye were called into the fellowship of His Son, Jesus Christ our Lord (verse 9).

How do we *know* that God was "faithful" when at our conversion He thus called us into the fellowship of God's people in Christ? We know it because, as the preceding verse says,

> Who [God] shall also *confirm* you unto the end, that ye may be blameless in the day of our Lord Jesus Christ (verse 8).

So, whom God saves He keeps; whom He converts He also "confirms" or *preserves*. Years ago, during the latter part of World War II, the mother of a friend of mine gave accommodation to a Polish military general who was stationed with his forces in Peebles, Scotland. After peace was declared the day came when he was leaving Peebles, and a comical little incident occurred. With customary Polish politeness he wanted to thank his kind hostess and say good-bye in his best English wording. Having carefully looked up his Polish-English dictionary, he bowed, shook hands, and said, "t'ank you, t'ank you, kind madam; and may you always be pickled!" She looked quizzically at him for a moment, wondering what on earth he meant. Then, of course, it dawned on her what had happened. His dictionary had given the English equivalent of the Polish word as "kept, preserved, pickled." It at once reminded me of a humorous yet serious remark which I heard a whimsical old Lancashire preacher make when I was just a boy. "Brethren, God never pickles His saints but He does *preserve* them." That witty remark really says something. God never quarantines or insulates or exempts us from risky contacts with this "present evil age" (Gal. 1:4). There is no artificial immunization of the saints, but there is a continuous, ever-watchful safeguard of us by that heavenly keeper who "neither slumbers nor sleeps" (Ps. 121:4). We are "kept by the power of God through faith unto salvation ready to be revealed in the last time" (1 Peter 1:5).

A dear old saint of some eighty-five years, in Glasgow, Scotland, was puttering about in his garden one day when a Christian friend of his passed by and called to him over the garden fence, "Hello there! How are you keeping?" Looking up from his hoeing the radiant old man replied, "Oh, thank you, thank you—and thank God, I'm not just 'keeping'; I'm *kept.*" Yes, thank God, we Christian believers are not just keeping, we are kept; and our almighty Guardian will never let us down, and never let us go, and never give us up. He will preserve, or "confirm" us right on until the promised consummation, even "the day of our Lord Jesus Christ."

> The soul that on Jesus has leaned for repose
> He will not, He will not desert to its foes;
> That soul, though all hell should endeavor to shake,
> He'll never, no *never*, no *NEVER* forsake.

How wonderful, then are these seven occurrences of "God is faithful" in the New Testament! See them now set out in their developing succession. As the sevenfold candelabrum in the old Israelite tabernacle had a flame of bright light shining from each of its seven branches, so does the faithfulness of our God shine out in seven aspects from these seven texts.

1 John 1:9,	Faithful in *pardoning.*
2 Thessalonians 3:3,	Faithful in *protecting.*
Hebrews 10:23,	Faithful in *promising.*
2 Corinthians 1:18,	Faithful in *performing.*
1 Thessalonians 5:23,24,	Faithful in *purifying.*
1 Corinthians 10:13,	Faithful in *permitting.*
1 Corinthians 1:8,9,	Faithful in *preserving.*

Next see the correspondence between those seven written guarantees and the seven pillars on which that sevenfold faithfulness of God rests.

The seven pillars.	*The seven texts.*
The divine *righteousness*	1 John 1:9—"Faithful and righteous to pardon our sins..."
The divine *omnipotence*	2 Thess. 3:3—"The Lord is faithful, who shall guard you from the evil one.
The divine *truth*	Hebrews 10:23—"He is faithful that promised" (for all His promises are truth).
The divine *immutability*	2 Cor. 10:18—"God is faithful... all the promises yea and Amen" (God never changes).

The divine *holiness*	1 Thess. 5:23,24—"He is faithful that calleth you" (i.e., to holiness).
The divine *wisdom*	1 Cor. 10:13—"God is faithful, who will not permit...above what you are able."
The divine *love*	1 Cor. 1:8,9—"God is faithful...who shall preserve you to the end" (His love never fails.)

What does this sevenfold biblical picture of God's faithfulness say to us as Christian believers today? What is its central meaning? Its overall message? Its central meaning is that the faithfulness of God, our "faithful Creator," has found its perfect expression in Christ. His faithfulness in creation and providence has become sublimatingly crowned by His faithfulness in redemption. Calvary is not only the crimson-sealed guarantee of this; it is the measure of it. Such redeeming faithfulness as that can never, never, never fail us as long as eternity lasts.

It says to us today, amid these "troublous times," that we need not agitatedly flutter like startled birds in a storm-shaken nest. In William Cowper's well-known lines it counsels us—

> Judge not the Lord by feeble sense,
> But trust His sovereign grace;
> Behind a frowning providence
> He hides a smiling face.
>
> His purposes now ripen fast,
> Unfolding hour by hour;
> The bud may have a bitter taste,
> But sweet will be the flower.
>
> Ye fearful saints, fresh courage take;
> The clouds ye so much dread
> Are big with mercy and shall break
> In blessings on your head.

Do I address some discouraged Christian, weighed down with a grievous burden, scourged by trials, beaten down by hard reverses, undergoing sickness, pain, privation, or weeping over cruel betrayal by loved ones, wondering if God has forgotten to be gracious? Such personal sufferings are far more acute and "on top of us" than the parlous international situation. What are we to say about them?

Well, there are no snap answers to the questions asked by broken hearts. There are no cheap and easy solutions to the poignant enigmas of the present. Yet with the light of biblical revelation streaming into our minds, we may say that back of it all is a faithful Creator who has already given us an interim answer by coming Himself to live and share and suffer with us in the person of His only-begotten Son, our Lord Jesus, Immanuel, "God with us." Also, in His written Word, that same faithful Creator has given us the pledge of a day to come when mysteries shall melt away in final solutions, and questions shall be supplanted by the glad exclamation,"He hath done all things well!" What He has already *done* for us in Christ is the guarantee of His all-sufficiency for us in the present, and the irrefrangible assurance of full and final answer in that coming day of cloudless joy. That day will surely come. "Instead of the thorn shall come up the fir tree, and instead of the brier shall come up the myrtle tree" (Isa. 55:13). "The desert shall rejoice, and blossom as the rose" (Isa. 36:1). "Night shall be no more." The last dark shadow shall "flee away," and "all tears" shall be dried.

Meanwhile, to those who know trial and trouble, and in particular to those who suffer "for conscience' sake," He gives the indwelling heavenly comforter, the Holy Spirit, to make inwardly real the faithfulness of the heavenly Father. Dear Christian with an aching heart, I say to you in the words of our opening text, "Let them that suffer according to the will of God commit the keeping of their souls to Him in well doing, as unto a *faithful Creator*." Think back over the gracious, sympathetic promises given to us in God's written Word— hundreds of them, and every one of them bearing the signature of that God whose faithfulness is as the everlasting mountains.

When my dear daughter was just a chubby, dimple-faced little girl, her uncle Sam made her a birthday present of a charming little wicker chair. Besides its pretty appearance, it had the auricular novelty that when sat upon it played a merry tune. It quickly became a great favorite. Our little Miriam would sit and stand, and sit and stand, and as she did so the music started and stopped, and started and stopped. It gave *so* much pleasure. (I do not mind telling you secretly that sometimes, when mommie and Mim were not around, *daddy* used to sit on that little chair. The one problem was that when *he* got up, the chair got up too!) But what I want to tell you is this: Again and again when our little one sat on that chair and the pleasant music started, an inner voice would whisper to me, "Sid, Sid, the promises of God are like that chair—they only play their music to those who *rest* in them!"

Fellow-believer, is it not time we began really to *rest* in those promises? Is it not time we learned to sing hosannas on the darkest days,and hallelujahs even through our tears? What a Bible we have! What a Savior! What a faithful heavenly Father! What an understanding, sympathizing, indwelling Paraclete! Let sighing become singing and doubting become trusting, and limping become leaping; for in the words of Romans 8:18, "The sufferings of this present time are not worthy to be compared with the glory which shall be revealed in us!" Ten thousand times ten thousand hallelujahs—

GOD IS FAITHFUL!

1 Perhaps someone may ask about Genesis 22:1, "And it came to pass after these things that God did tempt Abraham..." The word, "tempt" there, however, is merely a matter of translation. The Hebrew word is better rendered as "prove," which both British and American revisers adopted. Also the "proving" had nothing to do with sin, but with obedience in the yielding up of Isaac.

Scripture Index

Other books by J. Sidlow Baxter

Does God Still Guide?

If there is one thing more than another which our world needs, it is a guidance other than human. Baxter offers insights into questions such as: Which is the right way?, What's at the end?, Is there a sure guide?, Does God still guide?, How may I know? The Bible says yes, and Dr. Baxter sets forth a clear-cut presentation of that truth.

ISBN 0-8254-2199-3   **paperback**   **192 pp.**

Mark These Men

A treasure house of Bible biographies including Elisha, Elijah, King Saul, Daniel, Gideon, Balaam, and Nehemiah. Also included are such New Testament characters as the Apostle Paul, Lazarus, the rich young ruler, Ananias, Simon of Cyrene, and many others.

ISBN 0-8254-2197-7   **paperback**   **192 pp.**

The Strategic Grasp of the Bible

An extensive look into the origin, structure, and message of the Word of God. The pastor, teacher, and sincere Bible student will not only find rich gems and insights, but also challenging study to promote growth in their Christian life. A condensed version of the author's exemplary work *Explore the Book.*

ISBN 0-8254-2198-5   **paperback**   **406 pp.**

A New Call to Holiness

Volume one of the *Christian Sanctification Series*. An important contribution to the subject of Christian sanctification in which Baxter examines the basic question—"What is Holiness?" and how and to what extent can it be experienced.

ISBN 0-8254-2170-5 **paperback** **256 pp.**

His Deeper Work in Us

Volume two of the *Christian Sanctification Series*. Offers a clear and uncomplicated argument for the work of the Holy Spirit in the sanctification of the believer and will enlighten those confused by the various schools of thought frequently encountered today.

ISBN 0-8254-2172-1 **paperback** **256 pp.**

Our High Calling

Volume three of the *Christian Sanctification Series*. These devotional and practical studies affirm the need for personal sanctification and point to the New Testament's emphasis on the individual and the call to sanctification as an imperative.

ISBN 0-8254-2171-3 **paperback** **208 pp.**